COURTS AND POLITICS

The Federal Judicial System

COURTS AND POLITICS

The Federal Judicial System

HOWARD BALL

Mississippi State University

PRENTICE-HALL, Englewood Cliffs, New Jersey 07632

Library of Congress Cataloging in Publication Data

BALL, HOWARD, 1937-
   Courts and politics.

   Bibliography: p.
   Includes indexes.
     1.–Courts—United States. 2.–Judicial-process—
United States. 3.–Political questions and judicial
power—United States. 4.–Judges—United States
I.–Title.
KF8700.B33   347'.73   79-14748
ISBN 0-13-184655-8

Editorial/production supervision and interior
design by Dianne Poonarian
Cover design by Wanda Lubelska
Manufacturing buyer: Harry P. Baisley

Printed in the United States of America

10 9 8 7 6 5 4 3 2 1

PRENTICE-HALL INTERNATIONAL, INC., *London*
PRENTICE-HALL OF AUSTRALIA PTY. LIMITED, *Sydney*
PRENTICE-HALL OF CANADA, LTD., *Toronto*
PRENTICE-HALL OF INDIA PRIVATE LIMITED, *New Delhi*
PRENTICE-HALL OF JAPAN, INC., *Tokyo*
PRENTICE-HALL OF SOUTHEAST ASIA PTE. LTD., *Singapore*
WHITEHALL BOOKS LIMITED, *Wellington, New Zealand*

FOR CAROL

contents

preface

"My uncle on the farm behind the plowhorse (has to) understand every opinion I write."

Associate Justice Hugo L. Black
United States Supreme Court

The purpose of this book is to examine the federal judicial system in what I hope is a refreshing, nontechnical manner. The United States District Courts, the United States Circuit Courts of Appeals, and the United States Supreme Court hear and decide cases and controversies that have great impact on our daily lives. The judges and justices of these courts very often make political judgments much like those made by congressmen and presidents, but they make them in a manner characteristic of courts: through written orders based upon careful judicial review of the law and facts presented in court.

If you understand (1) the functions of the courts in our democratic political system, (2) the structure and dynamics of the judicial process, and (3) the politics of the judicial process in the federal system, then you will come to appreciate the effect the federal judiciary has had on the social, political, and economic development of our society. That is what this book is about. It presents these facts in three segments (in addition to a brief introduction and concluding statement). Part One, *Roles and Functions of the Federal Courts,* examines two basic and interrelated judicial activities: norm enforcement and policy making. Examining legal questions involving organized baseball, apple growers, crime control, and picketers on private property, the chapters will illustrate these two general characteristics of the federal courts.

Part Two, *The Structure and Dynamics of the Federal Judicial System,* presents information about the organization and jurisdiction of the federal courts and how a person or a group gains access to these courts. By closely examining the actions of organizations such as the Reservists Committee to Stop the War and the Sierra Club, you will get to know what kinds of conflicts courts can attempt to resolve and how a person or an organization gains access to the federal court system. Part Three, *The politics of the Federal Judiciary,* will focus on the kinds of people who are tapped for judicial service and also on the complexities of judicial decision making in the three constitutional federal courts. To make the examination of this segment more fascinating, several case studies have been incorporated. For example, there is an examination of the G. Harrold Carswell nomination to fill the Fortas vacancy on the Supreme Court that I hope will interest and inform the reader about the complexity of the selection process.

The book is about the federal courts and the persons who use and work in them. Its goal is to portray clearly the "goings on" in the federal judicial system, in great part through the use of illustrative case studies that form an integral part of the chapters. The book is aimed at those who, much like Justice Black's uncle, have not yet attended law school and who have little or no knowledge of the functions and dynamics of the federal courts in the political process.

acknowledgments

Many persons have assisted me in the preparation of this book. I sincerely appreciated their help. In particular, I would like to thank:

my children, Susan, Sheryl, and Melissa, for not bothering me too much while I was writing,

my colleagues at Mississippi State University for giving me some much needed advice and criticism,

my colleague and friend at Georgia State, Tom Lauth, for his comments,

my graduate assistant, Sam Dawkins, for his assistance throughout the research and writing phases,

my excellent secretaries, Stella Phillips and JoAnn Cohen, for their fine work in the preparation of the manuscript,

those anonymous Prentice-Hall reviewers who helped enormously through their critiques and suggestions,

my editor, Stan Wakefield, for posing some darn good questions about the scope and direction of this book,

and, last but not least,

my wife Carol, to whom the book is dedicated, for once again providing encouragement and support.

These people provided encouragement, support, criticism, and ideas; I alone am responsible for the end product, *Courts and Politics: The Federal Judicial System.* I have planned a book that will enable instructors in various courses that focus on the federal judicial system to introduce some basic concepts about judges and politics in an informal, easy to read style. I hope I have succeeded in this attempt. I would appreciate any and all comments you have about the book's style and substance.

HOWARD BALL

COURTS
AND POLITICS
The Federal
Judicial System

ROLES AND FUNCTIONS OF THE FEDERAL COURTS

Part I

*Scarcely any political question arises in the United States that
is not resolved, sooner or later, into a judicial question. Hence
all parties are obliged to borrow, in their daily controversies,
the ideas, and even the language, peculiar to judicial proceedings.*

Alexis deTocqueville,
Democracy in America, 1835

We Americans like to go to court. We have a passionate
love affair with courts and the law and we have been brought up to
believe that if "we take it to the judge" we can resolve conflicts we have
with our boss, our wife (or husband or, in some states, our lover), our
neighbor, and our government. In 1976 in the three primary federal
constitutional courts[1]—that is, the 91 United States Federal District
Courts (which are the trial courts of original jurisdiction in the federal
system), the 11 United States Courts of Appeals, and the United States
Supreme Court—there were 195,325 filings of complaints, briefs, petitions, and appeals before the 505 judges and justices by unhappy persons and groups. These people come to the courts because they believe

[1]Constitutional courts include the "general" courts (Federal District Courts, U.S.
Courts of Appeals, and the U.S. Supreme Court) and the "special" courts (U.S.
Court of Customs, U.S. Court of Claims, and U.S. Court of Customs and Patent
Appeals). Legislative courts, responsible for interpreting only statutory law (acts of
Congress) include the U.S. Court of Military Appeals and the three U.S. territorial
district courts in Guam, the Canal Zone, and the U.S. Virgin Islands.

that their problems can be resolved in the judicial system. They are able to use the federal courts because both the Constitution and the United States Congress gave these courts *jurisdiction,* i.e., legitimate powers, to hear certain kinds of cases and controversies.

The federal courts, however, are courts of *limited jurisdiction;* they can hear and decide only those kinds of controversies that are enumerated in Article III of the United States Constitution. If a person suffers a wrong not listed in the Article, the federal courts *lack the power* to hear and resolve that issue and therefore cannot devise a needed remedy. Article III of the Constitution, written in 1787, outlines the powers and the limits on power of the three branches of the national government. For any governmental action to be legitimate, it must be based on a grant of power found somewhere in the U.S. Constitution. Article III, the Judiciary article, enumerates the powers of the Supreme Court and all those "inferior courts as the Congress may from time to time ordain and establish." It describes in broad terms the *scope* of federal judicial power; this power encompasses:

1. all cases in law and equity arising under the Constitution, laws, and treaties of the United States;
2. all cases affecting ambassadors, other public ministers, and consuls;
3. all cases of admiralty and maritime jurisdiction;
4. controversies between two or more states;
5. controversies to which the United States is a party;
6. controversies between a state and citizens of another state;
7. controversies between citizens of different states;
8. controversies between citizens of the same state claiming lands under grants of different states; and
9. controversies between a state, or its citizens, and foreign states, citizens, or subjects.

As modified by the Eleventh Amendment, adopted in 1798, which prohibited constitutional courts to hear and decide controversies between a state by a citizen of another state or by citizens or subjects of any foreign state, the above list establishes the parameters of judicial power *if* the Congress confers this power on the courts through statutory grants of jurisdiction.

This "if" is an important condition of federal judicial power. While Article III enumerates the scope of federal judicial power it also reflects the eighteenth-century commitment to "checks and balances." Article III indicates quite clearly that, except for original jurisdiction conferred upon the Supreme Court of the United States by the Constitution, the Congress can, if it desires, grant to all the federal courts the power to hear cases and controversies.[2] In order for a person to be able to bring his/her case to a federal district court and appeal the judgment all the way up to the United States Supreme Court, the problem must (1) fall somewhere within the judicial powers of the Courts as defined in Article III, and (2) be covered by a statutory grant of power to the courts by the United States Congress.

With the passage of the first Judiciary Act in 1789 by the Congress, the federal courts have been given broadly defined grants of power by the national legislature. As will be pointed out in the chapter on jurisdiction, the power of the federal courts to hear cases and controversies, civil and criminal, is quite broad—too broad for many harried federal judges whose dockets are crowded and whose staff is small.

Because the federal courts have been given the power to hear cases arising under the Constitution and can also hear disputes that arise as a consequence of congressional legislation, the political impact of these legal agencies is great. The chapters in Part I will examine the basic functions of the federal courts, given the jurisdiction they have, and will point out the critical importance of the concept of judicial review. The first chapter will examine the concept of judicial review by the federal courts. Chapter 2 will (1) examine the norm enforcement function of the courts, and (2) discuss the policy-making role of the federal courts.

What emerges from an examination of the functions of the federal courts is a portrait of judges as political actors. Although the legal language in the federal judicial system is unfamiliar or alien to many people listening to arguments in a federal court, the outcome can be very political because these federal judges are being asked to examine and to interpret the language of the Constitution, statutes, administrative rulings, and so forth. Because the judges have jurisdiction to hear all cases "arising under the Constitution," the decisions they make fall into the realm of political jurisprudence. This is a fact of judicial life in America.

SUMMARY

An aggrieved person comes into the federal court system because he believes he can have his case heard by the federal judge. He has come to that conclusion either because he knows or because his counsel

---

[2]"In all cases affecting ambassadors, other public ministers, and consuls, and those in which a state shall be a party, the Supreme Court shall have original jurisdiction. In all the other cases before mentioned, the Supreme Court (and all other inferior courts created by the Congress) shall have appellate jurisdiction, both as to law and fact, with such exceptions and under such regulations as the Congress shall make."

has advised him that the federal court has *jurisdiction* to hear his problem by virtue of a particular section of the United States Code (USC) granting the federal court the power to hear that kind of dispute. Congress, in its wisdom, has decided that that particular kind of problem falls within the scope of federal judicial power, as enumerated in Article III, and it has legislated accordingly.

Given the jurisdiction it has and given the existence of "standing"[3] on the part of the person bringing the suit into the federal court system, judges must act to resolve the dispute. In the resolution of the conflict, the judges and justices in the federal judicial system continuously (1) legitimatize public policies that have come under attack in the courts, or (2) develop new policy through basic constitutional interpretation. In effect, by functioning in these two ways, the federal judges are continuously defining and redefining the boundaries of political authority. It is, to say the least, an extremely difficult and sensitive task.

[3]The concept of standing to sue will be discussed at length in chapter 4. Basically, it suggests that, in addition to the federal court having the power, i.e., jurisdiction, to hear the case, the person bringing the case into the federal judicial system must have personally suffered a direct, concrete injury. Federal Constitutional courts do not have the power to issue advice to people; they can only hear concrete cases and controversies and not hypothetical or abstract/friendly suits.

judicial review by the federal courts

1

Our Constitution "proclaims its own supremacy and the supremacy of the laws of Congress passed in pursuance of it. But," note the authors of a modern case book of constitutional law, "no precise line is drawn" regarding the outer limits of governmental powers.[1] Can a president withhold information from an inquiring congressional committee investigating impeachment charges? Can the Congress force a restaurant to integrate its facilities? Can New York State restrict the manner of usage of the American flag? Can the president claim executive privilege and thus deny requests from the special prosecutor for information allegedly material and relevant for a criminal trial? Can the government—the FBI—use wiretaps without search warrants? Can a state use the death penalty or is that "cruel and unusual punishment"? Can a school board order the use of busing to achieve the end to school segregation?

These are but a few of the many controversial questions that have been raised in the past few years regarding the issue of governmental abuses of power. These questions arise because, in part, the Constitution is vague as to the extent of the powers of the Congress or of the president, and some agency has had to resolve these dilemmas. "Applying standards drawn from these vague words (of the Constitution), the Supreme Court is the ultimate guardian of individual privilege and gov-

[1]Alfred Mason and William Beaney, *American Constitutional Law* (Englewood Cliffs, N.J.: Prentice-Hall, 1975), p. 12.

ernmental prerogative alike. It is, Woodrow Wilson observed, 'the balance wheel of our entire system.' "[2] That it is a *nonelected* governmental agency within a working democratic political system to which citizens *ultimately* turn to resolve major questions affecting them is the essence of the paradox of the United States Supreme Court.

POLICY MAKING IN A DEMOCRACY

Our political system—constitutional democracy—is based on a profoundly simple compound premise. Policies—public laws—are the outcome of intense, complex negotiations between political decision makers chosen in free elections and other interested groups representing various publics in America. In this energetic activity there will be the clash of wills, and the underlying theory of democracy posits majority rule as the method of resolving this kind of disagreement.

In a democratic system, majority rule is the only basis for choosing among alternative courses of action presented to and by policy makers.[3] It is the only feasible choice given the limited number of options for the making of public policy: majority rule, unanimity, or institutionalized minority rule. The last is tyranny, the middle is impossible to achieve, the remainder—majority rule—becomes the standard by process of elimination.[4]

In only one way is majority rule consistent with the other option, minority rule: there will always be a loser in the policy-making process. Policies—laws—discriminate because they are essentially categorizations and classifications of various segments of the community: You, Mr. Smith, pay Y dollars in taxes and you, Mr. Green, pay Z dollars; you, Mr. Stone, must report to the army whereas you, Mrs./Ms. Nathan, need not, etc. So long as the categorization is a valid one the policy is legitimate.

Remember, however, that the words of the Constitution—which grants powers to the president and to the Congress (as well as limiting their activities)—are vague and that there will be abuses of political power, both intentional and unintentional. The framers of the Constitution, mindful of this possibility, built certain correctives into the political system. First, majority rule itself is not without limitation. The popular will is constrained by the presence in the Constitution of certain vested rights that cannot be easily ignored by the popular majorities in

[2]Mason and Beaney, *Constitutional Law*, p. 13.
[3]James Madison's *Federalist Papers*, Number 10; see also Thomas Thorson, *The Logic of Democracy* (New York: Norton, 1967).
[4]Ibid.; see also, Howard Ball, *The Warren Court's Conceptions of Democracy* (Rutherford, N.J.: Fairleigh Dickinson University Press, 1971).

the Congress and in the executive branch. These "unceded rights" of speech, press, association, religion, and petition (among others) may not be violated by democratic government—even one that was elected by an overwhelming majority and voices the feelings and attitudes of the overwhelming majority of citizens in that constituency.[5]

In addition to basic protections within the body of the Constitution and the Bill of Rights for persons and citizens—applicable now to both national and state governments—there are other correctives in the Constitution to ensure that democracy, in the words of the late Clinton Rossiter, "will be carried on through safe, sober, predictable methods." There are the constitutional provisions for open and free elections where all people who meet minimal requirements can register and vote. And if a legislator is not representing the best interests of his constituency he can be removed from office at the next election.

The Constitution also provides, in James Madison's words, "auxiliary precautions" against the abuse of governmental powers. Madison meant by that phrase the "separation of powers," and "checks and balances," and the "federal" character of the political system itself. The institutions of government developed in the summer of 1787 reflected the idea that power had to be separated and fragmented.[6] Frightened of absolute power, distrustful of popular majorities, keenly aware of the need for some form of national government, but appreciative of the aphorism that power corrupts and absolute power corrupts absolutely, the men in Philadelphia skillfully created our constitutional pattern.

Their belief was that there would be sufficient checks on abuses of power by the various participants within the system by the other policy makers. But with the fragmentation brought on by separation and checks and federalism, questions and controversies arose. Does the Congress have exclusive control over interstate commerce? Can a state legislate in the absence of commercial legislation of Congress? Can the president commit armed forces in the absence of a declaration of war? Can Congress pass an income tax bill without regard to apportionment of population? Can the state tax products that are traveling in commerce? Do the federal courts have jurisdiction to hear lawsuits involving a state? Can the federal government lower the voting age of citizens in both federal and state elections? And so questions go on and on because of the fact that even where there are the "auxiliary precautions" there are the questions as to boundaries and limits of these checks.

[5]See Howard Ball, *The Vision and the Dream of Justice Hugo Black* (University, Ala.: University of Alabama Press, 1975) for a discussion of Thomas Jefferson's and Hugo Black's views on First Amendment rights. See also *Lucas v. 44th General Assembly, Colorado*, 1965.
[6]See *Federalist Papers*, Number 51.

The federal courts—from the very first problem of extent of governmental prerogatives[7] to the present—have been called upon to clarify the ambiguities in the Constitution that have created the dilemmas of power and responsibility. The power of "judicial review," an extraconstitutional power nowhere mentioned in the Constitution and developed by the Supreme Court itself in 1803,[8] has been used to clarify the words of the Constitution and in so doing has ameliorated the conflict that arose due to ambiguity. Judicial review has, in one sense, become the overarching, all-encompassing auxiliary precaution. The federal courts, especially the Supreme Court, have become the "balance wheel" of the political system.

THE PARADOX OF JUDICIAL REVIEW

Very early in our history the Supreme Court became the fulcrum of the constitutional system because citizens viewed the federal courts as the agent to resolve questions regarding abuses of power. Article III of the Constitution gave the Supreme Court and all other federal courts created by Congress the power to hear certain types of cases and controversies between specified parties arising "under the Constitution."

Concerning the application of these judicial powers, the framers of the Constitution suggested that the Supreme Court review acts of Congress at the appropriate time and, if necessary, check abuses of power. During a prolonged discussion in July of 1787, the members of the Constitutional convention on the judiciary committee debated the merits of having the president and the Court form an "offensive and defensive alliance against the legislature."[9] Their fear was legislative usurpation of powers and their concern focused on measures to be developed to prevent that eventuality. James Madison and others saw the executive-legislative alliance as a necessary "auxiliary precaution."[10] But arrayed against Madison were John Rutledge and Luther Martin who argued the danger of having the judiciary participate in such judgment *at that time.*

With respect to the question of the constitutionality of the laws passed by the Congress, Luther argued that "that point will come before the judges in their official character."[11] No need for the Court to act as

---

[7]*Chisholm v. Georgia,* 2 Dall 431 (1796).
[8]*Marbury v. Madison,* 1 Cranch 137 (1803).
[9]Saul K. Padover, *To Secure These Blessings, The Great Debates of the Constitutional Convention of 1787* (New York: Ridge Press, 1962), p. 417.
[10]Ibid., pp. 411ff.
[11]Ibid., p. 416.

a council of revision with the president because Article III gave the Court the reviewing power "in their official character." Rutledge "thought the judges of all men the most unfit to be concerned in the revisionary council. The judges ought never to give their opinion on a law *until* it comes before them."[12]

On July 21, 1787, the amendment attempting to join the judiciary to the executive in a veto power over the Congress was defeated, four to three. However, the notion that the judges of the Supreme Court would at a later time in the political process review the acts of the Congress—and all other actions that came under the judicial powers described in Article III—was presented and there was no disagreement noted in committee about that role of the Court.[13]

Two political scientists have written that there was little doubt that the framers intended the Supreme Court to have this power of judicial review.

> Unquestionably, 'the framers anticipated some sort of judicial review. . . .' Why, then, did the framers not specifically provide for judicial review? Probably because the power rested on certain general provisions that made specific statements unnecessary.[14]

In the 1803 U.S. Supreme Court opinion of *Marbury v. Madison,* Chief Justice John Marshall voiced the beliefs of the men of the 1787 convention when he said that it is "emphatically the province and the duty of the judicial department to say what the law is." And if a law is in conflict with the Constitution, then the "duty" of the judiciary is to declare that law void as being "repugnant to the Constitution, and that courts, as well as other departments, are bound by that instrument."

William Marbury "filed the most significant lawsuit in American history."[15] He was one of many "federalists" appointed by President John Adams just days before the federalist executive left office in March 1801. Marbury's nomination (to serve as Justice of the Peace in Washington, D.C.) had received the U.S. Senate's advice and consent, his commission of office had been signed by President Adams, and the great seal of the U.S. government had been affixed upon the document. However, when Thomas Jefferson assumed the presidency, the Marbury

---

[12]Ibid., p. 418.

[13]See Alexander Hamilton, *Federalist Paper, 78,* and also note Thomas Jefferson's views regarding judicial review in a letter written to James Madison in 1789: "In the arguments in favor of a declaration of rights, you omit one which has great weight with me: the legal check which is put in the hands of the judiciary. This is a body which, if rendered independent and kept strictly to their own department, merits great confidence for their learning and integrity."

[14]James MacGregor Burns and J.W. Peltason, *Government by the People* (Englewood Cliffs, N.J.: Prentice-Hall, Inc., 1975), p. 420.

[15]Leon Friedman, *Milestones* (St. Paul, Minn.: West Publishing Co., 1976), p. 73.

commission had not been delivered and the president, choosing to disregard this appointment, instructed his secretary of state, James Madison, not to deliver the document to the federalist. (Basic political movements therefore led to this watershed constitutional case being heard and resolved in 1803.) William Marbury, joined by three other men who had not been given their commissions by Madison, then asked the United States Supreme Court to issue a writ of mandamus commanding the secretary of state to deliver the signed and sealed commissions of appointment to these men.

Due to a congressional action that delayed the convening of the Supreme Court, the case was not heard until February 1803. When the opinion was announced one month later, it reflected the perception of judicial review discussed in the constitutional convention and in the *Federalist Papers.* John Marshall, for the Court, raised and answered three basic legal and political questions. (1) Did Marbury have the right to the commission? Answer: yes. (2) If he has a right, is there an available remedy to provide the injured person relief from the wrong? Answer: yes, there is a remedy-mandamus. (3) If there is a remedy, mandamus, can the Supreme Court issue the writ? It was this last question that led the Court to the conclusion that federal courts have broad, potent reviewing powers that they can exercise.

Marbury had asked the Supreme Court to issue the writ of mandamus under its original jurisdiction in light of Section 13 of Judiciary Act of 1789, 1 Stat 73 (which was the congressional act that established the U.S. federal courts and enumerated their jurisdiction). That section said, in part, that the Supreme Court was authorized to issue writs of mandamus "in cases warranted by the principles and usages of law, to any courts appointed, or persons holding office, under the authority of the United States." Congress, wrote the Chief Justice in this major opinion, was attempting to enlarge the original jurisdiction of the U.S. Supreme Court. However, it could not do this because Article III gave Congress control over only the appellate jurisdiction of the Supreme Court.

Marshall's opinion reached the height of judicial craftsmanship when he wrote that the Court could not provide the remedy because Section 13 of the Judiciary Act of 1789 gave the Court original jurisdiction. If the Constitution is the fundamental law of the land, can ordinary legislation modify its commands? asked Marshall. The "very essence of judicial duty" is to determine which of the conflicting rules "governs the case." Given the supreme, paramount character of the Constitution, Marshall was led to conclude that "a law repugnant to the Constitution is void."

It was in these paragraphs that the concept of judicial review, incipient in 1787 debates, broadsides, and brochures, emerged. Although there have been countless arguments devoted to the question of judicial usurpation, the point is that after *Marbury v. Madison* judicial review was a legal fact of life and it has long been accepted, although not without its critics, by society as a uniquely American characteristic of democratic government. Employing the power of judicial review, the Supreme Court (and other federal constitutional courts) has throughout our history performed two less than distinct functions: (1) validation of legislation passed by the Congress (and the states)—*norm enforcement*, and, (2) *policy making* through examination and interpretation of a statute or of the Constitution in a case or controversy properly before the Court.

By employing judicial review, the federal courts become policy makers and norm enforcers. The paradox lies there: The political system is democratic, yet a nonelected, lifetime appointed set of jurists are normatively and constitutionally committed to preserving and maximizing the contours of the democratic system. The federal court system is an oligarchic institution functioning within a democratic environment. Some of the judges and justices of these tribunals have been profoundly affected by the paradox and have sought to restrain the judiciary from taking too active a role in the policy-making process. Others have been less constrained by the paradox but all are aware of it.

More than any other justice, Felix Frankfurter as Justice of the Supreme Court of the United States reflects upon this paradox in most poignant terms. In a letter to Chief Justice Stone, written shortly before the Court announced its original opinion upholding the constitutionality of compulsory flag salute statutes, Frankfurter wrote: "There is for me, as I know also for you, a great makeweight for dealing with this problem, namely, that we are not the primary resolvers of the clash. We are not exercising an independent judgment; we are sitting in judgment upon the judgment of a legislature. . . . What weighs with me strongly is . . . that we do not exercise our judicial power unduly, and as though we ourselves were legislators by holding too tight a rein on the organs of popular government."[16]

When, three years later, the Supreme Court reversed its stand on the question of flag salutes, Justice Frankfurter was one of three dissenters and wrote what many believe to be the classic expression of judicial restraint and of the paradox of judicial review.

One who belongs to the most vilified and persecuted minority in history is not likely to be insensible to the freedoms guaranteed by our Constitution. Were my purely personal attitude relevant I should wholeheartedly associate myself with the great libertarian views in the Court's opinion,

[16]Quoted in Murphy and Pritchett, *Courts, Judges, and Politics* (New York: Random House, 1971), pp. 668–69.

representing as they do the thought and action of a lifetime. But as judges we are neither Jew nor Gentile, neither Catholic nor agnostic. . . . As a member of this Court I am not justified in writing my private notions of policy into the Constitution. . . . Our functions are not comparable to that of a legislature nor are we free to act as though we were a super legislature.[17]

Awareness of this apparent paradox between judicial review and democratic theory by the federal judges has been evident since the Supreme Court of John Marshall. In any event, "no matter what jurisprudential doctrines judges follow, as long as access to the courts remains open and as long as judges retain some measure of the power that they have historically possessed, it is inevitable that individuals, groups, and public officials will attempt to utilize the judicial process to achieve their policy aims." There will be cases and controversies that the federal judges will not hear because they do not want to hear them: judicial restraint by the judges to avoid the paradox. But then there are times when the justices cannot "escape the duty to judge, to choose between competing societal values. And that choice is what politics is all about."[18]

The paradox exists because the federal judges *choose* to examine a case or controversy brought to them under Article III by parties in conflict. Once the justices decide to hear a case they are faced with the fundamental existential dilemma all policy makers face: choosing among alternatives. In the case of judges they have to decide whether lines drawn by other policy makers—laws, statutes, regulations—were done in keeping with the Constitution and the laws of the land. "The words of the Constitution," wrote one justice, "gain meaning and content from the value judgments one puts into them. These value judgments are not those for robots."[19]

THE PARADOX ILLUSTRATED: THE PROBLEM OF RESIDENT ALIENS

The Constitution gives to the political departments—Congress and the executive—certain powers associated with the concept of national sovereignty, i.e., "the idea that there are certain powers which pertain to any sovereign nation and Congress as the incarnation of the national

[17]*West Virginia State Board of Education v. Barnette,* 319 *US* 624 (1943).
[18]Murphy and Pritchett, *Courts,* p. 685.
[19]Quoted in Ball, *The Warren Court,* p. 73.

sovereignty must have certain inherent powers."[20] Congress' power is enormous with respect to territories, Indian affairs, and foreign affairs, and it is "nowhere better illustrated than in cases involving Congress' power over aliens."[21]

Over the years Congress has energetically used its powers to regulate, control, and exclude certain classes of persons from entering America and from acquiring resident status or citizenship. Many of these actions of the Congress have been reviewed by the Supreme Court because the aliens adversely affected by restrictive legislation argued that the Congressional statute violated the due process clause of the Fifth Amendment.

In 1893, in the *Fong Yue Ting v. United States* opinion, the justices of the Supreme Court, employing judicial review, examined an 1892 Act of Congress excluding Chinese from entering America and requiring all those Chinese then living in America to acquire a residence certificate or face deportation. Ting did not have a certificate and was ordered deported. He appealed the order to the Supreme Court. He was turned down by the Court which said: "The right to exclude or expel all aliens or any class of aliens, absolutely or upon certain conditions, is an inherent right of every sovereign and independent nation. . . . The right of a nation to expel or deport foreigners who have not been naturalized is as absolute and unqualified as the right to prohibit and prevent their entrance into this country."[22] The 1892 Act was validated—an example of the Court acting as *norm enforcer*—and became the law by virtue of judicial approval.

In the 1940s and 1950s new restrictive immigration and naturalization statutes were passed by the Congress in response to the Communist menace and, in *Galvan v. Press,* a 1954 opinion, these were upheld by the Supreme Court. Justice Felix Frankfurter wrote the opinion which, reluctantly, upheld the portion of the Internal Security Act of 1950 relating to deportation of aliens who had contact with the Communist party regardless of the length of time spent in America as a resident alien. "Were we writing with a clean slate," noted Frankfurter, then the due process clause of the Fifth Amendment might very well qualify the activities of Congress regulating the entry and deportation of aliens. "But the slate is not clean."[23] Precedents of the Court were followed thereby allowing the congressional statute to stand.

In the late 1960s the Supreme Court again had occasion to examine

---

[20]Harold W. Chase and Craig Ducat, *Constitutional Interpretation* (St. Paul, Minn.: West, 1975), p. 143.
[21]Ibid., p. 142.
[22]*Fong Yue Ting v. United States,* 149 *US* 698 (1893).
[23]*Galvan v. Press,* 347 *US* 522 (1954).

sections of the Internal Security Act of 1950 relating to aliens and again the Court concluded that the Act had not violated the due process clause of the Fifth Amendment. One case involved a requirement that, prior to attaining naturalization, the applicant prove good moral character for the preceding five years. Berenyi was denied citizenship by the district court because he had lied about association with the Communist party while still living in Hungary during the 1950s. The denial was affirmed by the Supreme Court.[24]

In a second case, a Canadian alien was ordered deported because the Internal Security Act excluded "psychopathics" from entering this country. Boutilier had been arrested once for sodomy (charges which were later dropped) and had confessed that he was a homosexual. He challenged the deportation order on the grounds that the phrase was vague and his rights were taken without due process of law. The Supreme Court disagreed. It maintained that the Congress had plenary power to make rules and exclude classes of aliens.[25]

In 1976, two additional cases involving the rights of aliens living in the United States came to the attention of the United States Supreme Court. The first case, *Mathews v. Diaz,* raised the question of whether aliens could receive Medicare benefits. Under the Law, Volume 42 of the United States Codes, Section 1395, residents of the United States who were 65 or over and aliens who have resided in the United States for five or more years or who were admitted for permanent residence were made eligible for Medicare Supplemental Insurance Programs. Diaz, a Cuban alien who did not have five years in America or permanent resident status, challenged the constitutionality of the Congressional statute. He argued that it denied him due process of law. The lower federal courts struck down the section as unconstitutional (*all courts* have the power of judicial review) and the secretary of the Department of Health, Education, and Welfare appealed the judgment to the Supreme Court.

Justice John Stevens wrote the opinion for the Court that overturned the lower federal court and validated the section of the Public Law. Stevens maintained that while aliens do have protections under the due process clause "they are not entitled to enjoy all the advantages of citizenship. . . . The decision to share the nation's bounty was made by Congress." It is reasonable and legitimate—constitutional—for "the Congress to make an alien's eligibility depend on both the character and the duration of his residence." Congress had chosen certain criteria for

[24]*Berenyi v. District Director, Immigration and Naturalization,* 385 US 630 (1967).
[25]*Boutilier v. Immigration and Naturalization Service,* 387 US 118 (1967).

court concluded that there was no "considered evaluation" of the policy and that "national interests cannot provide an acceptable rationalization for such a determination by the Civil Service Commission. By *broadly* denying this class substantial opportunities for employment, the Civil Service Commission deprives its members of an aspect of liberty."[30] As there was no showing (by the president, Congress, or the Commission) of justifiable reasons for excluding an entire class of persons—aliens— the regulation was declared invalid. The Supreme Court, using judicial review, struck down an act of the federal government because it came into conflict with the Constitution.

These alien cases illustrate the essential qualities of the paradox of judicial review in a democratic society. Judicial review—or "judicial scrutiny" as Justice Stevens referred to the activity—occurred in all these cases. Judges in the district courts, courts of appeals, and the Supreme Court, *chose* to hear cases challenging the legality of various congressional statutes (enacted into law by the people's representatives) involving al- iens' rights and responsibilities in such areas as sexual behavior, medical care, loyalty, good moral character proofs, Communist party affiliation, and federal employment.

Lifetime appointed officials were judging the actions of represen- tatives of the people; they were judging the output of the democratic policy-making process in light of their perceived duty to ensure that the fundamental law was faithfully adhered to by the legislators. These nonelected judges were examining the actions of popularly elected of- ficials and appointees of these elected officials to determine whether the actions were legitimate or whether the rights of other classes had been violated in the name of the people. And they were using as a standard of measurement the very instrument used by the policy makers to pass the acts in dispute: the Constitution. In effect, judicial scrutiny in these alien cases focused on whether the Congress or the Commission acting on behalf of the people *had the power within the Constitution* to make the laws that affected aliens. These judicial actions were the manifestation of the perception Madison and others had of judicial review as the overarching "auxiliary precaution" against usurpation of powers by the political agencies.

As will be seen later on, most of the time the federal court will validate the actions of an agency; in the alien cases presented above, the courts in all but one dispute validated the act of the governmental agency. As *norm enforcer* the Court strengthened democratic policy-making processes by resolving the dispute in a way that supported the agency. In effect, the justices of the Court, when acting as norm enforcers, are

[30]Ibid.

eligibility. Diaz, the Court argued, was "inviting us to su
judgment for that of Congress. We decline the invitation."[26]

The second case announced in 1976 was the case of
Mow Sung Wong. The dispute involved Section 338.101(a) of t
States Civil Service Commission Regulations. That section bar
from employment in the federal competitive civil service. W
four other Chinese aliens living in San Francisco brought suil
Hampton, the Chairman of the Civil Service Commission. Th
argued that the Commission policy denied them the due proces:
law guaranteed them in the Fifth Amendment. The federal distric
upheld the regulation but, on appeal to the Ninth Circuit Col
Appeals,[27] the district court action was reversed and the regulatio
validated. The Commission then appealed to the Supreme Court o
United States.[28]

The Supreme Court, in an opinion again written by Justice Steve
overturned the regulation. It employed judicial review to examine
controversy and, having heard arguments on both sides and having re:
the lengthy briefs filed by the parties, reluctantly came to the conclusio
that the Constitutional guarantee of due process had been violated b
the government in this instance. "We do not agree with the federal
government's contention that federal power over aliens is so plenary
that *any* agent of the national government may arbitrarily subject *all*
resident aliens to different substantive rules than those applied to citizens" (italics added).

> We deal with a rule which deprives a discrete class of persons of an interest
> in liberty on a wholesale basis. By reason of the Fifth Amendment, such
> deprivation must be accompanied by Due Process. It follows that some
> judicial scrutiny of the deprivation is mandated by the Constitution.[29]

After examining the reasons given by the Commission for pro-
mulgating the regulation in 1883—diplomatic, economic, loyalty—the

---

[26]*Mathews v. Diaz*, 428 *US* 67 (1976).
[27]The federal judicial system consists, in essence, of 94 Federal District Courts, at
least one district court in each state and eleven Federal Judicial Circuits with their
respective circuit courts including the Court of Appeals that sits in Washington, D.C.
These circuits are regional, covering a number of states and a responsibility of the
Circuit Courts is to hear appeals from the various District Courts within that circuit.
The Ninth Circuit, mentioned above, is the far west circuit, and includes California,
Nevada, Oregon, Washington, Alaska, Hawaii, Idaho, and Montana. At the apex
of this organizational structure is the Supreme Court of the United States. Chapter
four will discuss access to these courts.
[28]*Hampton v. Mow Sung Wong*, 426 *US* 88 (1976).
[29]Ibid.

saying this: We recognize the importance of the dispute and we have heard the arguments both sides have made and, on balance, we believe that the Congress did act in accordance with the powers given to that political branch of government in the Constitution.

In those instances where the Supreme Court comes to the conclusion that the political agency has acted in a manner inconsistent with the grant of power in the Constitution—or has acted in a way that violated one of the prescriptions on that agency in the Constitution— the democratic process is strengthened when the act is declared null and void. The claim inherent in the Court's judgment is that the people's rights have been jeopardized by such political action. On behalf of the people, and consistent with the Constitution, the judiciary is invalidating what a majority of the justices believe to be an illegal and unconstitutional act.

As will be discussed later in the book, the action of the federal courts striking down an action of Congress is not irrevocable. Another court can modify, ignore, or overturn an earlier court action. The Congress can pass new legislation that takes account of Supreme Court objections to the old invalid legislation. For example, the Congress can modify the *Hampton* opinion of the Supreme Court by amending the statute establishing the Commission.

What does happen, however, after invalidation is an examination— by the agency adversely affected by the court judgment—of its actions in light of the constitutional bars and limits referred to by the court. The court is saying this when it overturns an act of Congress: We believe that the Constitution prohibits you from taking this action; we think you ought to reexamine the limits on power the Constitution places on the Congress and if and when you rewrite the legislation take into account these constitutional restraints.

THE NECESSITY OF THE PARADOX

Through application of judicial review, functioning as "auxiliary precaution" in the swirl and cacophany of participatory politics, the federal courts have the capacity to prevent the democratic policy-making process from going too far off track. The paradox discussed in this chapter suggests that this "undemocratic" institution aids and abets democratic majoritarianism by insisting that the political agencies act in keeping within the powers enumerated and implied in the Constitution.

Looking at cases and controversies the federal courts have examined and, in most cases, resolved by deciding one way or another, one is struck with the fact that judicial review had become a necessity in our political system. Judicial scrutiny of actions of the other branches of government, both federal and state, has over and over again brought the policy makers back to constitutional foundations. This scrutiny has had a centripetal effect on centrifugal forces—Congress, president, agency—that attempt to break loose of the moorings of federalism.

This is not to say that the federal judiciary is powerful enough to prevent a political agency from actively seeking to subvert the constitutional pattern. Indeed, judicial reality suggests that the federal courts are very limited in the face of concerted effort to intentionally—totally—redirect the constitutional pattern of checks and balances.

What is important to understand about the paradox and the necessity of the paradox is that the moral force of the federal courts can, along with other forces—auxiliary precautions—prevent the massive abuse of power in our democratic self-government.

The chapters that follow will examine in greater detail two types of consequences of judicial scrutiny: norm enforcement and policy making. In addition, the book will examine the quality of the men selected to sit on the Supreme Court and the politics of the selection process; organization of the federal judiciary and access to the federal courts and the nature of the judicial decision-making process.

The key to understanding what follows, however, lies in understanding the unique position of the federal courts, especially the United States Supreme Court, in our political system. What cases they scrutinize and how they decide to resolve the dilemmas the judges confront are certainly important and will be discussed in these upcoming chapters. But the fact that the federal courts *do* scrutinize, and that they *do* choose to hear the cases and controversies, and that they *do* choose to tell representatives of the people that they have acted inconsistent with the fundamental law—the Constitution—is most critical to an understanding of law, politics, and the federal courts in our democratic system of government.

basic functions
of the federal courts

2

When federal judges review cases they are doing more
than resolving conflicts between interested parties in that particular dispute. Federal judges characteristically perform basic functions in this
conflict-resolution activity: they act as either *norm enforcers* or, especially
at the appellate level, *policy makers*.

The *norm enforcement* function of federal (as well as state) judges
is an essential characteristic of the fair administration of justice in
America. The society's norms, that is, communal values expressed in the
form of legislative statutes that make up the criminal and civil law,
judicial precedents, and the customs and traditions of the community,
ought to be enforced by the federal judges in a fair manner. "Administering justice means that norms are enforced in an even handed way."[1]

When a case comes before the trial judge for equitable resolution,
the norm enforcement characteristic requires the jurist to apply the
existing norms to the instant case before him. He has to fit the law, as
he sees it, to the case before him. This enforcement of community
norms, therefore, does involve flexibility on the part of the trial judge.
It is a flexibility that is inherent in our judicial system: We expect that
a trial judge will fit the legal norms, as best he or she can, to the particular
factual circumstances in the case before the court.

Norm enforcement actions of the federal judges illustrated in this
chapter include: (1) umpiring the federal system; (2) validating national

[1]Herbert Jacob, *Justice in America* (Boston: Little, Brown, 1978), p. 23.

norms that have been challenged in the federal courts; (3) examining and validating federal administrative procedures and practices developed by federal bureaucrats; (4) construing congressional norms when these legislative enactments have been constructed in a vague or nebulous fashion; and (5) deferring to national norms.

The essential difference between norm enforcement and policy making lies in the basic fact that judicial policy making involves conscious intent on the part of the federal judges to reach decisions that have a prospective impact on the society. In this *policy-making* activity, the federal judge creates, consciously and intentionally, societal norms or "guide-posts for future action."[2] Through their interpretation of the Constitution, federal judges: (1) create fundamentally new public policies "with profound social consequences;"[3] (2) veto fundamental societal norms and replace the old socio-legal norm with a new set of these norms with the same profound social consequences; and (3) develop and *administer* new social and political norms, for example, court ordered and created reapportionment plans, school busing formulas devised by the federal judges, administration of prisons and mental institutions by federal judges. These various dimensions of the federal judicial functions will be examined in this chapter.

Although there may once have been a clear-cut distinction between the roles of the lower federal court judges and the duties of the United States Supreme Court justices, in recent decades the differences have blurred. Formerly, the argument was that the lower federal judges followed precedent and, in their legal activities, merely enforced norms that were in force at the time of the litigation. On the other hand, the justices of the Supreme Court were the policy makers, the changers of the future direction of the law in our society.

In recent years, however, as this chapter will suggest, lower federal court judges have played more of a policy-making role in many pressing social and political controversies. Frank M. Johnson, Sr., a U.S. District Court judge, presently sitting on the federal bench in Alabama (Middle District-Alabama), wrote as follows:

> In granting to the federal judiciary the power to decide constitutional cases, the framers fully recognized that the courts would be thrust into the political arena. . . . When squarely confronted with a properly presented constitutional issue, a federal court, as the ultimate interpreter of the Constitution, must act. . . . It is my firm belief, therefore, that the action on the part of federal judges which has generated criticism is in most instances not unwarranted policy making on the part of judges at

[2]Ibid., p. 33.
[3]Archibald Cox, *The Warren Court* (Cambridge, Mass: Harvard University Press, 1968), p. v.

all. Judges do not relish making hard decisions and certainly do not encourage litigation on social or political problems. But, I repeat, the federal judiciary in this country has the paramount and continuing duty to uphold the law. When a case or controversy is properly presented, . . . the courts are bound to take jurisdiction and decide the issues—even though these decisions result in criticism. The basic strength of the federal judiciary has been—and continues to be—its independence from political or social pressures, its ability to rise above the influence of popular clamor. And, finally, I submit that history has shown, with few exceptions, that decisions of the federal judiciary over a period of time have become accepted and revered as monuments memorializing the strength and stability of this nation.[4]

THE NORM ENFORCEMENT FUNCTIONS OF THE FEDERAL COURTS

Umpire of the Federal System

The fundamental norm of our society is the United States Constitution. That document established the nature of the governmental structure, the powers of the agencies of the government, and the basic limitations of the central and state governments. One of the most important functions of the federal judges is the enforcement of that supreme norm of political life.

Federalism is the legal-political term that is translated into a governmental operation with a fragmentation of powers between levels of government as well as a fragmentation or division of powers within a particular governmental system. In our federal system, powers are granted and restricted according to constitutional proscriptions. Certain powers of government are given to the national agencies—war making, conduct of foreign affairs, coining money. Other powers are reserved to the states. And both the national and the state governments are restricted by the Bill of Rights.

One fundamental problem, already suggested, is determining the extent and limits of national power and the extent and limits of state rights. Since the beginning of the federal system, the federal courts have been involved in resolving conflicts between the two separate yet interdependent systems of government, as well as resolving confrontations between two or more states. In this confrontation of sovereignties, the federal courts, acting as referee of the federal system, have used the Constitution as the rule book. Although there have been varied interpretations—for example, about the congressional power to regulate

---

[4]Frank M. Johnson, Sr., "Federal Judges: Policy Makers?," Speech, Mississippi State Prelaw Society, April 3, 1978.

commerce (located in Article I, Section 8)—there is one fairly categorical rule that guides the federal judges: the supremacy clause of Article VI. It reads, in part, as follows:

> This Constitution, and the Laws of the United States which shall be made in Pursuance thereof; and all treaties made, or which shall be made, under the Authority of the United States, shall be the Supreme Law of the Land; and the Judges in every state shall be bound thereby, any thing in the Constitution or Laws of any state to the Contrary not withstanding.

The Constitution, then, is the supreme law (norm). With the help of the federal courts, when a confrontation between the national and state sovereignties arises over an alleged misuse of power, the Constitution controls and determines the outcome. An example of such judicial refereeing would be the conflict between North Carolina, the apple growers in Washington State, and the commerce clause (Article I, Section 8).

Washington State Apples to North Carolina

The state of Washington is the largest producer of apples in America. It is a multimillion dollar business protected and enhanced by legislative action within the state.[5] Since the turn of the century, legislation has existed which has led to a strict, mandatory inspection system. The state Department of Agriculture has established a grading system that is at least the equivalent of the United States Department of Agriculture's standards. The various grades of Washington apples grown in the state are generally superior to the comparable grades developed by the USDA. The state produces 30 percent of all the apples consumed by Americans; nearly 50 percent of all those apples are shipped in closed containers in interstate commerce. This translates to more than 40 million closed containers shipped to the other states in a given year. These containers, as an economy measure, are preprinted with the Washington State grade on the outside of the box. The apples are packed in these containers, which are then placed in cold storage warehouses. There they keep until they need to be shipped; the ultimate destination of these apples is unknown at the time they are placed in the warehouses.

North Carolina receives about 1.25 percent of the apples shipped by the state of Washington, that is, about 500,000 containers. In 1973, in great part due to the lobbying pressures of North Carolina apple growers, the state passed legislation that called for all closed containers shipped or sold in the state of North Carolina to bear no grade "other

---

[5]Succeeding paragraphs are based on data from the Supreme Court opinion, *Hunt v. Washington Apple Advertising Commission,* 53 L Ed 2d No 2 (1977).

than the applicable United States (Department of Labor) grade or standard." All state grades were expressly prohibited. The Washington State Apple Advertising Commission, in 1973, requested the North Carolina legislature to amend the legislation in order to allow states such as Washington to display state grades that have been employed for many years and have been recognized by consumers. In response, the North Carolina legislature, in the name of consumer protection, passed an Amendment to the Act stating that only those containers bearing the "U.S. grade or unclassified not graded, or grade not determined" would be allowed into the state.

The Apple Advertising Commission then brought suit in the United States District Court, Eastern District, North Carolina. The Washington State commission was very concerned about the adverse impact of the North Carolina statute on the apple growers and distributors in the state. It argued that the North Carolina statute interfered with the free flow of interstate commerce because of the impact it had on distribution and packaging of the apples. The suit asked the three-judge district court[6] to issue a declaratory judgment that the statute violated the commerce clause and to then issue a permanent injunction against enforcement of the North Carolina statute.

North Carolina argued in federal court that the state, consistent with the powers inherent in the Tenth Amendment to the United States Constitution, had the right to protect its citizens/consumers against fraud, deception, and confusion by passing the regulation. Although the state had never established a grading or inspection system for its own growers and distributors and therefore the statute would have no effect whatsoever on local producers and distributors (who would use the USDA grade or nothing at all), lawyers were arguing that the state had the right to establish the goal of uniformity for all apples shipped or sold in containers: the USDA grade on the container or nothing at all. Whatever burden was placed on shippers was far outweighed by the local benefits and protection against fraud and deception that might be brought against the citizens of North Carolina.

The district court granted the requested relief asked for by the state of Washington. The judges found that the North Carolina statute discriminated against the Washington State growers and dealers in favor

[6]A three-judge United States District Court, usually consisting of one judge of the Federal Circuit Court of Appeals and two district court judges hears, in accordance with congressional statutes, certain questions of federalism. According to 28 USC Sections 2281 and 2282, any suit for a permanent injunction against enforcement of a state statute on the ground that is unconstitutional must be heard by a three-judge U.S. District Court. See chapter three for a more detailed discussion of this aspect of access to the federal courts.

of the local growers. The former were forced to alter long-established, quality control procedures, at substantial cost (5 to 15 cents to obliterate the writing from a single carton being shipped to North Carolina, or approximately $100,000 per shipment), thereby giving these containers a damaged appearance. Washington State could also repack the apples that had been stored in the warehouses, thereby running the risk of damaging the merchandise in the transhandling from marked to un-marked boxes, or simply lose the business (which, in 1974, netted the producers an excess of $2 million in sales in North Carolina). The statute, continued the district court opinion, not only discriminated against Washington State growers but placed an undue burden on the free flow of commerce even if it had been a neutral statute (affecting local and interstate producers and distributors in the same way).

The state of North Carolina then appealed this adverse judgment directly to the United States Supreme Court. The justices of the Supreme Court reviewed the history of the case and the meaning of the commerce clause. The essential conflict was between the state's use of the police powers inherent in the Tenth Amendment and the passive restraint of the commerce clause. The Court noted that while the commerce clause acts as a limitation upon state power even without congressional legis-lation, and while there is a residuum of state powers to make laws that protect its citizens that somehow affect commerce, the overriding con-sideration for the district court judges and the justices of the Supreme Court was this: the commerce clause's requirement of a "national com-mon market" for goods and products shipped between states. This was the paramount national interest; it clashed with the local North Caro-linian interest. And it was for the federal courts to resolve this dilemma of federalism.

The United States Supreme Court was of the unanimous opinion that the North Carolina statute unconstitutionally discriminated against the interstate shipments of Washington State apples. The North Car-olina statute raised the cost of doing business for outsiders who had established standards and grades, while at the same time the legislation shielded the local growers from the competition. The statute, the only one of its kind in America, also stripped the Washington apple industry of any advantages it had earned for itself through its over 60-year-old program of inspection and grading. Finally, the downgrading offered the local apple industry the protection against competing out of state products that the commerce clause was designed to prohibit.

Furthermore, with respect to consumers in the state of North Car-olina, the justices noted that legislation focused on the closed containers that only wholesalers and distributers in the state ever get to see. Consumers never come into contact with these boxes and the markings on them. With respect to the packaging of apples, the North Carolina wholesalers are the most knowledgeable people in the entire state and, reasoned the Supreme Court, these brokers and wholesalers did not need protection against fraud and deception.

Given these facts and given the constitutional-legal perceptions of the meaning of the commerce clause, the Supreme Court concluded that North Carolina had failed to meet the burden of justifying the discriminatory legislation. Chief Justice Warren Burger, writing for the Court, affirmed the judgment of the district court. In that judicial affirmation, we see the "umpire" function of the Supreme Court and the other federal courts.

All these federal judges were asked to resolve the conflict between constitutional intent and a particular state action. As umpires of the system they must determine the rules and then apply them in a fair, reasonable manner. Determining the rules means developing a perception of the meaning of the basic characteristics of the federal system: separation of powers, checks and balances, judicial deference to legitimate legislative and executive activities, and the meaning of basic phrases in the Constitution that relate to the federal system.

In the Washington State apples case, the commerce clause's parameters molded and shaped federal relationships between the central government and the states. Likewise, the tax power and general welfare clauses in Article I, Section 8 need constant clarification by the courts due to the fact that both the central and the state governments share these general governmental powers. It has fallen upon the federal courts to resolve these controversies. The goal of the federal judges is to deal with these conflicts in a rational manner. In effect, they determine, as in the apples case presented above, what falls within the power of the central government and what falls to the state to regulate, control, and prohibit.

Given the nature of the federal system, a most important responsibility of the federal courts is umpiring the process. The federal system would not fall apart if the Supreme Court could not review acts of Congress; it would be in grave danger if the Court were prohibited from reviewing and declaring unconstitutional those actions of the states that, in the estimate of the federal judges, go beyond the parameters of power granted to the state or that usurp powers that properly belong to the national government.[7]

[7]See Justice O.W. Holmes' Harvard Law School Association on Law and Courts address, February 15, 1913. Quoted in Charles Warren, *The Supreme Court in United States History*, Vol. 1 (Boston: Little, Brown, 1922), p. 17.

Validator of National Legislation

In the Washington apples case discussed above, the federal courts acted in the absence of federal legislation to overturn a state law that, by itself, disturbed the smooth flow of interstate commerce. There are, of course, many conflicts in our history where courts have had to resolve controversies between the national legislature and those states or citizens of the United States who believed that the national legislation passed by the Congress is unconstitutional. It may very well involve an act of Congress based on the commerce clause in which the courts, by hearing the issue, referee the federal system;[8] however, the added factor is that the federal courts, in so acting, may validate the federal law over the objections and legal arguments made by those that have challenged the national legislation. One such example of judicial validation of national legislation would be the 1965 Voting Rights Act case, *South Carolina v. Katzenbach.*

The National Response to Rioting in Selma, Alabama

The 1965 Voting Rights Act was a continuation, perhaps a culmination, of a policy developed by the national government with respect to racial discrimination in America. Given the terrible history of racial repression and based on Section 2 of the Fifteenth Amendment[9] which states that the Congress "shall have the power to enforce this Amendment by appropriate legislation," in 1965 the Congress passed the first substantive piece of voting rights legislation since the era of Reconstruction almost 90 years earlier.[10]

The Act, as passed by Congress, prohibited the use of literacy tests and other devices used to prevent registration in those states where less than 50 percent of the voting age population voted in the 1964 presidential election. In addition, examiners and observers (from the Department of Justice and the United States Civil Service Commission respectively) were sent to these states to ensure that black citizens would be registered and allowed to vote. (The southern states originally af-

---

[8]See for example *Perez v. United States,* 402 US 146 (1971), or *United States* v *Darby,* 312 US 100 (1941).

[9]The Fifteenth Amendment prohibits the states from denying or abridging on account of race, color, or previous condition of servitude, the voting rights of United States citizens. (The Fourteenth Amendment had conferred citizenship on blacks after the Civil War.)

[10]See Howard Ball, Dale Krane, and Thomas P. Lauth, Jr., "Judicial Impact on the Enforcement of Voting Rights Policy By Attorneys In the Department of Justice," Paper presented at the 1977 Annual Meeting of the Southern Political Science Association, New Orleans, Louisiana.

fected by the legislation were: Alabama, Georgia, Louisiana, Mississippi, South Carolina, Virginia, and portions of North Carolina.) Finally, Section 5 of the Voting Rights Act was enacted to "guard against ingenious actions by those bent on preventing negroes from voting."[11]

Section 5 was included in the 1965 Voting Rights Act because of the "acknowledged and anticipated inability of the Justice Department— given limited resources—to investigate independently all changes with respect to voting enacted by states and subdivisions covered by the act."[12] The section placed a burden on covered jurisdictions to submit all voting changes for prior approval by either the Department of Justice or the United States District Court in the District of Columbia. If Section 4 voided all old attempts to prevent the black citizen from registering and voting, Section 5 of the 1965 Act prevented the states from introducing any new processes, devices, or changes that would dilute or abridge the voting rights of the black citizen.

South Carolina, one of the seven deep south states covered under the automatic triggering mechanism within the Act, immediately proceeded to challenge the constitutionality of the 1965 Voting Rights Act. The basic argument of the state's legal counsel was that the Congress exceeded its powers within the Constitution "and encroached on an area reserved to the states."[13] Because the state had elections scheduled for June of 1966, it filed directly to the Supreme Court under the Court's original jurisdiction guidelines spelled out in the Constitution. Supported in its suit by the states of Alabama, Georgia, Louisiana, Mississippi, and Virginia, South Carolina contended that the Congress had reached out to invade areas of responsibility (voting requirements) that had traditionally been the responsibility of the state.

The automatic triggering device, their briefs argued, presumed discrimination and therefore denied the covered jurisdictions' due process and the equal protection of the laws. Guilt was assumed without any prior hearing and therefore the 1965 Voting Rights Act was, in effect, a bill of attainder. (A bill of attainder is a legislative act that applies to identifiable individuals or easily identifiable members of a group in such a way as to inflict punishment on them without a judicial trial. Article I, Section 9 prohibits the Congress from passing such legislation.) Also, the fact that the Act gave the Department of Justice the power to send federal registrars and Civil Service Commission personnel as observers denied "due process" to the states and interfered with normal judicial functions.

[11]*Allen v. Board of Education,* 393 *US* 544 (1968).
[12]*Perkins v. Matthews,* 400 *US* 379 (1971), p. 391.
[13]*South Carolina v. Katzenbach,* 383 *US* 301 (1966).

The Attorney General of the United States, supported by *amicus curiae* briefs[14] from 21 states, argued that Congress had acted legitimately; that the Fifteenth Amendment gave the national legislature the power to enforce the right to vote by "appropriate legislation"; and that the failure of the 1957, 1960, and 1964 civil rights acts to end voting discrimination in the south unalteringly led the Congress to develop more direct strategies with which to deal with racial discrimination. The procedural devices—the federal examiners and observers, and the reporting of all voting changes to the Department of Justice or the United States District Court in the District of Columbia—were "appropriate legislation" consistent with the Fifteenth Amendment.

The Supreme Court of the United States heard the case on the merits. It is unusual for the Court to hear cases under original jurisdiction because the justices like to have the case develop a record in lower court proceedings. Generally original jurisdiction appeals can also be brought into the federal district courts for argument and judgment; that is the normal pattern. This case was far from ordinary, however, and the Court invoked its original jurisdiction in order to hear the arguments without delay.

Chief Justice Earl Warren handed down the decision for a nearly unanimous Supreme Court (Justice Black dissented with respect to the constitutionality of Section 5 of the 1965 Voting Rights Act). The basic question for the federal justices was this: Has the Congress exercised its powers under the Fifteenth Amendment in an appropriate manner with relation to the states? In answering this question, the Court discussed a fundamental principle of government in the federal system: "As against the reserved powers of the states, the Congress may use any rational means to effectuate the constitutional prohibition of racial discrimination in voting." Quoting from Chief Justice John Marshall's *McCulloch v. Maryland* opinion, 1819, Warren pointed out that so long as "the end is legitimate . . . any means appropriate and adapted to that end are constitutional."

Congress was led to the necessity of "inventive" and direct voting rights legislation because of the (1) invidious evil of voting discrimination in the south due to the "unremitting and ingenious defiance of the Constitution" by the southern states, and because (2) earlier efforts by Congress in 1957, 1960, and 1964 did not work to rid the society of the evils of racial discrimination in voting. Whatever legislation was adapted to carry out the object the Fifteenth Amendment had in view (voting

[14]*Amicus curiae* is a "friend of the court" brief. With the permission of the court, an interested party (not part of the lawsuit) can file a legal brief to aid the judges in gaining information necessary in making a correct judgment in the proceedings before the court.

equity for all citizens), if not specifically prohibited by the Constitution itself, was within the domain of congressional power. The remedial legislation of the Congress, passed to "banish the blight of racial discrimination" in America, was upheld by the Supreme Court justices.

The South Carolina argument, that the Congress could do no more than forbid, in general terms, the states to violate the Fifteenth Amendment was rejected out of hand by the Court. The congressional power, the judges said, is complete in itself and may be exercised to its limit, and the only limitation upon the congressional exercise of power is that written into the Constitution itself. The remedies developed by the Congress (i.e., ending of literacy test requirements, sending of federal examiners and observers, and the preclearance of all new voting changes) are reasonable and appropriate ones. They are valid means for carrying out the commands of the Fifteenth Amendment.

In this case the federal judges acted to validate a piece of national legislation challenged by the states as unconstitutional. While it was acting as an umpire or referee, the federal Court, was, as officials do all the time, benefitting one side and depriving the other side in the dispute. In so acting, the federal judges, as referees, often validate the statutory enactment of the Congress. As we will see in another segment, occasionally the judges in the federal courts have to interpret or construe the meaning of the statutory language when they validate the legislation. In this example, there was no need to interpret or construe the language. The statute, the 1965 Voting Rights Act, was clear and unequivocal with respect to the issue of racial discrimination: it had to end as quickly as possible.

Examiner of Administrative Procedures and Practices Developed by Bureaucrats in Government

We live in the "bureaucratic era."[15] In the course of our political development since the 1787 constitutional convention, American legislators and executives have come to rely very heavily on the organized bureaucracy to formulate, activate, and implement public policy passed by the legislature and signed into law by the executive. The bureaucracy is a natural phenomenon in modern society that provides continuity of program enforcement regardless of the political winds that blow in Washington, D.C. and elsewhere. As the government developed more plans and programs of social engineering for the society, agencies within

---

[15]Guy Benveniste, *Bureaucracy* (San Francisco: Boyd and Fraser, 1977), p. xi.

the executive department and independent of it were developed to do the work of implementing these programs.

Executive departments of the national government, e.g., the State, Defense, Treasury, Interior, Agriculture, Justice, Health, Education and Welfare, Housing and Urban Development, etc., have been created since the presidency of George Washington. Regulatory agencies, independent of the president, have been in existence since the 1880s and, since the 1930s, there has come into being the Executive Office of the President. Today there are hundreds of federal agencies within these three areas with over 2.3 million employees working in these many agencies all across America.[16]

A primary responsibility of the various agencies of the national government is to implement efficiently and effectively the legislation passed by the Congress. Doing so means that these bureaucracies must develop regulations to be followed by those persons in society affected by that agency. For example, the Department of Labor will develop guidelines and regulations, consistent (the bureaucrat would argue) with congressional instructions couched in general language of the statute, with respect to employee-employer relations. With the development of such regulations and guidelines comes the enforcement of these procedures and, finally, appeals from adverse judgments by the agency to the federal courts. The Congress has given the federal courts of appeal initial responsibility for hearing appeals from executive agencies and independent regulatory agencies.

The federal courts hear hundreds of appeals from rulings by administrative agencies in a given year. To a large extent these federal judges affirm the decisions of these federal agencies;[17] to that extent the federal judges validate these agency decisions much in the same manner they validate legislative statutes or executive orders.

Norm enforcement of agency decisions does not take place all the time however. For example, a classic case in which a federal court revoked such an agency decision would be the WLBT case involving a television station in Jackson, Mississippi. The case was *United Church of Christ, Aaron Henry, Robert L. T. Smith and United Church of Christ at Tougaloo v. Federal Communications Commission,* 359 F2d 994 (1966). The FCC had mildly rebuked but had not revoked the license of the television station even though the record was replete with facts pointing to the racial bias of the station. The Federal Court of Appeals directed the FCC to review the facts and, after the FCC still did not deal with the

[16]See Hugh Heclo, *A Government of Strangers* (Washington, D.C.: Brookings Institute, 1977).
[17]See Leonard Weiss and Allyn Strickland, *Regulation: A Case Approach* (New York: McGraw-Hill, 1976).

matter, the federal judge, Warren E. Burger "for the first time in history . . . ordered a license to be terminated." The FCC followed the instructions of the Court.[18]

An example of judicial response to federal agency activity would be the way in which the Supreme Court responded to the Department of Justice's Civil Rights Division promulgation of the regulations that would implement the 1965 Voting Rights Act.

The Justice Department's Effort to Develop Voting Change Preclearance Guidelines

We have already discussed the validation of the 1965 Voting Rights Act by the Supreme Court in *South Carolina v. Katzenbach*. This segment will illustrate how the United States Supreme Court (1) encouraged a reluctant bureaucracy, the Civil Rights Division of the United States Department of Justice, to formulate a series of regulations so that the jurisdictions covered by the voting legislation could preclear all new voting changes with the Department of Justice (in accordance with Section 5 of the Voting Rights Act); and (2) examined some of these regulations and decisions based on the guidelines and validated both the regulations themselves as well as the decisions based upon them reached by the lawyers in the voting section of the Justice Department's Civil Rights Division.[19]

If the 1966 case involving South Carolina validated Section 5 of the Voting Rights Act, then the 1969 Supreme Court option of *Allen v. State Board of Elections* afforded the federal judges the opportunity to define the *scope* of Section 5 (in the absence of Department of Justice regulations). The Supreme Court, in a case that combined Virginia and Mississippi litigation involving voting procedures, concluded that "the 1965 Voting Rights Act was aimed to the subtle, as well as the obvious, state regulations which have the effect of denying citizens their right to vote because of their race." The federal judges maintained that the preclearance requirement should be liberally construed to protect the voting rights of blacks in the covered states and counties.

The Court addressed the issue of preclearance submission procedures. Both states had argued that since no formal preclearance submission procedures were required by the Department of Justice (the regulations were not promulgated by the Justice Department until September 1971), their Section 5 obligations were fulfilled whenever the United States Attorney General became aware of voting changes made

[18]Fred Friendly, *The Good Guys, The Bad Guys, and the First Amendment* (New York: Vintage Books, 1977), pp. 100–101.
[19]Ball et al., "Judicial Impact," p. 17.

by the covered jurisdictions. After taking notice of the absence of formal procedures, the Court rejected the contention of the states by stating that Section 5 of the Voting Rights Act of 1965 "required that the state in some unambiguous and recordable manner submit any legislation or regulation . . . directly to the Attorney General with a request for his consideration."

The impact of this judicial decision on the Department of Justice was great. *Allen v. State Board of Elections,* along with *Perkins v. Matthews,* a 1971 opinion, outlined at least seven basic types of voting changes that were subject to Section 5 preclearance by federal judges or bureaucrats: (1) redistricting, (2) annexations, (3) polling places, (4) precinct changes, (5) reregistrations, (6) incorporations, and (7) changes in election laws such as filing fees, at large elections to replace single-member district elections, etc. Within days after the *Allen* opinion, according to a bureaucrat in the U.S. Department of Justice at that time, work got underway by staff attorneys in the Civil Rights Division's Voting Section to develop more formal guidelines for the enforcement of Section 5. The federal judges had prodded bureaucrats into action.[20]

The regulations that quickly followed were developed by the Department of Justice, with considerable urging by southern leaders in Congress and the Nixon administration.[21] They were then circulated to these officials and to civil rights groups for their comments and suggestions. The regulations, after much consultation and deliberation, were released in September 1971. At that point, the federal judges had to determine, in cases and controversies brought into the courts, whether the regulations were valid. Such judicial examination of agency regulations and actions based on these written guidelines is another basic function of the federal courts in America.

After the regulations were developed, the implementers of the guidelines, the attorneys in the voting section of the Civil Rights Division in the Department of Justice, faced two analytically distinct but operationally inseparable problems of implementation. The first issue concerned the mechanics of implementing the preclearance procedures; the second involved the substantive issue of the meaning of discriminatory purpose and effect. As written, the guidelines stated (Section 51.4) that a covered jurisdiction that sought to enact a voting change "must first obtain either a judicial or an executive determination that denial or abridgment of the right to vote on account of race or color is not the purpose and will not be the effect of the change." The Supreme Court has gotten involved with the first question, but the involvement

[20]Ibid., p. 19.
[21]Ibid.

has been minimal and has not affected bureaucratic behavior. Instead, it has validated those procedures developed and carried out by the Department of Justice.[22] The Court has also heard appeals from states who argued that the objections filed by the Department of Justice against voting changes they had prepared were unconstitutional.

The fundamental substantive problem confronted by the voting section staff attorney bureaucrat was this: Under what circumstances and given what characteristics will a voting change proposed by a state covered by the Voting Rights Act be objected to by the Department of Justice? The bureaucrat in the federal agency came up with a basic set of pragmatic guidelines when examining proposed voting changes submitted to the Department of Justice. Essentially a voting change will fail to gain preclearance from the agency if (1) the purpose of the change is obviously discriminatory, (2) the effect is obviously discriminatory, or (3) there is a retrogression of black voting strength after the voting change. Using these unwritten parameters, the federal agency has, through 1978, precleared over 95 percent of all the submissions received by the Department of Justice. United States Supreme Court opinions, especially *Richmond v. United States,* have legitimized the perceptions of the meaning of discriminatory purpose and effect held by the agency bureaucrats in the Department of Justice.

Richmond v. United States was heard and decided in the 1975 term of the U.S. Supreme Court. It involved an annexation of land adjacent to Richmond, Virginia, that would have had the effect of decreasing the black population in the enlarged city from 52 percent to 42 percent. In a series of discussions, informal bargaining and negotiations, the city officials and the Department of Justice arrived at an arrangement by which the annexation would not be objected to by the department if the city went to ward elections.[23] The city then modified its plan to show a nine-ward enlarged city in which four were predominantly white, four were predominantly black, and one was 60 percent white and 40 percent black. However, in a separate suit brought by a black resident of Richmond, Virginia, the United States District Court in the District of Columbia ruled that the plan diluted the voting strength of the black population and therefore had the purpose and effect of denying black voters their Fifteenth Amendment rights. On appeal to the Supreme Court, the question raised by Virginia (and [implicitly] by a very interested Department of Justice) was this: did the annexation have either the purpose or effect of denying or abridging the right to vote?

Associate Justice Byron White for the Supreme Court majority of

[22]Ibid.
[23]Ibid., p. 20–21.

five (three dissented and one justice, Lewis Powell of Virginia, did not participate) answered the question. For Justice White the controlling factor in the case was whether or not the latest annexation could be sustained on sound "objectively verifiable legitimate" economic or administrative grounds and, a corollary factor, whether the ward system as developed by the city in consultation with the Department of Justice fairly reflected the strength of the black community after the annexation. If the annexation was for a legitimate, verifiable purpose and if it did reflect the true strength of the black community afterwards, then the annexation did not, in purpose or effect, dilute black voting strength.

So long as black voting power in the new city is not "undervalued, the Negros will not be underrepresented on the council," then the Court "cannot hold that the effect of the annexation is to deny or abridge the right to vote." Congress did not intend to have blacks assigned a proportion of the decision-making procedures regardless of legitimate annexations or incorporations. If there is no undervaluation of black voting strength in the new city now or in the future, then the annexation could stand. The plan developed through bargaining and negotiation between the city and the Department of Justice was "in our view" a plan that "did not undervalue the black strength in the community after annexation; and we hold that the annexation in this contest does not have the effect of denying or abridging the right to vote within the meaning of Section 5."

The Supreme Court majority, in effect, affirmed the practice that had been developed by the bureaucrats in the Justice Department's Civil Rights Division. The parameters established by the voting section attorneys and enforced by that agency during the Richmond, Virginia, discussions and development of the voting plan were legitimized by the United States Supreme Court in *Richmond v. United States*. Although there are critics of the Justice Department's working guidelines for determining the meaning of discriminatory purpose and effect, and although there were dissenting voices on the Supreme Court, the outcome is that federal judges legitimized (controversial) norms of an executive agency.

Construer or Interpreter of Congressional Legislation

Another common function of federal judges is the interpretation of legislative statutes that have been written in such a general way as to call for classification by these jurists when cases and controversies come to the federal bar. For various reasons (necessary political compromise being a major one)[24] the national legislators very frequently paint legislation in broad strokes. For example, when the Congress passed the White Slave Traffic Act (referred to as the Mann Act) in 1910, which forbade the transportation of women in interstate commerce for the purpose of prostitution, it used the following language:

> prostitution, *debauchery,* or . . . *any other immoral purpose.* Anyone inducing, enticing, or compelling such woman or girl to become a prostitute, or to give herself up to debauchery, or to engage in any other immoral practice . . . shall be deemed guilty of a felony.

Does that statute mean that a prostitute and her pimp cannot travel in interstate commerce at all? Even if they are visiting Yellowstone National Park?[25] Federal courts have been responsible for giving meaning to general terms such as those found in the Mann Act.

Most of the time these federal judges validate the national legislation that has been challenged in the federal courts. The courts deal with these difficult questions by: (1) referring to the legislative text and to textual exegesis, (2) going to the congressional debates, (3) using committee reports and other information to define the meaning of the general words (including the use of expert grammarians from time to time).[26] Based on such data as can be collected and developed by the judges and by opposing counsel, the courts make their decision regarding the meaning and intent of the national legislation. The judges do so with the view toward validating national legislation unless the statute is patently unconstitutional.[27] If the interpretation of the statute by the federal bench is incorrect, Congress always has the clear option of rebuking the judiciary and clarifying the statute through the new legislation.

The Judicial Dilemma Surrounding the Omnibus Crime Control Act of 1968

The first major national legislation in the area of crime control was the Omnibus Crime Control and Safe Streets Act of 1968. Introduced by President Lyndon Johnson and a reluctant Attorney General Ramsey Clark,[28] it was a catch-all piece of legislation, with portions in it that

[24]See Arthur S. Miller, "Statutory Language and the Purposive Use of Ambiguity," *Virginia Law Review,* vol. 42, no. 2 (1956).
[25]*Mortensen v. United States,* 322 *US* 369 (1944).
[26]Interview with Associate Justice Potter Stewart, United States Supreme Court, March 2, 1976.
[27]Ibid.
[28]See Richard Harris, *The Fear of Crime* (New York: Praeger & Co., 1969).

benefitted the many legislators who had pet grievances and concerns about crime and lawlessness and were able to introduce into the omnibus bill these many (overlapping) and constitutionally suspect prohibitions.[29] Many of these suggestions turned into law without any committee discussion, much less deliberate debate on the floor of the House or Senate. The 1968 bill was created in response to violence and political pressure on the Democratic administration.[30] The important thing for politicians, evidently, was just getting the legislation passed. So ably understated by the United States government in the case that will be discussed below, the Act was "not a model of logic or clarity."

One section, Title VII of the Act, gave federal courts particular difficulty. Section 1202 (a) (1) of the Title read as follows:

> Any person who has been convicted by a Court of the United States or of a state or any political subdivision thereof of a felony . . . *and who receives, possesses, or transports in commerce or affecting commerce* . . . any firearm shall be fined not more than $10,000 or imprisoned for not more than two years, or both. (italics added)

In the two years between passage of the legislation and judicial review of the statute by the Supreme Court of the United States, 6 of the 11 United States Courts of Appeals had examined the meaning of that section in addition to federal district courts in the states of Indiana and Tennessee. These lower federal courts had come up with two different interpretations of the statutory language.[31]

One definition of the statute, the argument of all the federal prosecutors in the many federal courts, went as follows: There need be no connection drawn between receipt and possession of a firearm and "commerce or affecting commerce." The statute, however, did say that a connection must be developed at the trial between transporting and "commerce or affecting commerce." In short, the governmental interpretation of the Title was a very broad one: Anyone who had a record of felonious conviction could not receive or possess any firearm. The congressional prohibition was broad and prohibited any person with a prior felony conviction in any jurisdiction in America from possessing or receiving a handgun.

The second definition of the statute, presented by counsel for those persons arrested and charged with violating Title VII, was that the Section did not cover receipt or possession of firearms *not shown* to have been in "commerce or affecting commerce." This was a narrow view of that

---

[29]Ibid.
[30]Theodore H. White, *The Making of the President, 1968* (New York: Doubleday, 1969).
[31]The following discussion is based on *United States v. Bass,* 404 *US* 336 (1971).

Section of the crime control legislation, a view that emphasized that a connection must be made between not only transportation but also receipt and possession and "commerce or affecting commerce." Counsel (and judges) also argued that if the statute was as broad as the government argued in court, then it should be struck down as a vague and unconstitutional piece of legislation.

These views had been presented to the federal judges in a number of cases heard across the country between 1969 and 1971. Five of the courts of appeals had opted for the broad definition of the Section in the crime control legislation. One federal court of appeals and a number of United States district courts had, in cases argued before the federal judges, accepted the narrow view of the statute. And so it was that the United States Supreme Court, in the 1971 case of *United States v. Bass*, attempted to clear away the misunderstanding in the lower federal courts and to do so by trying to decipher the meaning of the Section at issue.

Associate Justice Thurgood Marshall wrote the opinion for the Supreme Court majority. First, the Court noted the ambiguity in the statute. The Court pointed out that ambiguity existed because of the haste with which the Congress adopted this particular Section of the crime control legislation. Looking at the Title itself and based upon grammatical experts as well as on "the natural construction of the language," the majority opinion suggested that the clause "in commerce or affecting commerce" probably (though not with any degree of certainty) qualifies all three antecedents in the list (receipt, possession, and transportation). The "language of the statute did seem to provide support for" the narrow interpretation of the Section of the crime control statute. However, Marshall warned, the argument is certainly "neither overwhelming nor decisive."

"We cannot pretend," continued Justice Marshall, "that all statutes are model statutes." This Section was added at the last moment, with "little discussion, no hearings, and no report." The legislative history of the act "hardly speaks with that clarity of purpose which Congress supposedly furnishes courts in order to enable them to enforce its true will." The courts were left with an ambiguous statute. Given these circumstances, Justice Marshall pointed to "two wise principles" federal courts have long followed. Followed in this case, the Supreme Court adoption of the narrower interpretation of Section 1202 (a) (1) took place.

The first principle of judicial deference to legislative actions (discussed further in the next segment of the chapter) is that federal courts should resolve ambiguity in criminal statutes "in favor of lenity." Where there are doubts due to ambiguity in criminal statutes, these "doubts are resolved in favor of the defendant. . . . Here we conclude that Congress has not plainly and unmistakenly made it a federal crime for a convicted felon simply to possess a gun absent some demonstrated nexus with interstate commerce."

The second general principle referred to by the Court majority was that whenever there was legislative statutory ambiguity, the congressional legislation "will not be deemed to have significantly changed the federal-state balance." To accept the broad governmental definition of the statute "renders traditional local criminal conduct a matter for federal enforcement and would also involve a substantial extension of federal police resources." Having rejected the broad, governmental position, the Supreme Court affirmed the judgment of the court of appeals in the *Bass* case. Bass had been arrested in New York and convicted of possession of firearms. (The federal prosecutors, given their interpretation of Section 1202 (a) (1) did not bother showing any nexus or connection with "commerce or affecting commerce." The government attorneys did not even attempt to show that the firearm had previously traveled in interstate commerce, a showing that would have met the narrow interpretation given the Section by the Supreme Court majority.)

Here then is an example of legislative ambiguity variously defined by federal judges in cases before them. Due to the confusion and conflict in the lower federal courts, the Supreme Court heard the case. (This is a basic reason for the United States Supreme Court deciding to hear a case on the merits and will be discussed in another chapter.) In hearing the case, the federal court employed judicial review. Carefully and tactfully the Court attempted to interpret the statute so as not to declare it unconstitutional.

The bottom line in such an activity, as one of the dissenting justices in the *Bass* case noted, is that the Court might very well engage in "judicial transfiguration" of congressional intent. However, if that is the case and if the Court has misread the beclouded intentions of the congressional majorities, then the Congress can eradicate the judicial error by responding with clearly worded legislation. With respect to Section 1201 (a) (1), the Congress has not modified the *Bass* majority's interpretation. We can assume one of two things from this legislative inaction: (1) Congress did not mind what the Court majority did to the Section, or (2) Congress did mind but has not quite gotten around to revising that particular ambiguous Section 1202 (a) (1).

Judicial Deference As Norm Enforcement

Another example of the norm enforcement judicial function would be judicial deference to the desires and values of the political branches of government: the legislative and the executive. Another chapter in the book will discuss the "political questions" doctrine and the concept of judicial parsimony. For now, it is important to understand that when a court does act in a parsimonious manner, it is deferring to the wishes of the other branches of government. In so acting, federal courts are enforcing the existing societal norms as defined by national legislators and executives (or, in the case below, as defined by federal judges with the approval of the national legislature for over fifty years).

Baseball and the Sherman Antitrust Act

The following case study involves federal antitrust legislation aimed at breaking down monopolies in restraint of trade, and whether or not organized sports in America (all or just one) are exempt from such regulations. It is a highly unusual case illustration in that the initial agency that answered this question was the United States Supreme Court rather than the Congress of the United States! However, the Congress has, through its silence on the constitutional question for over a half a century, adopted the judicial understanding of the federal legislation even though on numerous occasions the Supreme Court has encouraged the Congress to change the substantive law on the issue by passing appropriate legislation. This positive inaction of the Congress has been interpreted by the Supreme Court as congressional policy and, even though the recent development of the law has been illogical, the justices of the Court have refused to overturn early Court opinions out of deference to this legislative silence!

The Sherman Antitrust Act, passed in 1890, was one of the first legislative attempts to curb excessive conspiratorial action that had the effect of restraining or monopolizing interstate commerce. The Act provided in part (15 USC Section 1) that:

> Every contract, combination in the form of trust or otherwise, or conspiracy, in restraint of trade or commerce among the several states . . . is declared to be illegal.

Section Two of the Act (15 USC Section 2) provided that:

> every person who shall monopolize, or attempt to monopolize, or combine or conspire with any other person or persons, to monopolize any part of the trade or commerce among the several states . . . shall be deemed guilty of a misdemeanor.

In 1922 the United States Supreme Court, in the case of *Federal Baseball Club v. National League*,[32] a unanimous decision, argued that the Sherman Antitrust Act did not apply to organized baseball. The Federal

[32]*Federal Baseball Club v. National League*, 259 US 200 (1922).

League was in competition for customers with the National League. It claimed that the latter organization had systematically destroyed the Federal League by buying up some of the clubs and by coercing all the others except the plaintiff to leave the Federal League. The justices of the Court pointed out that the character of the business of baseball was sports competition which had "attained the great popularity they have achieved" by arranging competitions between clubs from different cities and states.

The Court argued that transporting the teams is "a mere incident" to the playing of the game. Furthermore, the Court contended that "the competition could not be called trade or commerce in the commonly accepted use of those words."

> That which in its consummation is not commerce does not become commerce among the states because the transportation that we have mentioned takes place.[33]

With this decision, the Supreme Court carved out for baseball a very broad exemption from the federal antitrust statutes—unless the Congress chose to override the judicial pronouncement of 1922.[34] This the Congress did not choose to do. By 1953, the Court was able to say that

> Congress has had the ruling under consideration but has not seen fit to bring such business under these laws by legislation having prospective effect. . . . We think that if there are evils in this field which now warrant application to it of the antitrust laws it should be by legislation.[35]

In 1972, 50 years after the *Federal Baseball* decision of the Court, the federal courts once again confronted the antitrust statutes and organized baseball. In October 1969, center fielder Curt Flood of the St. Louis Cardinals was traded, without his consent or knowledge, to the Philadelphia Phillies. After failing to work out a negotiated compromise with the baseball commissioner, Bowie Kuhn, Flood hired former Supreme Court Justice Arthur Goldberg to bring suit in federal court challenging baseball's "reserve clause" as being violative of the Sherman Antitrust Act. Goldberg was to argue that the reserve clause, which confines a player to a particular ball club and which allows the club to reassign the player's contract to another club with the player's permission, was a monopolistic practice in violation of Sections 1 and 2 of the Sher-

---

[33]Ibid.
[34]See John R. Allison, "Professional Sports and the Antitrust Laws: Status of the Reserve System," *Baylor Law Review* vol. 25, no. 1 (Winter 1973), p. 1.
[35]*Toolson v. New York Yankees*, 346 *US* 356 (1953).

man Act. The lower federal courts dismissed the suit and Flood appealed to the Supreme Court.[36]

In Flood's case,[37] the Supreme Court deferred to the Congress of the United States. Justice Harry Blackmun wrote the opinion for the court. While admitting the exceptional and anomalous situation surrounding baseball's exemption, calling it "unrealistic, inconsistent, illogical," Blackmun then stated that the "aberration is an established one . . . with us now for half a century." Congress has never acted to change or modify the 1922 decision of the Court and the Court "has concluded that Congress as yet has had no intention to subject baseball's reserve system to the reach of the antitrust statutes. This, obviously, has been deemed to be something other than mere congressional silence and passivity."

The Court was simply unwilling to do by judicial action "when Congress by its positive inaction has allowed these decisions to stand for so long and, far beyond mere inference and implication, has clearly evinced a desire not to disapprove them legislatively." Upholding the judgment of the lower federal courts (based on the prior decisions of the federal courts), Blackmun concluded by stating that

> if there is any inconsistency or illogic in all this, it is an inconsistency and illogic of long standing that is to be remedied by the Congress and not by this Court.

Here is the classic case of judicial deference to the political branches of the government. In the absence of any action by the Congress, the Court was unwilling to overturn a prior judicial decision that reflected a view of commerce that was legally buried in the 1941 case of *United States v. Darby Lumber Company*.[38] The majority admitted that illogical and unreasonable features were present in the case but it was unwilling to act in the absence of congressional action. The norm enforcement role is clear: Congress' position with respect to baseball and the Sherman Act was passive. This nonaction was a decision or value judgment of the legislature. By not striking down an earlier ruling, the Court in 1972 was merely enforcing the congressional (norm) judgment on the question of baseball and antitrust regulations.

In this segment of the chapter we have discussed and illustrated five not too distinct norm enforcement functions of the federal courts. Throughout our history federal courts have played a fundamentally

[36]Allison, "Professional Sports."
[37]*Flood v. Kuhn*, 407 *US* 258 (1972).
[38]See Howard Ball, *Judicial Craftsmanship or Fiat? Direct Overturn By the United States Supreme Court* (Westport, Ct: Greenwood Press, 1978).

important role in determining the parameters and limits of power by acting as:

1. *umpire* or *referee* of the federal system,
2. *validator* of national legislation,
3. *examiner* of administrative procedures and regulations,
4. *interpreter* of the meaning of legislative words, and
5. *deferrer* to national legislative wishes and values.

However, these have not been the only roles the federal courts have played in our history. The next segment of this chapter focuses on the functions of the federal courts and will examine the policy-making role of the federal courts. This does not mean that the courts, as norm enforcers, do not make or clarify existing policy. The federal judges do indeed act as political policy makers but do so through validation of legislation that has been challenged in the courtrooms. The policy-making role is distinguished because of the far-reaching thrusts of judicial officers. The significant difference is that, as policy maker, the federal judge creates policy *de novo* rather than commenting or observing and validating the legislation challenged in the federal court.

THE POLICY-MAKING FUNCTION OF THE FEDERAL COURTS

Creation of Public Policy by the Federal Courts through Constitutional Interpretation

Throughout our history federal judges have had to examine and interpret the Constitution of the United States. Such action is generally not taken lightly by the judges for there has developed a reverential quality to the document—interpreting the Constitution has been likened to the high priests interpreting holy books. Judges have never been considered in this light and have been very reluctant to go to the Constitution to decide a case or controversy before the federal courts. This general reluctance has led to the development, by the federal judges themselves, of rules of judicial parsimony that outline restrictions on constitutional interpretation.[39]

There are those occasions, however, when the federal judges, in order to properly dispose of the case or controversy, must turn to the document and determine the meaning of its words. To that extent we in America are under a Constitution, but the document is what the

[39]See *Ashwander v. TVA*, 297 *US* 288 (1936), for example.

judges say it means. Such an action is the most difficult responsibility the judges in the federal system shoulder. As has been noted in the previous segments, federal courts will try to deal with the legal questions raised in the litigation by attempting to construe or interpret the statutory language in a certain way. But there are those times when the avoidance of the constitutional question cannot be put off—where there is no alternative but to open the Constitution and attempt to resolve the legal question by deciphering the words written in 1787.

In the effort to understand the meaning of the terms of the Constitution relevant to the legal dispute, federal judges try to discern the intent of the framers, analyze the language of the Constitution, uncover the meaning of certain words as used in the eighteenth century, and so forth. The bottom line is (1) the perception the federal judge has of the role and function of the federal courts in the process, and (2) the meaning he places on the terms that have been questioned in the case or controversy. Essentially, the judge's philosophical, ideological, and professional background prepare him to make a judgment on the meaning of the constitutional words. It is a very hard judgment to make. The impact of such constitutional judgments has been profound in many social and political ways.[40]

In recent years, federal courts have interpreted phrases such as "due process" and "equal protection of the laws" to mean an end to a fundamental social policy, Jim Crowism;[41] an end to sexual discrimination in employment in both the public and private sectors;[42] an end to unequal treatment in the criminal justice system by calling for assistance of counsel in all criminal cases where there is the jeopardy of imprisonment;[43] and an end to certain state practices that denied persons the right to marital privacy.[44] In this same period of time, federal courts have given new meaning to words such as "freedom of religion," "freedom of speech," "due process of law," "cruel and unusual punishment," "freedom of the press," and "unreasonable searches and seizures," among others.[45]

Religious Picketers in a Company Owned Town

Freedom of speech (and expression), one of the central tenets in the First Amendment of the United States Constitution, is the foun-

[40]See C. Herman Pritchett, *The Federal System in Constitutional Law* (Englewood Cliffs, N.J.: Prentice-Hall, 1978).
[41]*Brown v. Board of Education*, 347 *US* 483 (1954).
[42]*Frontierro v. Richardson*, 411 *US* 677 (1973).
[43]*Gideon v. Wainright*, 372 *US* 335 (1963).
[44]*Griswold v. Connecticut*, 381 *US* 479 (1965).
[45]Ann Fagen Ginger, *The Law, The Supreme Court, and the People's Rights* (New York: Barron Publishing Company, 1973).

dation block of a viable, dynamic, democratic system. In recent decades the federal courts have been asked by petitioners to determine the scope and dimensions of the free speech guarantee. Recent cases have raised such interesting questions as: Is draft card burning free speech? Is burning the American flag free speech? Is the wearing of long hair, by an American Indian high school youth, an expression protected by the First Amendment? Is a silent protest, through the use of black armbands by public school children, free speech? Years earlier the issues that confronted the federal judges were less exotic; they involved heretical groups who had been denied free speech rights by local communities.

In a 1939 case involving discrimination by a city in New Jersey against organized labor organizations, the Supreme Court rejected the local prohibition and said that

> wherever the title of streets and parks may rest, they have immemorially been held in trust for the use of the public and, time out of mind, have been used for purposes of assembly, communicating thoughts between citizens, and discussing public questions. Such use of the streets and public places has from ancient times been a part of the privileges, immunities, rights, and liberties of citizens.[46]

The federal courts since that time have interpreted the First Amendment as giving protesters the right to use the public streets. In the case discussed below, the right to protest was not at issue, the *place of protest* was the issue that called for resolution by the courts.

Grace Marsh was a member of the Jehovah's Witnesses, a small, extremely fundamental religious sect that seemed to work best in small towns with large traditional Christian populations. She was arrested for preaching her views on the streets of a *privately* owned company town, Chickasaw, Alabama. The managers of the town, employees of the Gulf Shipbuilding Corporation, had refused to allow Marsh to use the streets. She did and was arrested by a deputy sheriff, paid by the private corporation to serve as the town's policeman, for violating the state's trespass statute. Convicted of trespass, and upheld on appeal by the state's highest court, she appealed the judgment to the United States Supreme Court.[47]

The question for the Court was whether or not the imposition of the criminal penalty for free speech was in violation of the First and Fourteenth Amendments. The intervening complexity was the fact that it was a company owned town—private property. Justice Hugo Black, a true believer in the primacy of the First Amendment, wrote the opinion for the Court in the case of *Marsh v. Alabama*. The arrest and conviction

[46]*Hague v. CIO,* 307 *US* 496 (1939).
[47]*Marsh v. Alabama,* 326 *US* 501 (1946).

was not consistent with the First and Fourteenth Amendments. If a public municipality cannot block freedom of speech and expression then can a private town act any differently?

The answer was that if the private town "has all the characteristics of any other American town" and "if it did not function differently from any other town"—except that the legal title to the property belonged to a private corporation—then that private town must be seen as the equivalent of the public municipality and was subject to the same constitutional restraints. Black then noted that the private town was the "functional equivalent" of the public town and no town, public or private, can govern "so as to restrict the citizens' fundamental liberties." The managers of the town were performing the "full spectrum of municipal services and stood in the shoes of the state," concluded Justice Black. The First Amendment was held to bar private property owners from interfering with peaceful protestation on their streets.[48]

The Court had created a policy with respect to free speech and private property. None had existed before the 1945 case of *Marsh v. Alabama.* In *Marsh,* the federal courts now had precedent to guide them if cases came to them that had similar fact situations. As will be seen in the following segment, federal courts can employ precedent in many different ways, broadly or narrowly, based on the judgments of the federal judges. *Hudgens v. National Labor Relations Board* (1976) is a case in which the federal courts dramatically narrowed a public policy created by the federal courts. In so doing, the federal judges substantially affected economic and political rights of persons in our society.

Judicial Negation of Public Policy

There have been occasions in our history when the United States Supreme Court, by negating earlier judicial or legislative norms, has affected social, political, and economic policies by replacing one public policy with another. The 1857 Supreme Court opinion that invalidated the Missouri compromise of 1850, *Dred Scott v. Sanford,* had a profound effect on the political imbroglio that had been developing in our society between the north and south. When the Court ruled in that case that a black person born in the United States was not a citizen but an article of property not protected by the Constitution, it created a socioeconomic/ ethical policy that inflamed already raw emotions in the society.

Unlike the policy making of the courts in the preceding segment, judicial negation is a clear rejection of existing policy and a substitution

[48]See Howard Ball, "Careless Justice," *Polity* vol. XI, no. 2 (December 1978), pp. 200–228.

by the judiciary of another value. For example, when the Court invalidated the 1916 Child Labor Act of the Congress, which prohibited the use of children in certain types of employment for more than 60 hours a week, it negated a broad based social policy of the national legislature. Instead, in *Hammer v. Dagenhart* (1918), the federal judges substituted their policy views, which narrowly defined the meaning of the commerce clause of the Constitution, for those of the national legislators.[49] In the case described below, which illustrates the negative impact of judicial acts, the federal judges negated an earlier policy statement of the federal courts.

Can Picketers Protest on Private Shopping Center Property?

We have already discussed *Marsh v. Alabama,* the 1945 opinion of the Supreme Court that extended the coverage of the First Amendment to free speech on private town streets. In a 1968 judgment of the Supreme Court, *Amalgamated Food Employees Union Local 590 v. Logan Valley Plaza,* another court majority creatively extended the *Marsh* rationale to cover freedom of expression on the privately owned shopping center. "The shopping center here," wrote Justice Thurgood Marshall, "is clearly the 'functional equivalent' of the business district in Marsh." With that decision, the Court extended the policy created by the 1945 jurists to cover peaceful picketing on shopping center property. As a consequence of this judicially created policy, lower federal courts in New York, Washington State, and other jurisdictions allowed economic, political, and religious protestors to hand out their material in shopping centers. The judicially created policy created a constitutional easement on private property open to the public within which citizens could use their First Amendment rights of free speech and expression.[50] Less than a decade later, the justices of the Supreme Court negated the *Logan Valley* policy. In a case involving labor union picketing of a shoe store in an Atlanta, Georgia, shopping center,[51] the Supreme Court overturned the 1968 opinion of the Court. Justice Potter Stewart (who voted the other way in 1968) stated that the private shopping center did not have all the characteristics of the public municipality and therefore still retained its essential private character. "The present state of the law was that private property becomes public when it takes on all the attributes of a town." If it does not rise to that level of state action, argued Stewart, then it remains constitutionally protected private property.

49Ball, *Judicial Craftsmanship.*
50*Ibid.*
51*Hudgens v. National Labor Relations Board,* 424 *US* 507 (1976).

The First Amendment, he argued (noticeably narrowing the parameters of that important civil liberties statement), restrains state and federal action and the actions of their agents acting under color of law. The Amendment does not restrain the property owner unless he becomes an agent of the state or his property assumes *all* the characteristics of a public town. The "right of the private property owner to control the use of his property predominated over free expression in *Hudgens*."

The federal judges, in this 1976 case, very dramatically narrowed the parameters of the First Amendment by stating that an earlier public policy was incorrect. By saying "no" the Court majority created a public policy radically different from the one that had been in force. Saying no can be as forceful as positively creating public policy by an expansive meaning of the First Amendment.

Courts as Bureaucrats Creating and Administering Public Policy

In the past decade or so federal judges have begun to play a new and different role. With the *Brown v. Board of Education* decisions in 1954 and especially in 1955, these federal judges began to create and judicially administer school integration programs. This led to the implementation by local school officials of plans drawn up by judicial officers.[52] Judges thereafter began hearing cases and issuing orders with respect to busing of students, prison reform, reapportionment, and other major social and political issues that traditionally had been the responsibility of the elected and appointed political officers of the state.[53]

The judge acting as bureaucrat has become a function of the courts and has led many to wonder whether or not such a new responsibility properly belongs to federal judges. (One national news weekly devoted a front cover and an extensive essay to the question: "Too Much Law?") So long as the case is properly before the court and so long as the federal judges believe the issue is a justiciable one, i.e., a case or controversy that the judiciary can hear and help resolve without damage to fundamental principles of comity, federalism, and separation of power, then federal judges will function—in certain situations—as bureaucrats.

[52]See Jack Peltason, *58 Lonely Men* (Chicago: University of Chicago Press, 1960).
[53]See Jerold Footlick, "Too Much Law," *Newsweek*, January 10, 1977, pp. 42–47. For a critical view see Robert J. Harris, "The Intrusion of the Federal Courts into Administration," paper presented at the Southern Political Science Association meeting, New Orleans, Louisiana, November, 1977.

A Federal Judge Oversees Conditions At State Mental Hospitals

In 1971, Ricky Wyatt was involuntarily committed to an Alabama state mental hospital by and through his legal guardian, Mrs. Rawlins. He instituted legal proceedings in the United States District Court, Middle District-Alabama, against the state's Commissioner of Mental Health, Dr. Stonewall B. Stickney.[54] Wyatt was confined in Bryce Hospital, located in Tuscaloosa, Alabama. The hospital held almost 5,000 patients. Due to budget cuts in 1970 the staff was reduced to 17 physicians, 850 psychiatric aides, and 21 registered nurses, and 12 psychologists. However, "of the employees remaining whose duties involved direct patient care in the hospital therapeutic program, there are only one Ph.D. clinical psychologist, three medical doctors with some psychiatric training, and two MSW social workers."

There was gross overcrowding; in this hospital there were almost 1,600 geriatric patients who were not mentally ill and did not need mental care. Violence abounded in these facilities; "treatment from trained authorities was no better: one patient was kept in a straitjacket for nine years to keep him from sucking his hands and fingers."[55] At the time of the litigation, Alabama ranked fiftieth among all states in per patient expenditures per day. In short, a pattern of abuse and neglect "even more shocking than in the state's prisons"[56] was revealed in the litigation before the federal district court. The claim made by the petitioners was a simple one: They had received no satisfactory mental health treatment and care and had been, as a consequence, denied due process of law due to this set of poor conditions.

Wyatt v. Stickney (1971)[57] came before Chief Judge Frank M. Johnson who has been referred to by one news weekly as the new Atticus Finch (the lawyer/hero in the classic novel of southern justice *To Kill A Mockingbird*). When patients were committed to such facilities without the constitutional protections afforded defendants in criminal proceedings, "they unquestionably have a constitutional right to receive such individual treatment as will give each of them a realistic opportunity to be cured or to improve his or her mental condition," stated Judge Johnson after reviewing the record of neglect in the mental facilities.

The purpose of such involuntary commitment is *treatment* and not mere custodial care or punishment. The patient, stated the federal

[54]*Wyatt v. Stickney*, 325 F Supp 781 (1971).
[55]Lawrence Wright, "Atticus Finch Goes to Washington," *New Times*, December 9, 1977, p. 31.
[56]Ibid.
[57]*Wyatt v. Stickney* (1971, 1972).

judge, has the right to such treatment. There is "no legal (moral) justification" for the state failing to afford treatment.

> To deprive any citizen of his or her liberty upon the altruistic theory that the confinement is for humane therapeutic reasons and then fail to provide adequate treatment violates the very fundamentals of due process.

Judge Johnson issued an order giving the state officials six months to promulgate and implement proper standards for adequate mental care of the patients at the Bryce Hospital (and the other mental health facilities in Alabama). Failure to implement such a plan would, noted Johnson:

> necessitate further court action, including an order requiring full inspection of the existing facilities, a study of the operational and treatment practices and programs and recommendations that will enable this court to determine what will be necessary in order to render the Bryce facilities a mental health unit providing adequate and effective treatment, in a constitutional sense, for the patients who have been involuntarily committed and are confined there.

The district court order concluded by stating that "this court specifically retains jurisdiction of this case."

Alabama filed the report but the judge found that the institutions continued to infringe upon the plaintiff's constitutionally protected rights by failing to provide a proper physical and psychological environment, sufficient numbers of qualified staff, or individual treatment plans. Johnson then conducted extensive hearings at which national medical organizations, civil liberties organizations, and other amici (plural of *amicus curiae*, or "friend of the court") as well as individual experts testified.[58] All these witnesses concluded that the following conditions prevailed: (1) overcrowding; (2) lack of basic sanitary, fire, and safety measures which led to patient deaths; (3) use of nontherapeutic personnel or uncompensated patient labor; (4) serious understaffing, i.e., one psychiatrist for about 1,000 patients; (5) underqualifications of existing staff; and (6) absence of written individual treatment plans.[59]

The federal district court then issued its final decree. It contained 74 guidelines for attaining as quickly as possible a constitutionally adequate level of treatment. It articulated "minimum medical and constitutional requirements to be met with dispatch." Among the 74 requirements established by Judge Johnson were standards guaranteeing

---

[58]Case comment, "Wyatt v. Stickney and the Right of Civilly Committed Mental Patients To Adequate Treatment," *Harvard Law Review*, 86 (1973), 1282, at p. 1283.
[59]Ibid., p. 1283, fn 4.

basic patient rights to privacy, presumption of competency, communication with outsiders, compensation for labor, freedom from unnecessary medication or restraint, and freedom from treatment or experimentation without informed consent. Requirements were established governing staff to patient ratios, educational opportunities, floor space, sanitary facilities and nutrition. The court also ordered individual treatment plans be developed, that written medication and restraint orders be filed and that these be periodically reviewed.[60]

Johnson issued a final order requiring the state to submit progress reports, declaring that "a lack of financial resources would not excuse noncompliance," and appointed "permanent outside committees to review treatment and implement patients' rights under the order."

Of all his decisions, Johnson considers *Wyatt v. Stickney,* 1971/1972 his most important.[61] The impact on the state mental health officials was dramatic. They were under court order to dramatically revamp mental health facilities and to report back periodically to the federal judge who was supervising the reorganization. The Fifth Circuit Court of Appeals upheld this judgment of Judge Johnson (along with another order he issued concerning lack of medical facilities for prisoners in Alabama prisons) on November 8, 1974. Here then is a classic case of a federal judge overseeing the activity of an agency of the state: reviewing existing conditions, asking experts for advice, developing standards for the mental health officials, and, finally, overseeing the way in which the state officials implemented these judicially ordered and constructed plans.

SUMMARY

Throughout this chapter, we have shown the many basic functions of the federal courts. Courts have two overarching functions in our political system that are consistent with the basic judicial responsibility for resolving disputes. Under the umbrella of norm enforcement, courts examine and interpret and construe the output of legislators, executives, bureaucrats on both the state and national levels of government. They umpire the federal system when they resolve disputes between states' rights and powers of the national government. Norm enforcement has come to mean deferral to legislative values on many occasions in our history.

As policy maker, the federal courts have had tremendous impact on the social, economic, and cultural development of our society. Ex-

[60]*Wyatt v. Stickney,* 1972.
[61]Statement by Judge Frank Johnson, January 17, 1978.

amining the constitutional language or developing a plan for mental health facilities, the federal judges have affected the lives of millions of Americans. The federal courts have been applauded and condemned for their actions but, consistent with the admonition Chief Justice John Marshall laid upon the federal judges, "it is emphatically the duty of the judges to say what the law is."[62] Despite all the shouts and criticism, the federal judges will continue to play these roles in the future.

[62]*Marbury v. Madison,* 1 Cranch 37 (1803).

THE STRUCTURE
AND DYNAMICS
OF THE FEDERAL
JUDICIAL SYSTEM

Part II

I submit that we (federal judges) are being smothered with confidence.

Chief Judge Irving H. Kaufman,
United States Court of Appeals,
Second Circuit, 1973

The complaint of Judge Kaufman, voiced at a meeting of the Commission on Revision of the Federal Court Appellate System (appointed by the Congress), is a far cry from the early days of the federal courts. After the federal court system was created in 1789 in the first congressional Judiciary Act, the federal judges were not a very busy group of men. The newly created U.S. district courts had very limited jurisdiction and the biggest crisis for the U.S. Supreme Court justices was their discomfort in having to "ride the circuit." Although the Judiciary Act of 1789 created federal circuit courts, it did not provide these circuits with sitting judges. Therefore, U.S. Supreme Court justices had to ride to these circuits and, with the help of a U.S. district court judge, hear cases. This was one basic reason why a job as a justice of the Supreme Court was not considered a plum in 1789. American justice has come a long way since 1789. Indeed, as was indicated in the previous chapter, the cry today is that we have "too much law" created by the judges in the federal courts.

In Part II we will examine organizational development and jurisdictional politics of the federal courts since 1789. Since the 1789 Judiciary Act there have been many developments in the organization of the federal judiciary, and Chapter 3 will examine these events, including the most recent suggestion that another intermediary court, the National Court of Appeals, be created to relieve the burden on the United States Supreme Court. In addition, the chapter will examine the nature and the extent of the jurisdiction of the federal courts.

Chapter 4 will focus on the ways in which federal judges have responded to petitions presented to them by litigants. If jurisdiction is the legal authority to hear and decide cases and controversies, then it is the federal judge who determines whether there is a legitimate case or controversy before the court.

Chapter 4 will focus on issues such as standing to sue, concepts such as justiciability and "political questions." Finally the chapter will underscore the melding of legal process and political/ideological views in the judicial determination of whether a case falls within the jurisdiction of the court and, if it does, whether it is justiciable, nonjusticiable, or a "political question." If the situation is a nonjusticiable one, then the federal court will not hear that case or controversy and will dismiss the suit. The decision to dismiss is a value judgment of the federal judge and it clearly illustrates the merger of law and politics.

Chapter 5 focuses on the selection of federal judges. It is important to understand the joining of law and politics in the federal judicial system. An examination of the judicial selection process brings out the essentially political/ideological characteristics of the federal judiciary.

Gaining access to the federal judiciary, especially the U.S. Supreme Court (because of its commitment to hearing and developing broad legal policy for the entire society), is a difficult venture. It is based, to a large extent, upon the judge's perception of the arguments in the jurisdictional briefs. As will be pointed out it takes a "vote of four" to bring a case to the United States Supreme Court. The federal judges will vote to hear the case if they believe it is an important public policy/legal dilemma. This is essentially a subjective decision made by the federal judges. Who they are (and what their backgrounds are) will largely determine what cases they will hear and what cases will be dismissed or denied.

Selection, then, of the federal judges not only determines the outcome of trials in the district courts, it determines what kinds of cases will come into the federal appellate process. Selection of the federal judges is inextricably bound to access and jurisdiction. Together, these aspects create the dynamics of the judicial process. Part II will present this information, using illustrative issues and cases to lay out the legal/political nature of the federal court system.

organization and jurisdiction of the federal courts

3

It (Judiciary Act, 1789) swallows up every shadow of a state judiciary.

James Jackson, Georgia, 1789

It is necessary that the National tribunal possess the power of protecting those (Federal government constitutional) rights from such (state court) invasion.

Roger Sherman, Connecticut, 1789

To understand how the federal judges operate, how decisions are handed down, it is necessary to understand the environment in which they operate. The organization of the federal judicial system is a reflection of the dilemmas of an emergent nation after the revolutionary period. The organizational framework, from the very beginning of our political and judicial system, reflects the impact and continued vital presence of federalism.

FEDERAL COURT ORGANIZATION

The dispensation of justice in America has been handled by two sets of courts and court systems that exist side by side and have existed in rough and tumble equilibrium since the very first Congress met in 1789. The society has two separate systems: state judicial systems and the federal judicial system. The relationships between these two systems have been carved from constitutional interpretations, statutory enactments, political and legal practices, and the force of politics, tradition, and legal custom. If there is today in America a fairly clear set of parameters as to which jurisdiction belongs to the state courts and which falls under federal jurisdiction, this was not the case during the formative constitutional period of our history.

The Formative Years of the Federal Judiciary, 1789–1801

Article III of the United States Constitution states that the "judicial power of the United States shall be vested in one Supreme court and in such inferior courts as the Congress *may* from time to time ordain and establish." The language, although simple, did conceal a great debate that took place at the Constitutional Convention held in Philadelphia in the summer of 1787. Article III was the subject "of more severe criticism and greater apprehension than any other portion of the Constitution."[1] The basic reason for this dramatic confrontation over the court system was because of the fact that state judges and state courts were in existence and in use by Americans, and the states' rights advocates concern was the obvious threat to these court systems from a new federal system of courts.

The "monstrous appearance"[2] of a new system of courts was a real threat to the jurisdiction and power of state courts. The creation of a national system of courts was a manifest threat to those at the Constitutional Convention who believed in the prominence of state power in the new system of government. Antifederalists at the 1787 Convention felt that the state courts could continue the business of dispensing justice and that the judges in the state systems would enforce federal legislation fairly. One representative, Luther Martin, believed that the creation of inferior federal tribunals "would create jealousies and oppositions in the state tribunals with the jurisdiction of which they will interfere."[3]

The nationalists (federalists) at the 1787 Convention argued that the success of the new system "depended on the existence of a supreme

---

[1]Charles Warren, *The Supreme Court in United States History*, vol. 1 (Boston: Little, Brown, 1926), p. 7.
[2]Ibid., p. 8.
[3]Ibid.

national tribunal, free from local bias or prejudice, vested with power to give an interpretation to Federal laws and treaties which should be uniform throughout the land, . . . and to control State aggression on the Federal domain."[4] The bottom line for those delegates who believed in the necessity of federal courts was distrust of state courts: "The courts of the states cannot be trusted with the administration of the national laws. The objects of jurisdiction are such as will often place the general and local policy at variance."[5]

The mediated response took two directions and the Constitution as drawn up and accepted by the delegates to the convention reflected these views. Article VI, the supremacy clause, stated that the Constitution and the federal laws and treaties were the "Supreme Law of the Land," and that "the judges in every state shall be bound thereby, any thing in the Constitution or laws of any state to the contrary notwithstanding." The general judicial relationship was set in this Article. All officials, including the state judges, were bound to follow the laws of the land, including the fundamental law: the United States Constitution. (As will be noted in the Jurisdiction segment, Section 25 of the Judiciary Act of 1789 gave the United States Supreme Court the jurisdiction to review, on writ of error,[6] certain acts of state supreme courts that involved federal questions.)

The second response, dictated by the need to develop some sort of document that was acceptable or minimally tolerable to a majority of the delegates at the Constitutional Convention, was Article III, which said, in part, "The judicial power of the United States, shall be vested in one Supreme Court, and in such inferior courts as the Congress may from time to time ordain and establish." The specifics of the federal judicial system were left to the soon-to-be-seated Congress to develop and operationalize. The first Congress, which met in 1789, was given "a task of the most delicate nature."[7]

The newly elected national legislators had to determine the composition of the Supreme Court, erect those inferior tribunals referred to in Article III, frame procedures for these courts, and establish the jurisdiction of the Supreme Court as well as the inferior courts they were to create. The fundamental differences of opinion that existed at the Constitutional Convention two years earlier manifested themselves

[4]Ibid., p. 9.
[5]Ibid.
[6]A *writ of error* is an order of an appellate court to a lower court to send up the record in the case so that the appeal court could determine whether or not errors of law, as alleged, do in fact exist on the record. After 1925 the writ of certiorari replaced the writ of error.
[7]Warren, *The Supreme Court*, p. 7.

during the debates from April 7, 1789, to September 24, 1789, in the Congress. Federalist opposed antifederalist and out of this intensely partisan discussion the Judiciary Act of 1789 emerged.

Two basic questions arose during these extended debates between the nationalists and the defenders of state sovereignty. (1) Should those inferior federal tribunals be created at all? (2) What kinds of jurisdictional limits should be constructed so that the federal courts would not "swallow up" the state legal systems? Two legislators, Oliver Ellsworth of Connecticut and William Patterson of New Jersey, led the fight in Congress for the creation of a federal judicial system.[8] Compromise ensued in Congress and the result was a federal judicial system that was acceptable by the nationalists while at the same time tolerated by the states' rights advocates.

Although a system of inferior courts was created (see Table 3-1), the jurisdiction of these courts was severely limited (and would remain so for another century). Although federal trial courts were created to hear cases and controversies, these U.S. district courts followed existing state lines; the federal judges would be selected and, with the advice and consent of the United States Senate, would then preside in court in those states in which they had been born, reared, and educated, and in which they practiced law and had participated in state politics.

As passed by the Congress, Senate Bill 1, 1 Stat 73, the Judiciary Act of 1789 established the federal judiciary system that, in essence, we have in America today. There were 13 federal district courts created with a federal district court judge assigned to each district. Also created were three federal circuit courts—the southern, middle, and eastern circuits. However, the Congress used district court judges and Supreme Court justices to staff the circuits. One district court judge and two Supreme Court justices rode each of these three circuits to hear appeals. Finally, the Congress determined that there would be a Chief Justice of the United States and five Associate Justices who would comprise the Supreme Court of the United States.

Organizational Development, 1801–1891

As early as 1791 the pronationalists in the national government were attempting to change the organization of the federal judicial system.[9] The major organizational problem was the circuit-riding respon-

---

[8]See generally Warren, ibid. for a history of this important period of constitutional development.
[9]See generally Richard J. Richardson and Kenneth N. Vines, *The Politics of Federal Courts* (Boston: Little, Brown, 1970).

TABLE 3-1   FEDERAL JUDICIAL ORGANIZATION, 1789

UNITED STATES SUPREME COURT

*(U.S. Constitution,
Article III, Section One.)*

Chief Justice Jay (1789)
Associate Justice Rutledge (1789)
Associate Justice Cushing (1789)
Associate Justice Wilson (1789)
Associate Justice Blair (1789)
Associate Justice Iredell (1790)
          (1 Stat 73, 1789 Judiciary Act)

UNITED STATES CIRCUIT COURTS

*(1 Stat 73,
1789 Judiciary Act)*

Southern Circuit—no sitting federal judges
Middle Circuit—no sitting federal judges
Eastern Circuit—no sitting federal judges

Two justices of the United States Supreme Court and one judge from the United States district court would serve as circuit judges.
(Section 2, 1 Stat 73)

UNITED STATES DISTRICT COURTS

*(1 Stat 73,
1789 Judiciary Act)*

13 District Courts (1 district court in each of the 11 states in the Union at that time. The states of North Carolina and Rhode Island, which had not ratified the Constitution when the 1789 Judiciary Act was signed into law in September 1789, each received a U.S. district court after they entered the Union. Two other district courts were created for Maine, then part of Massachusetts, and for Kentucky, then still part of Virginia.)

sibilities of the federal justices of the Supreme Court. In 1799 the federalist administration of President John Adams introduced legislation that was passed in February 1801 (2 Stat 89). In addition to enlarging the jurisdiction of the federal courts (discussed later in the chapter), the Judiciary Act of 1801 eliminated the burdensome circuit-riding responsibilities of the Supreme Court justices, created 6 circuit courts of appeals, and created 16 resident circuit judges.[10]

Unfortunately for the nationalists, as soon as the new Jeffersonian administration and Congress were in power, the 1801 Judiciary Act was repealed by passage of the Circuit Court Act of 1802 (2 Stat 132). "It is generally expected," wrote a colleague of the new president, "that among the first acts of the next Congress will be a repeal of the extraordinary judicial bill, the design of which was too palpable to elude com-

[10]Warren, *The Supreme Court*, pp. 31–67, passim.

mon observation."[11] President Jefferson's justification of the repeal was basically political: The "Federalists have retired into the Judiciary as a stronghold . . . and from that battery all the works of republicanism are to be beaten down and erased."[12]

Not too unexpectedly for the Jeffersonians, in 1803 the United States Supreme Court, composed of federalist justices, validated the repeal statute in the case of *Stuart v. Laird,* 1 *Cranch* 299 (1803). Prior to the 1803 decision the federal judges had tacitly accepted the statute's constitutionality by agreeing to ride circuit after the 1801 Judiciary Act had been repealed. "No more striking example of the non-partisanship of the American Judiciary can be found than this decision by a Court composed wholly of Federalists, upholding, contrary to its personal and political views, a detested Republican measure," wrote a constitutional scholar of this judicial opinion.[13]

With the judicial validation of the 1802 Circuit Court Act, the organizational makeup of the federal judiciary, except for increases in numbers of district and circuit courts and increases in the size of the United States Supreme Court, remained essentially unchanged for 90 years until the passage of the Circuit Court of Appeals Act of 1891. This is not to suggest, however, that the issue had been muted with the repeal. Periodically (1848, 1854, 1965), bills were introduced with respect to the creation of circuit courts of appeals with resident judges and substantial jurisdiction to hear cases and controversies (thereby alleviating some of the workload of the United States Supreme Court), but these efforts failed.

The creation of the federal courts of appeals was "one of the most enduring political struggles in American political history."[14] The battle was fought by the same forces over the same issues: nationalists opposed by states' righters; localists versus nationalists. Until the 1891 legislation took effect, United States district court judges handled the jury trial, and would then (acting as circuit court judge—a consequence of the 1802 repeal statute) hear appeals from their courts. The justices of the Supreme Court also received all routine appeals from these judges.

If the 1802 repeal act reduced the circuit-riding duties of the Supreme Court justices, it did not relieve them of the burden of hearing the mundane civil and criminal cases that wound their way up from the lower federal court. By 1890, the docket of the Supreme Court contained over 1,800 cases.[15] This was a very high figure considering the fact that

[11]Ibid., p. 203.
[12]Ibid., p. 201.
[13]Ibid., p. 272.
[14]Lawrence M. Friedman, *A History of American Law* (New York: Touchstone, 1973), p. 120.
[15]Richardson and Vines, *Federal Courts,* p. 30.

the national legislation had not created many areas of litigation for the courts. These cases reflected the fact that there was no intermediate court to hear appeals from the trial court and therefore the U.S. Supreme Court had to hear them.

The pro-state forces in the Congress wanted to reduce even further the appellate powers of the federal courts by repealing Section 25 of the 1789 Judiciary Act which gave the Supreme Court the power to review certain decisions of state supreme courts. Not content with reducing the jurisdiction power of the U.S. Supreme Court, they wished to reduce the jurisdiction of all the federal courts. As one Congressman stated, repeating the 1789 argument: "I cannot be in favor of extending all over this country a system which takes from state tribunals and from state domination what properly belongs to it."[16]

A break developed in the battle between the nationalists and pro-staters when, in 1875, federal courts were given extensive jurisdictional powers (to be discussed in a later segment of this chapter). This modification went along with the 1869 legislation that created nine federal judgeships for the federal circuit courts. Thus, by 1875, there were nine circuit court judges hearing some of the cases that were appealed from the federal district courts. However, since there was the automatic right of appeal to the Supreme Court, the addition of the judges did not lessen the caseload of the Supreme Court.

In 1890 a new legislative attempt to develop the intermediate courts was introduced by the nationalists. It was ultimately to be accepted by Congress. The original plan abolished the old circuit court and created, instead, nine intermediate courts of appeal with jurisdiction that allowed these courts to end the flood of litigation to the Supreme Court. Each new circuit court of appeals would have three federal judges.[17] The jurisdiction (discussed below) of these new courts was such as to allow most appeals to end in these courts, subject to discretionary review by the Supreme Court using a writ of certiorari.[18] After debates, a compromise bill was passed by the Congress on February 28, 1891, and signed into law on March 3, 1891.

The changes, which became part of the statute, continued the old circuit courts, but provided for the new circuit courts of appeals to hear most of the appeals from the district courts. The personnel makeup of these new courts of appeals was as follows: one circuit court judge, one circuit court of appeal judge, one district court judge, and a Supreme

[16]Ibid., p. 29.
[17]Ibid., p. 30.
[18]*Writ of certiorari:* a request from a litigant to an appeal court which, if granted by that court, commands the lower court to certify and transmit the record of the case so that the superior court can determine where legal irregularities took place. It replaced, after the Judge's Bill of 1925, the writ of error.

Court justice. Two judges made up a quorum in these new federal courts.[19] In 1891, 90 years after the repeal of the 1801 act that had created a similar intermediary body of the federal judges and courts, the United States Circuit Courts of Appeals network was created (see Figure 3-1).

From 1891 to the Call for a U.S. National Court of Appeals in 1974

Except for the circuit courts in 1891, the eighteenth century organizational structure of the federal judiciary remains in existence today. By 1911 the growth of the recently created courts of appeals had led to the demise of the old circuit courts. The Congress passed the 1911 Judicial Code which abolished these tribunals and left the federal system with the trial courts (the U.S. district courts), the lower appellate courts (the U.S. courts of appeals), and the United States Supreme Court. In the 1920s organized bar association lobbying and nationalist forces in the Congress, aided and abetted by the Chief Justice of the U.S. Supreme Court, William H. Taft, expanded the jurisdiction of the federal courts, especially the Supreme Court, and dramatically improved the administration of a very decentralized federal judiciary. The Congress accomplished this by (1) authorizing the chief justice to assign federal judges to temporary duty anywhere in the federal system, and by (2) creating the conference of Senior Circuit Judges (later called the Judicial Conference) which would meet annually in the nation's capital to discuss common judicial administrative problems.

In 1937 there was the unsuccessful attempt by President Franklin D. Roosevelt to "pack the Supreme Court" through national legislation authorizing him to appoint a new justice for every sitting justice over 70 years of age. If successful, the legislation would have given Roosevelt six new Supreme Court seats to fill. The legislation was killed in the Senate but the justices of the Supreme Court received the presidential message. Very shortly thereafter, the Supreme Court began to validate New Deal programs that had been challenged in federal courts.

In 1939, at the behest of the Judicial Conference, the Administrative Office of the United States Courts was created by the Congress. The basic function of the Office is to collect statistics on the caseload and related judicial activities of the federal courts. The director of the Office was charged with responsibility for issuing an annual *Management Statistics for United States Courts for the Chief Justice of the United States* to the chairmen and members of the Judicial Councils of the Circuits (also

---

[19]Richardson and Vines, *Federal Courts,* pp. 30–31.

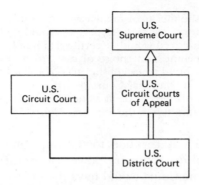

FIG. 3-1   FEDERAL JUDICIAL ORGANIZATION, 1891

created in 1939) and to the chief judges and judges of the United States courts. This report provides the judges and administrators with extremely useful data to be used for judicial administration reform, preparation of budgets, etc.

These and other administrative initiatives introduced since 1925 have tended to reduce judicial autonomy.[20] Federal Judicial Administrators and court executives as well as closer control of the federal judiciary by administratively oriented Chief Justices of the United States Supreme Court have somewhat curtailed the traditional judicial independence of federal judges.

In the 1970s, renewed concern over the increased workload of the federal courts, especially the U.S. Supreme Court (fostered in part by speeches and lobbying activities of the chief justice, Warren Earl Burger), led to the debate over the creation of another federal court situated between the U.S. Court of Appeals and the Supreme Court, the National Court of Appeals.

In arguments reminiscent of the nineteenth-century arguments made for the creation of the courts of appeals, the *Federal Judicial Center Report of the Study Group on the Case Load of the Supreme Court,* chaired by Professor Paul A. Freund (and commonly referred to as the Freund Report), called for the creation of this new tribunal to ease the workload of the Supreme Court. Composed of seven U.S. circuit judges who would be assigned to the court for limited staggered terms of three years and who would sit in Washington, D.C., the new court would receive all cases (except original jurisdiction) presently petitioned to the U.S. Supreme Court.

> We recommend creation of a National Court of Appeals which would screen all petitions for review now filed in the Supreme Court, and hear

[20]See Walter Early, *Constitutional Courts of the U.S.* (Totowa, N.J.: Littlefield, Adams, 1976).

and decide on the merits of many cases of conflicts between circuits. . . . The great majority, it is to be expected, would be finally denied by that court. Several hundred would be certified annually to the Supreme Court for further screening and choice of cases to be heard and adjudicated there. Petitions found to establish a true conflict between circuits would be granted by the National Court of Appeals and the cases heard and finally disposed of there, except as to those petitions deemed important enough for certification to the Supreme Court.[21]

Once the case was certified to the Supreme Court, the justices would use their full discretionary powers to grant or deny review. In addition the Supreme Court would have the power "to make rules governing the practice in the National Court of Appeals."[22] The Freund Report concluded by stating that "relief is imperative, and among possible remedies, none of which is perfect, this appears to us to be the least problematic."

This has not been the case. The suggestion of the Freund Committee has met with severe criticism from many legal circles, including justices of the U.S. Supreme Court William O. Douglas and William J. Brennan. Critics of the proposed National Court of Appeals do not agree with Chief Justice Burger's contention that the "Supreme Court is in trouble." They do not believe that there is the severe workload dilemma that, according to the chief justice, "calls urgently for a solution."[23] As one critic pointed out, one cannot talk about a court being overworked for it is the individual justices of the court that do the work. Justice Douglas would continue to climb mountains and write books with twice the volume of cases to examine whereas Justice Harry Blackmun would still burn the midnight oil with half the case load he works on at the present time![24] More important, criticism of the proposal has noted how the organizational addition would very dramatically change the nature and potency of Supreme Court decision making (a subject discussed in another chapter of the book).

As a consequence of the outcry against the proposed National Court of Appeals, the debate has been stilled. In 1975 Chief Justice Burger shifted gears and began campaigning not for a new court but for remedial legislation that would reduce "the load on nine mortal Justices."[25] During that year, 1975, another study group examined

---

[21]In Walter Murphy and C. Herman Pritchett, *Courts, Judges, and Politics* (New York: Random House, 1975), pp. 83–84.

[22]Ibid.

[23]Warren E. Burger, "Reducing the Load on 'Nine Mortal Justices,' " *New York Times*, August 14, 1975.

[24]See Nathan Levin, "Helping The Court With Its Work," quoted in Murphy and Pritchett, *Courts, Judges*, pp. 87–93.

[25]Burger, "Reducing the Load." See also his 1976 *Annual Report on the State of the Judiciary*, 96 *Supreme Court Reporter*, no. 9 (March 1, 1976), pp. 1–11.

whether or not "the Supreme Court is adequately fulfilling its role of providing authoritative guidance for the resolution of disputes involving questions of federal law."[26] The *Commission on Revision of Federal Court Appellate System* (called the Hruska Commission because former Republican United States Senator Roman L. Hruska chaired the commission meetings) concluded that due to the increased caseload another federal appeal court was necessary: a National Court of Appeals. However, unlike the Freund study group position on the function of the new court, the Hruska Commission urged that the new court "furnish additional authoritative decisions on issues of national law through the adjudication of cases referred *to it* by the (Supreme) Court."[27]

In December 1978, Chief Justice Burger added a statement to a case that had been denied certiorari, *Brown Transport v. Atcon*, No. 77–1581 (certiorari denied, 58 *L Ed 2* 687, 1978). In it, he pointed out that the Court was "accepting more cases for plenary review than [we] can cope with in the manner they deserve." In this very unusual statement from the Court, the Chief Justice called for the reexamination of the Freund committee recommendations. "The additional judgeships (created in 1978) may solve short-term problems, but the long-term problems of the Supreme Court analyzed by the Freund committee . . . remain as they were a decade ago."

Justice White, with Blackmun joining, dissented from denial of certiorari in this case: "Although I dissent from denial of certiorari, it must be acknowledged that this case is no more deserving of plenary consideration than many other cases in which certiorari has been denied this term." Illustrating this point by listing no less than 25 other important cases that had been denied certiorari, he concluded by stating that "there is grave doubt (given the increased workload of the Supreme Court) that the appellate system has the capacity to function in the manner contemplated by the Constitution." Both the Burger statement and the White dissent called for the immediate adoption of the Freund committee recommendations. So the discussion regarding the creation of a new intermediate appellate federal court still continues. However, not all of the justices agree with Burger, White, and Blackmun: Justice Brennan added a short statement reaffirming that he was "completely unpersuaded . . . that there is any need for a new National Court."

For the forseeable future, the organizational structure of the federal courts will remain the same as it has been since 1911.[28] But, as with

[26]Arthur D. Hellman, "The Business of the Supreme Court Under the Judiciary Act of 1925: The Plenary Docket in the 1970's," 91 *Harvard Law Review*, No. 8, June 1978, p. 1714.

[27]*Ibid.*, pp. 1716–1717.

[28]Toward the close of the 95th Congress (October 1978), the Congress passed legislation that created 152 new federal judgships: 117 new district court judgships

the circuit court of appeals debates and arguments for almost a century, if the need exists and the idea catches on in legal and political circles, then there will be renewed interest in the National Court of Appeals.

The Three-Judge U.S. District Courts

In 1903 the Congress passed legislation creating special three-judge U.S. district courts that would be required to hear suits filed by the Attorney General under the Sherman Antitrust Act or the Interstate Commerce Act. All cases involving violations of the Interstate Commerce Commission regulations were to be heard by the special district court—made up of two judges from the circuit's court of appeals and one judge from the U.S. district court in that area—with *appeals as of right* directly to the U.S. Supreme Court.[29]

The Mann-Elkins Act of 1910 empowered these special courts to hear cases brought by private individuals, involving the constitutionality of state or federal statutes and to issue injunctions to prevent enforcement of these challenged statutes. In the civil rights era (1960–1970) many petitions to the federal courts were initiated in these three-judge district courts because civil rights groups such as the NAACP were challenging the constitutionality of state statutes and seeking injunctions to prohibit their enforcement.

Prior to the decades of intense civil rights litigation, three-judge U.S. district courts "were a rarity."[30] In 1956 there were 50 cases in these courts; in 1963 there were 129 cases; in 1976 however there were 208 cases (including 161 civil rights trials, 25 I.C.C. cases, and 5 reapportionment hearings).[31] The primary problem was that judgments from three-judge district courts have direct appeal to the U.S. Supreme Court as a matter of right. The theory was that there should be "immediate Supreme Court review" of federal judicial actions that enjoin a state or federal statute.[32] In reality, the procedure created a caseload problem for the U.S. Supreme Court that has been bitterly criticized by Chief Justice Warren Burger. Consistent with his desire for the National Court of Appeals, Chief Justice Burger has also insisted on the abolition of these three-judge district courts because of their poor use of judicial

---

and 35 new court of appeals judgships. This will give President Jimmy Carter (D) a dramatic opportunity to remold the federal judiciary.

[29]See generally Felix Frankfurter and James Landis, *The Business of the Supreme Court* (New York: Macmillan, 1927).

[30]Burger, "Reducing The Load."

[31]*Annual Report of the Director of the Administrative Office of the United States Courts, 1976* (Washington, D.C.: Government Printing Office, 1976), p. 208.

[32]Richardson and Vines, *Federal Courts*, p. 32.

personnel and because the Supreme Court's discretion was limited insofar as reviewing cases that came to the court from the three-judge district courts.[33] In 1976 the Congress passed legislation, the Act of August 12, 1976 (28 USC Section 2284), which greatly restricted the use of three-judge district courts. One of the reasons stated by Congress for the restriction was "to relieve the burden of three-judge court cases (which have) caused a considerable strain on the workload of federal judges."[34]

United States Magistrates

Ideally, as one author wrote, "a litigant should have his case heard and decided within a reasonable time by an unhurried, highly qualified, judicial officer."[35] However the reality of the federal judiciary, as will be discussed at length in the next section on jurisdiction, is that the caseload of federal district courts has increased from 98,000 criminal and civil filings in 1964 to over 171,000 filings in 1976. The average number of cases heard by the federal district court judges was 339 in 1964 and was over 430 in 1977.[36] One remedy that has been developed to resolve the dilemma of time and caseload versus justice, outside the narrowing-of-jurisdiction remedy and the addition-of-new-judges remedy, was to "make use of a resource which is already authorized and available— the United States Magistrate."[37]

In 1968 the Congress passed the Federal Magistrates Act which established the office of U.S. magistrate. The office was created to "provide a new first echelon of judicial officers in the federal judicial system and to alleviate the increased workload of United States District Courts."[38] These magistrates, appointed and supervised by the federal district court judges, relieve the federal judges of certain routine duties. In this manner, the judges are freed to hear and monitor the cases that go to trial while the magistrate handles the various pretrial activities. Rather than enlarge the court system, the 1968 legislation attempted to "attack the current problems of judicial administration" by modifying the existing system.[39]

[33]Burger, "Reducing the Load"; and 96 *S Ct* 1976, pp. 4–5.
[34]C. H. Pritchett, *The American Constitution* (New York: McGraw-Hill, 1977), p. 93.
[35]Comment, "An Expanding Civil Role for United States Magistrates," *American University Law Review,* 26 (1975), 66.
[36]*Annual Report,* pp. 169ff.
[37]Comment, "Expanding Civil Role," p. 67.
[38]Steven Puro, "United States Magistrates: A New Federal Judicial Officer," *Justice System Journal,* 2 (Winter 1976), 141.
[39]Comment, "Expanding Civil Role," p. 68.

The magistrate performs certain functions—pretrial and post-trial—in both civil and criminal cases. These duties are both ministerial (taking depositions, administering oaths) and advisory, adjudicative, and quasi-judicial (hearing petty offenses, issuing search warrants, receiving prisoner petitions, disposing of motions, conducting postindictment arraignments). Magistrates must be members of the state bar; they are appointed by the judges in the district for an eight-year term during which they can be removed from the office only for "good cause" (see Figure 3-2).

There are still many unresolved constitutional problems surrounding the office of U.S. magistrate. Although the magistrates perform quasi-judicial tasks and are within the judicial branch of government, they are not Article III judges. At what time does the involvement of the magistrate in the case at hand and in its resolution "impinge upon

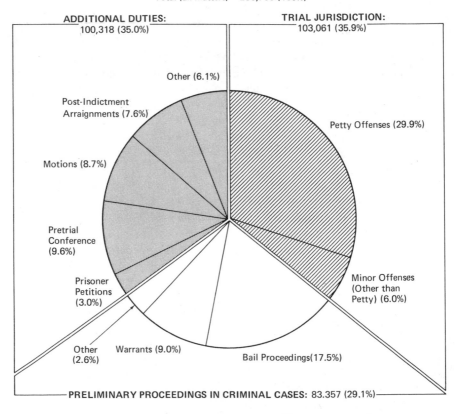

12 MONTHS ENDED JUNE 30, 1977

Total (all matters) = 286,736 (100%)

ADDITIONAL DUTIES: 100,318 (35.0%)

TRIAL JURISDICTION: 103,061 (35.9%)

Other (6.1%)

Post-Indictment Arraignments (7.6%)

Motions (8.7%)

Petty Offenses (29.9%)

Pretrial Conference (9.6%)

Prisoner Petitions (3.0%)

Minor Offenses (Other than Petty) (6.0%)

Other (2.6%)   Warrants (9.0%)

Bail Proceedings (17.5%)

PRELIMINARY PROCEEDINGS IN CRIMINAL CASES: 83.357 (29.1%)

FIG. 3-2   DUTIES PERFORMED BY UNITED STATES MAGISTRATES
Source: *Puro, "United States Magistrates," p. 147.*

or actually exercise the 'judicial power of the United States?' "[40] This and other questions are still to be answered by the Congress and by the federal courts themselves. What is important to consider is that there are now over 560 full- and part-time U.S. magistrates functioning in the federal courts. These quasi-judicial officers "are fast becoming an integral and important part of the federal judiciary."[41] For many who use the federal courts these federal agents are the only federal personnel they see because their cases are resolved at the pretrial stage or before the district court judge gets involved.

The Specialized Federal Courts

In addition to the federal courts described above, there are a number of specialized federal courts created by the Congress since 1855 that perform certain highly specialized functions that aid the Congress in fulfilling its legislative powers. There are a few basic differences between these special courts and the others. Jurisdiction of the three basic federal courts is determined in part by the constitutional requirements of Article III; tenure for these federal judges in the District, Appeal, and Supreme Court is lifetime. Salaries cannot be lowered and these judges can only be removed through a successful impeachment.

Judges—often called commissioners—on the "special" constitutional courts discussed below have the lifetime tenure and salary security that other Article III judges have; but they do not have their broad responsibilities. Congress has established these courts, staffed by jurists with expertise in those areas of concern—commerce, tax, customs, claims—in order to provide specialization in these problems and to relieve the other federal courts of increased and burdensome caseloads. It should be noted that all decisions handed down by these specialized courts can be reviewed, on appeal, by the United States Supreme Court (see Figure 3-3).

The U.S. Court of Claims

The Court of Claims was created in 1855; it has a chief judge and six associate judges who sit in Washington, D.C. The court adjudicates nontort action[42] claims against the United States. While the court does have some limited jurisdiction to review certain tort actions against the United States government, it primarily handles claims arising out of

---

[40]Ibid., pp. 107–8.
[41]Puro, "United States Magistrates," p. 161.
[42]Tort action is a suit brought into court because one party allegedly breached legal responsibility or duty to another party resulting, as a consequence of the breach, in damages to the second party.

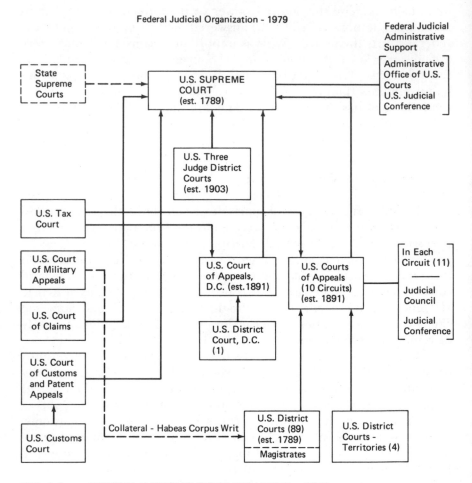

Federal Judicial Organization - 1979

FIG. 3-3   FEDERAL JUDICIAL ORGANIZATION—1979

public contracts where individuals holding these public contracts with the government bring suit against the U.S. government for back pay, refund of taxes, etc.

The U.S. Customs Court

The U.S. Customs Court, located in New York City, consists of a chief judge and eight associate judges. It was created by the Congress to hear cases involving civil rulings by U.S. customs collectors. It is the trial court for disputes between private citizens and corporations and the government involving amount of customs duties, value of imported goods, and exclusion of merchandise from the country.

The U.S. Court of Customs and Patent Appeals

This court is composed of a chief judge and four associate judges. It was created by the Congress in 1909, and acts as an appeal court for these litigants who have lost their arguments before the U.S. Customs Court; it also reviews decisions of the U.S. Patent Office.

The U.S. Tax Court

This institution, composed of a chief judge and 15 associate judges, is not really a court but an agency within the executive branch of government. It has been charged by the Congress to hear and review all disputes concerning tax decisions of the Internal Revenue Service challenged by citizens of the United States. Its judgment, like those of the rest of these specialized courts, is reviewable by the United States Supreme Court.

The U.S. Court of Military Appeals: An Article I Tribunal

This court, composed of three civilian judges appointed for 15-year terms, was created by Congress in 1950 when the legislature passed the Uniform Code of Military Justice. This special *non-Article III court* has been charged with reviewing and resolving all appeals from military courts martial. The court is charged with applying the military law, which is different from the rest of the federal laws and which does not feature many of those protections ordinarily found in criminal and civil procedures.

Consistent with its powers to "make rules" for the land and naval forces (Article 1, § 8), the U.S. Congress has created military tribunals, including the U.S. Court of Military Appeals, and a system and "uniform military code" of military justice that is somewhat different from ordinary civilian justice and civilian judicial processes. Because these military courts are "Article I" courts, there is no direct review of their actions by the federal courts. (Other Article I tribunals are the three territorial U.S. district courts located in Guam, the Canal Zone, and the U.S. Virgin Islands.)

There is, however, the possibility of collateral attacks of military court judgment through the use of the writ of habeas corpus by a person convicted in the military justice system. This writ provides the basic vehicle for review of military court action by federal judges. The federal courts including the Supreme Court, however, can review only questions of jurisdiction or questions relating to the constitutionality or alleged unconstitutionality of military court action or nonaction.

From 1789 to the present, the organizational development of the federal courts has been a consequence of political and workload pressures. Since the 1787 Constitution was written, there has been slow evolutionary growth of the federal court system; there have been innovations that have succeeded (the use of the U.S. magistrates) and those that have failed (the U.S. Commerce Court, created in 1910 and abolished in 1913). However, as Figure 3–4 indicates, while the contemporary federal court system has been greatly enlarged since the 1789 Judiciary Act, the early deference to the "state's rights" position continues. State boundaries still limit the scope of federal judicial power with respect to these two lower federal court systems. The only federal court that has broad national jurisdiction is the United States Supreme Court.

As the workload of the federal courts increases—due in part to new legislation creating new areas of jurisdiction as well as the way in which the federal courts determine the scope of their activities—the organizational growth dilemmas will not continue. Perhaps that is as it should be for a viable democracy is one in which the judiciary plays a vital role in the maintenance of the liberties and rights of the citizens. A growing federal judiciary signifies continued vitality of the American democratic system.

THE JURISDICTION OF THE FEDERAL COURTS

> Categories (of jurisdiction) establish the potential the judiciary has for intervention in American politics. . . . Jurisdiction opens the way for consideration (by the judiciary) of national political questions. . . .[43]

Article III of the United States Constitution enumerates the "judicial power" of the United States Supreme Court and those inferior federal courts created by the U.S. Congress. As already noted, this Article suggests the kinds of cases and controversies the federal courts *may* hear—*if* the Congress of the United States assigns the federal courts these responsibilities. The single exception to this pattern is the original jurisdiction of the Supreme Court because that particular authority of the Supreme Court to hear cases and controversies is specifically spelled out in Article III. Therefore, although the Constitutional description of judicial power includes, for example, cases "arising under the laws of the United States," the national legislature must delegate this constitutional responsibility to the federal courts, including the United States Supreme Court, through the passage of legislation before the federal judges can actually and legitimately hear and decide a particular

[43]Richardson and Vines, *Federal Courts,* p. 35.

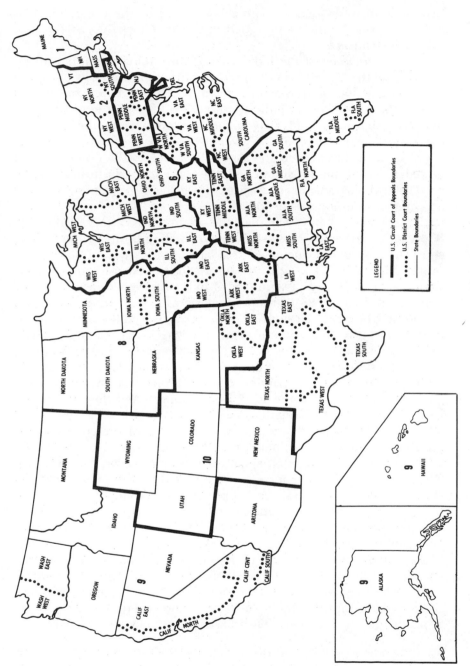

FIG. 3-4   UNITED STATES COURTS OF APPEALS AND UNITED STATES DISTRICT COURTS

Source: *Administrative Office of the United States Courts April 1975*

case or controversy dealing with a law passed by the Congress. This legislation, when passed and signed into law, defines the *jurisdiction* of the federal courts.

The *jurisdiction* of the federal courts, including the appellate jurisdiction of the United States Supreme Court, is the authority of a court to exercise its judicial power in a given case. If the U.S. Constitution defines the parameters of judicial power, it is the U.S. Congress which defines, determines, and assigns the responsibility to these federal courts. Jurisdiction need not be given to the federal courts by the Congress—or it might be given and then taken away by the Congress—but no federal court can, consistent with the concept of constitutionalism,[44] act outside the parameters of Article III (which means that no court can act without statutory jurisdiction).

Jurisdiction then (other than the original jurisdiction of the U.S. Supreme Court) is the *legislatively* determined authority of the federal courts to hear and decide cases. It is based on the judicial powers described in Article III *as actually assigned* to the federal courts by the Congress. This general assignment of judicial power to hear the cases is found in Volume 28 of the United States Codes. Inherent in this relationship between Constitution, federal courts, and the U.S. Congress are the concepts of "constitutionalism" and "checks and balances." These ideas were dominant during the constitutional period of American history (along with separation of powers and other "auxiliary precautions" thought necessary to the maintenance of a republican form of government by the framers of the 1787 Constitution)[45] and they are, in the latter decades of the twentieth century, still viable doctrines.

Constitutionalism suggests limits on powers of the governmental actors. No agent of government can act in a manner that is inconsistent with the grant of power that agency has received in the Constitution. The agency of government can use its powers (enumerated, inherent, or implied) to the maximum extent possible but it cannot use the power of the agency if the Constitution *does not grant the power* or if the Constitution *specifically prohibits* the agency from so acting. For example, although the president of the United States is charged with the defense of the nation, he may not order his agents to tap telephones of suspected enemies of the state without first receiving a warrant from a magistrate authorizing these wiretaps.[46] If the president acts in a manner inconsistent with the constitutionally authorized powers of the office, he would be acting unconstitutionally. The idea of constitutionalism reaffirms the

---

[44]See generally Arthur Sutherland, *Constitutionalism in America* (New York: Blaisdell, 1965).
[45]See generally *The Federalist Papers*, for a detailed discussion of these basic themes in our constitutional history.
[46]*U.S. v. U.S. District Court*, 407 *US* 297, 1972.

eighteenth-century notion of limits on the powers of the governors: thus far and no further *unless* the agent of government, the servant of the people, is willing to "breach the faith" the community has placed in him and in the office.[47]

Another auxiliary precaution discussed by James Madison and others during the constitutional period is the concept of "checks and balances." This concept is a pervasive notion that reflects the constitution makers' commitment to limited government. Theoretically, checks and balances refers to a sharing of powers by separated governmental agencies. Greatly concerned about the prospect of political tyranny, the men at the 1787 Constitutional Convention sought to prohibit it by developing a governmental operation that, in theory, would prevent one governmental agency from acquiring total political power. Checks and balances in our government is, in essence, a concept that optimally leads to a state of political equilibrium between president, congress, and courts. As James Madison stated, in the *Federalist Papers* (No. 51): Ambition must counteract ambition. The constitutional answer was in the form of a perpetual equilibrium (if the system was working) that we have come to call "checks and balances."

With regard to the jurisdiction of the federal courts, this "checks and balances" concept is readily apparent. The Constitution defines the parameters of judicial power; however, it is the Congress that decides the jurisdiction of the federal courts. Without that congressional legislation which has over the centuries become a part of 28 USC, the courts are powerless to act to resolve a legal dispute. This congressional authority (found in Article I, Section 8 and Article III, Section 3) to control the jurisdiction of the federal courts is a classic example of checks and balances at work in the federal system. As will be noted in the next chapter, there are other considerations beside jurisdiction that a federal judge will note and evaluate before hearing a case at trial or on appeal. Without *jurisdiction,* however, the process of determining access to the judicial branch doesn't begin!

The jurisdiction of the federal courts, described in Article III of the Constitution and a part of 28 USC, can be grouped in two basic categories. Federal courts can hear certain cases and controversies[48] according to the *subject matter* of the case. For example, federal courts

---

[47]See generally Theodore White, *Breach of Faith: The Fall of Richard Nixon* (New York: Atheneum, 1975).
[48]Cases and controversies: These words, common terms in any discussion of judicial activity, refer to an actual dispute over a real issue rather than an abstract discussion. As will be seen in the next chapter, concrete adversarial conditions are necessary preconditions for adjudication in federal courts. "If the two words are distinguishable at all, it is possibly because 'controversies' are confined to suits of a civil nature." See *Muskrat v. U.S.*, 219 *US* 346, 1911.

can hear a case "arising under the Constitution." Generally, subject matter jurisdiction cases involve questions of federalism: Under legislative guidance, discussed in the segments below, those questions that arise dealing with the law of the Constitution, the acts of Congress, or treaties entered into by the national government, fall within the jurisdiction of the federal courts. In addition to these "federal questions," the subject matter character of federal jurisdiction extends to those admiralty and maritime laws passed by the national legislature that are challenged by litigants.

The second category of cases and controversies that has come under the jurisdiction of the federal courts includes those that can be grouped according to the makeup of the *parties* to the dispute. The Constitution's Article III extends the "judicial power to the adjudication of disputes if: (1) the United States, or (2) one or more of the states, or (3) citizens of different states, or (4) foreign ambassadors, are involved in a legal dispute. Before examining the jurisdiction of the federal courts, a clarification of some additional basic legal terms is necessary.

In the discussions that follow there will be discussion of "original" and "appellate" jurisdiction, "civil" and "criminal" filings, and "exclusive" and "concurrent" jurisdiction of the federal courts. *Original jurisdiction* refers to those courts of first instance where the legal action originates. The U.S. District Courts are basically the trial courts in the federal judicial system. Although some of the jurisdiction of the U.S. Courts of Appeals is original and the U.S. Supreme Court's original jurisdiction is enumerated in the Constitution itself, they are not considered courts of first instance. As will be noted below in the discussion of district courts, these lower courts are the original jurisdiction agencies of the federal court system; Congress has given to the federal district courts only original jurisdiction.

Appellate jurisdiction is the power of federal courts to review and, if necessary, to correct errors of law that might have occurred in the court of original jurisdiction. If errors of law are found, the appellate court has the power to issue orders to the lower court to retry the individual and to change the general practice found to be in violation of the law by the appellate court. The primary appellate courts in the federal judicial system are the United States Courts of Appeals and the United States Supreme Court. The Congress of the United States, consistent with Article III of the Constitution, has the power to determine the parameters of the appellate jurisdiction of these federal courts and has used it to delegate power to these judicial tribunals.

The terms *exclusive jurisdiction* and *concurrent jurisdiction* have to be understood in the context of federalism. We have two sets of judicial systems in America. Some of the jurisdictional problems—and possible solutions—associated with the existence of a dual judicial system have already been discussed; other problems and solutions will be examined later on in this chapter. *Exclusive jurisdiction* is that power that only federal courts have to hear cases and controversies that arise in our society. This kind of jurisdiction will be discussed in the segments that follow. It is important to understand that exclusive jurisdiction means that only one set of courts can hear and resolve legal controversies. *Concurrent jurisdiction,* on the other hand, means that certain cases and controversies can be heard originally in either a federal or a state court. For example, if a citizen living in New York wishes to sue an individual living in Mississippi, he can either go into state court to initiate proceedings for recovery of damages, or to the federal district court if the amount involved is more than $10,000. In short, concurrent jurisdiction, where it exists, allows different courts to exercise jurisdiction over the same subject matter within the same geographical area.

The federal courts have jurisdiction over civil and criminal cases arising under the federal laws, treaties, and the Constitution itself as well as in those situations arising due to the nature and character of the parties to the dispute. *Civil filings* are all those actions (in 1977 there were over 130,000 civil cases that commenced in the federal district courts) instituted by individuals and corporations in order to protect a private civil right or to compel, through court order, a civil remedy to right a wrong they have suffered. Personal injury, habeas corpus, tax suits, social security claims, property, contract, and civil rights suits are typical of the civil suits initiated in state and federal courts.

Criminal actions, on the other hand, are those legal disputes instituted on behalf of the state or federal government against individuals charged with the commission of a criminal act against the state such as burglary, homicide, robbery, embezzlement, auto theft, selective service (draft) violations, narcotics violations, and immigration violations. In criminal proceedings the state or federal prosecutor asks the court to enforce the penalty and mete out the punishment as described in the criminal statutes.

In sum, the jurisdiction of the federal courts is characterized and identifiable according to:

1. subject matter;
2. parties to the dispute,
3. guidelines established by the Congress according to the parameters of Article III of the United States Constitution.

The jurisdiction is:

4. concurrent, or

5. exclusive, and, based on the decision of the litigant and his counsel, disputes will enter federal courts that have:
6. original jurisdiction.

These judgments of the trial court of the federal system (generally the U.S. District Court) can be appealed (over 90 percent of the cases never go beyond the court of original jurisdiction) and, if there is an appeal, it is taken to the federal court that has:

7. appellate jurisdiction (generally the U.S. Court of Appeals in the same circuit in which the district court is located). In the federal judicial system there is a possibility of two appellate reviews; one by the Court of Appeals and the second by the U.S. Supreme Court—if it wishes to hear the appeal.

What now follows is an examination of the nature of the jurisdiction of the three federal courts: the U.S. District Courts, the U.S. Courts of Appeals, and the United States Supreme Court.

The Jurisdiction of the District Courts

There were, in 1978, 94 U.S. District Courts in the 50 states and the territories of the United States. Eighty-nine of the courts are located within the 50 states; there is also 1 district court in the District of Columbia and 4 territorial district courts located in the Canal Zone, Guam, Puerto Rico, and the Virgin Islands. At the end of 1977 there were 399 federal district court judges assigned to these 94 courts who had to grapple with over 172,000 civil and criminal cases involving federal law filed during that year.[49] This is a dramatic change in workload from the initial decades of the republic.

These "local courts"[50] were created by Congress in 1789 when the national legislature passed the first Judiciary Act. However, as discussed in the preceding section, the pressures against creation of a national judicial system, much less a judicial system with substantive jurisdictional powers, were so great that it was not until 1875 that the district courts were given the general jurisdiction they have today. "In Congress, a strong states rights bloc was hostile to the federal courts. . . . Again and again, reform proposals became entangled in sectional battles or battles between the Congress and the President, and went down to defeat."[51]

[49]At the end of 1977, however, there were only about 380 actually sitting in the district courts.
[50]Chief Justice Warren E. Burger, personal communication, August 20, 1970.
[51]Friedman, *American Law,* p. 125.

Until the 1875 legislation was passed, the primary activities of the U.S. District Courts involved the settlement of disputes involving federal questions and admiralty.[52] The 1789 Judiciary Act's Section 34 was a basic restriction on the federal courts jurisdiction. It stated that the laws of the states "shall be regarded as rules of decision in trials at common law in the courts of the United States in cases where they apply" except for the federal questions. In 1793, the states rights forces in the Congress passed legislation that prohibited the federal courts from enjoining (staying) proceedings in the state courts.[53]

Obviously, in addition to the concern about the organizational development of a federal court system that would infringe upon the jurisdiction of the state court system, the opponents of the federal judicial system were very concerned about the nature of federal jurisdiction. States' righters would have preferred not to have created a federal judiciary at all since, under that circumstance, the state courts would have had original jurisdiction on federal questions as well as questions of state law. Since there was no serious prospect of denying the national legislature the opportunity to create the federal judicial organization, the natural response on the part of the states' rights political elites was to dramatically limit the jurisdiction of these new federal courts.

Although the Removal Act of March 3, 1875, did change the jurisdictional powers of the lower federal courts quite dramatically, there had been other removal acts prior to 1875. These earlier removal acts "had grown out of a fear of prejudice in state courts against the national government" and were passed as a consequence of a state-national dispute.[54] The 1815 and 1816 removal acts grew out of opposition of the New England states to the War of 1812. The Removal Act of 1833 grew out of the nullification battles between South Carolina and the Union, and the 1866 and 1867 removal acts passed by the Congress grew out of conditions in the southern states after the Civil War ended.[55]

What the Removal Act of 1875 accomplished was this: *Any action* asserting a federal right could begin in a federal court or, if begun in the state court, could be removed through writ of habeas corpus to the federal courts.[56] This Act "opened wide a flood of totally new business

---

[52]Richardson and Vines, *Federal Courts,* pp. 28–30. The 1789 Act also gave the District Courts concurrent jurisdiction (with state courts) "of all suits of a civil nature . . . where the matter in dispute exceeds the sum or value of $500, and the suit is between a citizen of a state where the suit is brought, and a citizen of another state." This jurisdiction, referred to as "diversity citizenship" is a major portion of the contemporary district court's workload.

[53]Warren, vol. I, pp. 48–67.

[54]Warren, vol. II, p. 685.

[55]Ibid.

[56]Habeas corpus: perhaps the most famous of the writs of law and equity that

for the federal courts."[57] Since that time the workload of the federal courts has increased dramatically. As seen in the following pages, the jurisdiction—civil and criminal—is as pervasive and as broad as are the legislative actions—substantive and procedural, state and federal—that preceded jurisdictional enlargements.

District Court Jurisdiction in Civil Actions

Of the more than 170,000 filings in the U.S. District Courts in 1977, more than 130,000 were civil cases (see Figures 3-5 and 3-6). These

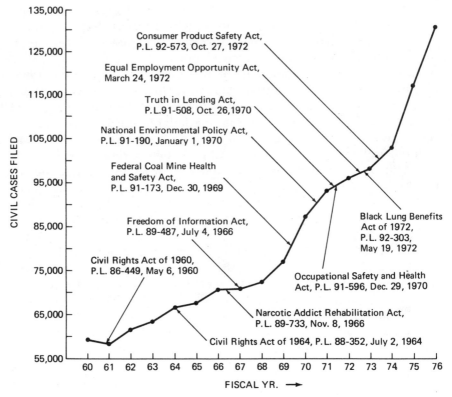

FIG. 3-5   CIVIL CASES FILED IN THE U.S. DISTRICT COURTS FISCAL YEARS 1960–1976

Source: *Annual Report of the Director of the Administrative Office of the U.S. Courts, 1976,* p. 120.

developed in England. It is a basic procedure for obtaining a judicial determination of the legality of the person in custody. Federal habeas corpus, when granted, allows federal judges to test the constitutionality of a state criminal conviction. Simply put, granting of the writ offers immediate relief from illegal confinement or unlawful custody.

[57]Friedman, *American Law,* p. 337.

were suits initiated to enforce a right or seek payment for a wrong committed against an individual. The jurisdiction of the federal district courts falls into a few general areas determined by Congress and placed into law (28 United States Codes, Sections 1331–1359): federal questions; diversity of citizenship; actions under statutes passed by Congress such as Antitrust, Social Security, Truth in Lending, and Civil Rights; bankruptcy; passports; and naturalization.

ACTIONS UNDER FEDERAL STATUTES   A private citizen can enter the U.S. District Court and initiate proceedings when the matter in controversy arises, in his judgment, under the Constitution, laws, or treaties of the

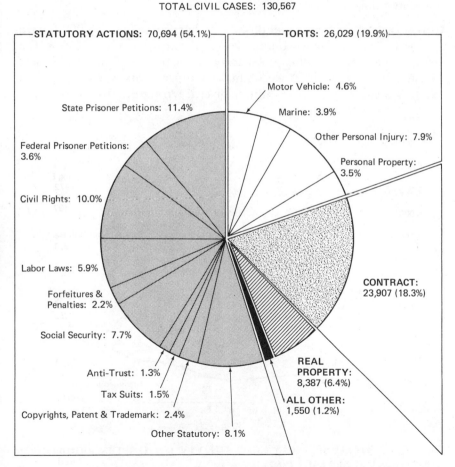

TOTAL CIVIL CASES: 130,567

STATUTORY ACTIONS: 70,694 (54.1%)

TORTS: 26,029 (19.9%)

State Prisoner Petitions: 11.4%

Federal Prisoner Petitions: 3.6%

Civil Rights: 10.0%

Labor Laws: 5.9%

Forfeitures & Penalties: 2.2%

Social Security: 7.7%

Anti-Trust: 1.3%

Tax Suits: 1.5%

Copyrights, Patent & Trademark: 2.4%

Other Statutory: 8.1%

Motor Vehicle: 4.6%

Marine: 3.9%

Other Personal Injury: 7.9%

Personal Property: 3.5%

CONTRACT: 23,907 (18.3%)

REAL PROPERTY: 8,387 (6.4%)

ALL OTHER: 1,550 (1.2%)

FIG. 3-6   TYPE OF CIVIL CASES COMMENCED (12 MONTHS ENDED JUNE 30, 1977)

Source: *Administrative Office of the United States Courts.*

United States. If there is a federal question involved—that is, if the person argues that he or she has a civil right or immunity protected by federal law, treaty, or the Constitution itself that has allegedly been denied to that individual—resolution of that legal dispute can be had in the federal courts. In this characteristic jurisdictional area, citizenship and/or financial amount are not relevant. In recent years there has been a dramatic increase in the number of civil filings of this nature, due to the passage of social welfare policies by the Congress that extended the civil rights and privileges of persons residing in the United States. As Figures 3-7 through 3-11 illustrate, the district courts have heard diverse federal questions associated with such issues as black lung disease, sexual discrimination in employment, occupational safety and health, and racial integration.

FEDERAL QUESTIONS   At the end of 1976 there were over 56,000 federal questions cases that had commenced in the district courts during that year. As Figure 3-12 illustrates, the growth of the "federal question" case has been constant since financial requirements were changed in 1958. A person who alleges injury or civil wrong due to a civil action

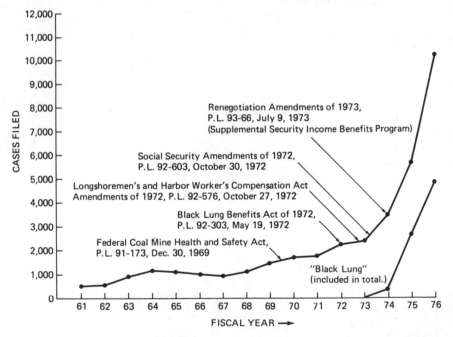

FIG. 3-7   SOCIAL SECURITY CASES FILED IN THE U.S. DISTRICT COURTS, FISCAL YEARS 1961–1976

Source: *Administrative Office of the United States Courts.*

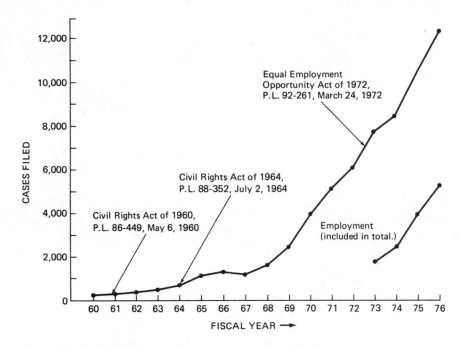

FIG. 3-8   CIVIL RIGHTS CASES FILED IN THE U.S. DISTRICT COURTS, FISCAL
YEARS 1960–1976

Source: *Administrative Office of the United States Courts.*

arising under the laws, treaties, or the United States Constitution, and whose claim is in excess of $10,000 may have the case heard in a federal district court if he or she so desires (See 28 USC, Section 1331). For example, if there was an injury or damages to property in excess of $10,000 and the injured party argued that the injury was a result of application of a federal statute or a provision of the Constitution, given the fact that the Congress granted jurisdiction to federal district courts to hear these cases, the party could bring suit in the federal district court.

DIVERSITY OF JURISDICTION   Section 1332 of 28 USC gives the district courts jurisdiction, if the claim is in excess of $10,000, to hear civil cases involving citizens suing each other who reside in different states, or between a citizen of a state and an alien. At the end of 1976 there were 31,675 such diversity jurisdiction civil actions that had commenced in that year (see Figure 3-13). Opposing parties must come from different states and the amount in question must exceed $10,000 for the district court to have jurisdiction. The diversity jurisdiction power is one of the

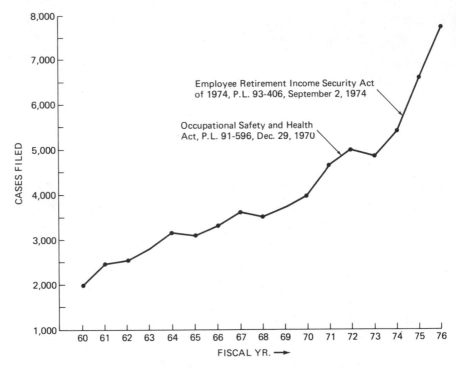

**FIG. 3-9 LABOR SUITS FILED IN THE U.S. DISTRICT COURTS, FISCAL
YEARS 1960–1976**

Source: *Administrative Office of the United States Courts.*

oldest of jurisdictional powers (along with the federal question power)
of the federal courts. There was a fear on the part of the nationalists
who drew up the 1789 Judiciary Act that citizens who brought suit in
a foreign state against a citizen of that foreign state would not receive
a fair hearing. Therefore the federal district court became the tribunal
to hear these cases because it was felt that there would be greater impartiality and complete justice dispensed in that federal district court.
(In recent years there has been a concerted effort, on the part of judges
as well as legislators, to do away with this diversity jurisdiction of the
district courts or at the very least to raise the minimum amount necessary
to get the case into the federal district court.)[58]

BANKRUPTCY PROCEEDINGS   Section 1334 of USC gives to the district
courts the power, exclusive of the courts of the states, to hear and resolve

[58]See the *Annual Report of the Chief Justice of the United States,* in *96 S Ct No 9,* March
1976.

88

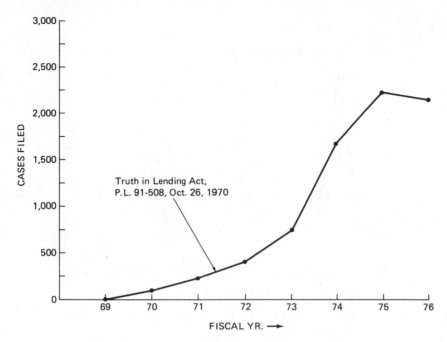

FIG. 3-10   TRUTH IN LENDING CASES FILED IN THE U.S. DISTRICT COURTS, FISCAL YEARS 1969–1976

Source: *Administrative Office of the United States Courts.*

all matters and proceedings in bankruptcy. At the end of 1976, there were 246,549 Bankruptcy Act filings that had commenced in that year (see Figure 3-14). (In addition to bankruptcy proceedings, the district courts also have jurisdiction over passport application and naturalization proceedings.)

PRISONER PETITIONS   One very interesting area of district court jurisdiction is covered by Sections 2242–2254 of 28 USC and that is the area of petitions from prisoners incarcerated in both federal and state penitentiaries. Prisoners, alleging that they were incarcerated in violation of federal laws, often ask the district courts to grant writs of habeas corpus. Others might ask for review because their civil rights were violated. The number of petitions presented to federal district courts by state and federal prisoners has climbed from about 3,500 filings in 1960 to over 19,000 filings at the end of 1976 (see Figure 3-15).

In summary, the major areas of civil jurisdiction for the federal district courts are:

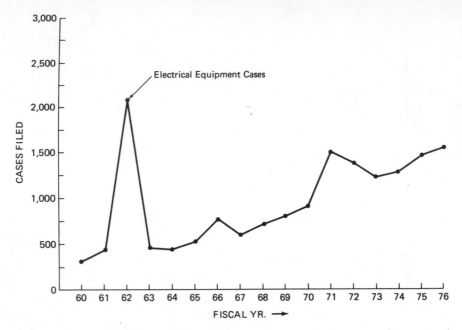

Electrical Equipment Cases

FIG. 3-11   ANTITRUST CASES FILED IN THE U.S. DISTRICT COURTS, FISCAL YEARS 1960–1976

Source: *Administrative Office of the United States Courts.*

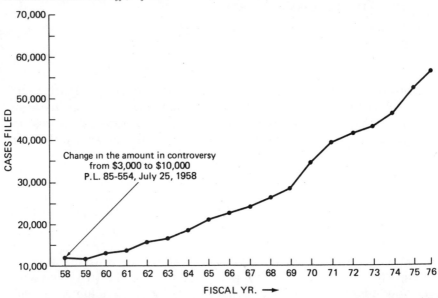

Change in the amount in controversy
from $3,000 to $10,000
P.L. 85-554, July 25, 1958

FIG. 3-12   CIVIL CASES FILED UNDER FEDERAL QUESTION JURISDICTION IN THE UNITED STATES DISTRICT COURTS, FISCAL YEARS 1958–1976

Source: *Administrative Office of the United States Courts.*

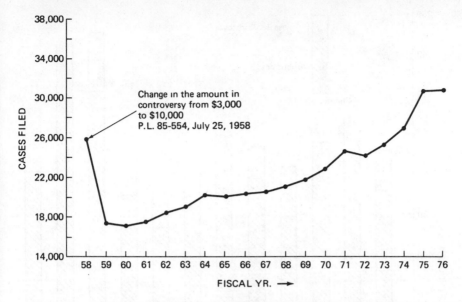

FIG. 3-13   CIVIL CASES FILED UNDER DIVERSITY JURISDICTION IN THE UNITED STATES DISTRICT COURTS, FISCAL YEARS 1958–1976

Source: *Administrative Office of the United States Courts.*

1. federal questions,
2. diversity of citizenship,
3. actions under federal statutes,
4. bankruptcy, patent, and copyright claims.

While there are other areas of civil jurisdiction such as federal postal law cases, interpleader, Interstate Commerce Commission orders, and so forth (See Sections 1331–1359 of 28 USC), the major areas are those that have been discussed above. (There is one other area of district court jurisdiction, removal of actions from state courts to the federal district courts. This particular area of jurisdiction will be discussed in the segment that will cover relationships between state and federal court systems.)

District Court Jurisdiction in Criminal Matters

At the end of 1976 there had commenced in the district courts 39,147 criminal cases. As already noted, this jurisdiction of the federal district courts is based on congressional legislation that established penalties for persons who committed actions that have been labeled as criminal. For example (see Figures 3-16 and 3-17 for the entire range of federal criminal statutes), the Drug Abuse Prevention and Control Act,

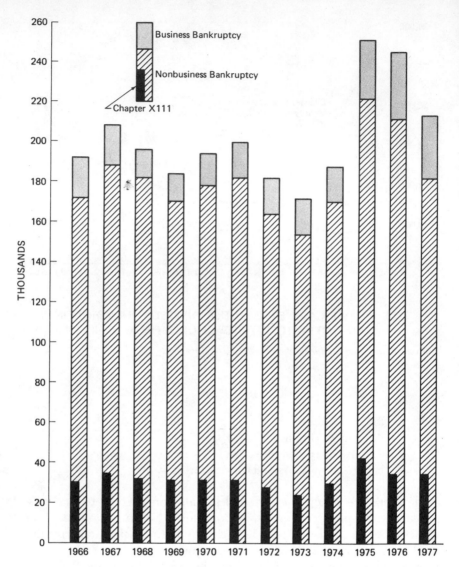

FIG. 3-14   BANKRUPTCY CASES COMMENCED BUSINESS AND NONBUSI-NESS (INCL. CHAPTER XIII); YEARS 1966–1977

Source: *Administrative Office of the United States Courts.*

passed in 1971 by the Congress, has led to the filing of almost 6,000 indictments and informations by federal U.S. Attorneys in U.S. District Courts in 1976.[59]

[59]An *indictment* is a formal written accusation to a federal grand jury, prepared by the U.S. Attorney, which, if accepted by the grand jurors, would lead to a criminal trial in the district court. The grand jurors, finding probable cause that a crime had

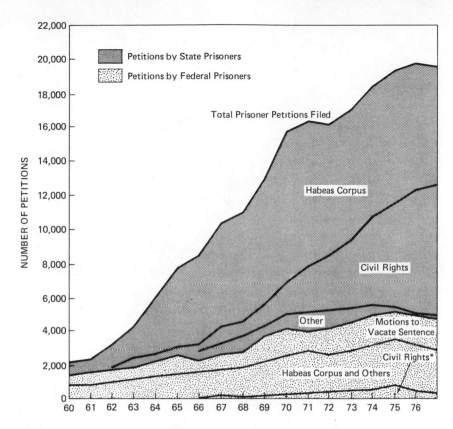

*"Civil Rights" prior to 1966 are included in "Other Prisoner Petitions".

FIG. 3-15   PETITIONS FILED BY STATE AND FEDERAL PRISONERS, 12 MONTHS ENDED JUNE 30, 1960–1977

Source: *United States District Courts.*

It must also be pointed out that criminal prosecutions and the maintenance of domestic tranquility with respect to the traditional domestic criminal activities have traditionally been a responsibility of the local communities in our society. As a consequence, criminal filings had never been a major jurisdictional area of the federal district courts. It has only been in the decades since the Roosevelt administration that

been committed, would indorse the indictment. This indorsement is referred to as a *true bill. Information* is a written accusation drawn up by the U.S. Attorney and presented to a judge rather than to a grand jury. If accepted, probable cause is inferred and the criminal trial would be scheduled. The United States Attorney is the major prosecuting attorney for the United States government. There is a U.S. Attorney in each of the 94 district courts. He or she is appointed by the president of the United States and serves at his pleasure. As will be noted in the chapter on the selection of judges, this is an important political appointment.

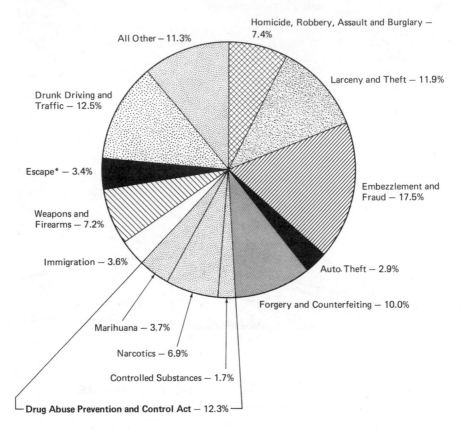

TOTAL CRIMINAL CASES: 39,786

Homicide, Robbery, Assault and Burglary — 7.4%

All Other — 11.3%

Larceny and Theft — 11.9%

Drunk Driving and Traffic — 12.5%

Embezzlement and Fraud — 17.5%

Escape* — 3.4%

Weapons and Firearms — 7.2%

Immigration — 3.6%

Auto. Theft — 2.9%

Forgery and Counterfeiting — 10.0%

Marihuana — 3.7%

Narcotics — 6.9%

Controlled Substances — 1.7%

Drug Abuse Prevention and Control Act — 12.3%

*Escape from custody, aiding or abetting an escape, failure to appear in court and bail jumping.

FIG. 3-16   ALL CRIMINAL CASES COMMENCED BY OFFENSE[1], 12 MONTHS ENDED JUNE 30, 1977

Source: *United States District Courts.*

there has been an explosion of federal criminal law and its consequence—criminal filings in the federal district courts.

National legislation defines crimes against the United States and expands the jurisdiction of the federal district courts. In recent years the national government has been dramatically concerned about the spread of organized crime in America; drug abuse; disturbances in the armed forces selection process; interstate crimes such as automobile theft, embezzlement, and robbery; and criminal violations of the immigration laws. As a consequence, major pieces of legislation were passed

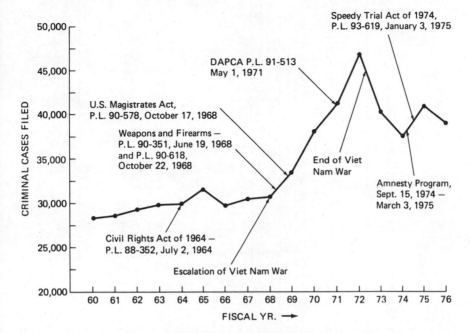

FIG. 3-17   CRIMINAL CASES FILED IN THE U.S. DISTRICT COURTS (ORIGINAL PROCEEDINGS ONLY), FISCAL YEARS 1960–1976

Source: *Administrative Office of the United States Courts.*

such as the Omnibus Crime Control and Safe Streets Act of 1968[60] and the Drug Abuse and Prevention Control Act of 1971. Revisions were made in the Selective Service Act to cover certain activities of antiwar protesters that were deemed inconsistent with national security. With respect to civil rights acts, there are criminal statutes on the books dating back to 1868[61] that make it a crime, punishable by a term in prison and/or a fine, for individuals to conspire to take away the rights and liberties of individual citizens of the United States. The major areas of criminal jurisdiction (see Table 3-2) for the federal district courts in the 1970s are as follows:

1. robbery
2. assault
3. burglary
4. narcotics offenses
5. immigration violations.

[60]See, generally, Richard Harris, *The Fear of Crime* (New York, Praeger and Co., 1969).
[61]See Section 1982, 42 USC.

TABLE 3-2 CRIMINAL CASES FILED BY NATURE OF OFFENSE, (EXCLUDES TRANSFERS), FISCAL YEARS 1968 THROUGH 1976

NATURE OF OFFENSE	FISCAL YEAR 1968	FISCAL YEAR 1969	FISCAL YEAR 1970	FISCAL YEAR 1971	FISCAL YEAR 1972	FISCAL YEAR 1973	FISCAL YEAR 1974	FISCAL YEAR 1975	FISCAL YEAR 1976 ALL OFFENSES	FISCAL YEAR 1976 FELONIES & MISDEMEANORS
Total	30,714	33,585	38,102	41,290	47,043	40,367	37,667	41,108	39,147	34,113
Homicide	206	197	275	237	309	144	160	149	158	158
Robbery	1,279	1,570	1,580	1,955	2,422	1,568	1,556	2,616	2,042	2,035
Bank	869	1,012	1,038	1,337	1,455	1,379	1,468	2,032	1,905	1,900
Postal	23	21	25	44	56	43	42	63	68	68
Other	387	537	517	574	911	146	46	71	69	67
Assault	477	594	684	655	646	695	710	833	832	778
Burglary	669	605	529	482	357	269	271	411	354	354
Larceny and theft	2,637	2,758	3,226	3,685	3,742	3,516	3,565	4,626	4,006	3,576
Embezzlement	1,419	1,712	1,932	2,250	1,810	1,571	1,612	1,870	1,778	1,711
Fraud	1,878	1,531	1,783	2,062	2,748	3,076	3,073	3,666	3,930	3,609
Auto theft	4,722	4,130	4,090	2,408	2,350	1,960	1,790	1,591	1,430	1,419
Forgery and counterfeiting	3,464	3,113	3,862	4,242	4,685	4,104	4,360	4,607	3,972	3,935
Sex offenses	229	224	241	206	274	180	189	176	127	124
Narcotic laws	2,860	3,458	3,511	4,679	6,758	8,817	7,374	7,331	6,198	6,007
Miscellaneous general offenses	1,862	2,152	3,478	4,393	5,066	5,020	6,021	7,230	7,971	5,740

Weapons and firearms	400	494	1,547	2,036	2,377	2,224	2,911	3,165	2,847	2,800
Escape[1]	783	894	1,024	1,245	1,415	1,377	1,505	1,497	1,433	1,384
Drunk driving & traffic	59	50	60	88	124	211	531	1,220	2,587	516
Other misc. general offenses	679	764	907	1,112	1,274	1,419	1,605	2,568	1,104	1,040
Immigration laws	2,609	4,107	4,614	5,027	5,904	2,208	1,921	1,947	2,070	1,782
Liquor, Internal Revenue	1,945	1,409	1,358	1,171	1,254	901	641	349	187	178
Federal statutes	4,458	6,016	6,939	7,838	8,718	6,338	4,424	4,156	4,092	2,707
Civil rights[2]	74	81	192	156	91	136	134	127	85	66
Food and Drug Acts	555	515	499	445	211	108	116	85	61	45
Migratory bird laws	485	426	685	400	389	232	253	361	944	223
Motor Carrier Act	495	476	401	324	230	252	225	146	113	91
Selective Service Act	1,826	3,305	3,712	4,539	5,142	3,043	1,008	274	120	119
Other Federal statutes	1,023	1,213	1,450	1,974	2,655	2,567	2,688	3,163	2,769	2,163

[1]Includes escape from custody, aiding and abetting an escape, failure to appear in court and bail jumping.

[2]These are principally cases removed from State courts under provisions of the Civil Rights Act, 28 U.S.C. 1443.

Source: *Administrative Office of the United States Courts.*

Federal district court jurisdiction will continue to grow so long as the national legislature enacts criminal statutes. There must be a court in which U.S. Attorneys can prosecute violators of the criminal statutes, and the United States District Court, the trial court of the federal judicial system, has the power to hear and try these criminal cases.

The Jurisdiction of the Courts of Appeals

The jurisdiction of the courts of appeals for the 11 federal circuits is completely determined by the U.S. Congress. There are essentially two kinds of case clusters that these appellate courts can review and decide: appeals from the federal district courts, and reviews of decisions of federal administrative boards and commissions. As the latter kind of case initially enters the federal judicial system at the court of appeals level, these take on the aura of "original" jurisdiction legal disputes.

In 1976 there were 18,408 cases docketed in the 11 U.S. Courts of Appeals (see Table 3-3). One major problem facing the judges in these federal appellate courts is the caseload. In 1976 there was a 10

TABLE 3-3   **APPEALS FILED, TERMINATED, AND PENDING IN THE U.S. COURTS OF APPEALS FISCAL YEARS 1962 THROUGH 1976**

FISCAL YEAR	NUMBER OF JUDGSHIPS AS OF JUNE 30	APPEALS			INCREASE IN APPEALS PENDING
		Filed	Terminated	Pending	
1962	78	4,823	4,167	3,031	656
1963	78	5,437	5,011	3,457	426
1964	78	6,023	5,700	3,780	323
1965	78	6,766	5,771	4,775	995
1966	88	7,183	6,571	5,387	612
1967	88	7,903	7,527	5,763	376
1968	97	9,116	8,264	6,615	852
1969	97	10,248	9,014	7,849	1,234
1970	97	11,662	10,699	8,812	963
1971	97	12,788	12,368	9,232	420
1972	97	14,535	13,828	9,939	707
1973	97	15,629	15,112	10,456	517
1974	97	16,436	15,422	11,470	1,014
1975	97	16,658	16,000	12,128	658
1976	97	18,408	16,426	14,110	1,982
Percent change 1976 over					
1962	—	281.7	294.2	365.5	—
1968	—	101.9	98.8	113.3	—
1975	—	10.5	2.7	16.3	—

Source: *Administrative Office of the United States Courts.*

percent increase in the number of cases filed with the courts of appeals; there were 2,000 more cases filed than disposed of by the federal judges in that year. (One reason for the increase is that the Congress, in 1975, passed legislation that took away jurisdiction of the three-judge district courts to hear Interstate Commerce Commission appeals and gave this responsibility to the courts of appeals.)

Appeals from District Courts

Litigants disappointed with the *final* district court judgment against them in the federal district court can take their appeal to the federal court of appeals in that jurisdiction by filing a simple notice of appeal with the district court within 30 days after judgment in the case was reached (28 USC, Section 1291). When the United States is a party in the federal district court case, there is a 60-day period within which the party must file a notice of appeal with the district court. There are no other restrictions outside the time factor; one does not have to meet a monetary amount, nor raise a federal question, nor claim diversity of citizenship. If the case was heard and decided in the lower trial court, it can be appealed to the U.S. Court of Appeals of the circuit in which the federal district court is located.

In 1976 less than 10 percent of the approximately 170,000 federal district court filings were appealed to the courts of appeals (15,054). Of this number of filings from district court judgments, 69 percent or 10,404 were appeals from civil actions and 31 percent or 4,650 were appeals from adverse criminal law judgments (see Table 3-4).

The civil cases appealed to the courts of appeals fell primarily into three areas. There were 3,327 cases involving the U.S. government directly as either plaintiff or defendant. Another 5,267 cases appealed to these federal appeal courts involved federal questions, and 1,714 cases were filed that had invoked diversity of citizenship jurisdiction in the federal district courts. The major area of criminal filing appeals was requested for reviewing adverse decisions in the area of narcotics. Of the 4,650 criminal filings, 1,388 were appeals of narcotics convictions.

Appeals from Federal Administrative Agencies and Commissions

In addition to hearing appeals from the federal district courts, which takes up the bulk of the workload of the federal courts of appeals, these appellate courts have also been given jurisdiction to take appeals from certain administrative agencies. In 1976, fewer than 20 percent (2,515) of the cases docketed in the federal courts of appeals came to these courts from various federal administrative agencies. Of this num-

TABLE 3-4   NATURE OF SUIT OR OFFENSE OF APPEALS FROM THE U.S. DISTRICT COURTS FILED IN THE U.S. COURTS OF APPEALS DURING THE STATISTICAL YEARS 1971-1977

NATURE OF SUIT OR OFFENSE	STATISTICAL YEAR							PERCENT CHANGE[1]	
	1971	1972	1973	1974	1975	1976	1977	1977 over 1971	1977 over 1976
Total cases	10,798	12,379	13,329	13,491	13,679	15,054	15,718	45.6	4.4
Total civil cases	7,601	8,399	8,876	9,424	9,492	10,404	10,980	44.5	5.5
U.S. cases	2,367	2,604	2,704	3,267	2,981	3,327	3,622	53.0	8.9
U.S. plaintiff	363	399	388	510	513	407	449	23.7	10.3
Contract actions	28	45	34	45	57	41	24	-14.3	-41.5
Real property actions	81	70	66	95	73	67	73	-9.9	9.0
Civil rights	34	38	22	62	42	44	55	61.8	25.0
Labor laws	67	83	75	82	65	59	52	-22.4	-11.9
All other	153	163	191	226	276	196	245	60.1	25.0
U.S. defendant	2,004	2,205	2,316	2,757	2,468	2,920	3,173	58.3	8.7
Contract actions	155	138	129	156	115	134	107	-31.0	20.1
Real property actions	19	45	51	40	40	33	32	-	-
Tort actions	119	162	165	163	146	162	181	52.1	11.7
Motions to vacate sentence	474	504	579	684	509	526	502	5.9	-4.6
Habeas corpus	261	234	261	261	207	206	242	-7.3	17.5
Prisoner civil rights	36	39	53	53	61	64	71	97.2	10.9
Other prisoner petitions	99	113	108	225	103	99	60	-39.4	-39.4
Selective Service Act	145	88	14	6	2	-	3	-97.9	-
Social security laws	130	210	193	246	247	293	478	267.7	63.1
Tax suits	220	260	213	233	220	212	193	-12.3	-9.0
All other	346	412	550	690	818	1,191	1,304	276.9	9.5
Private cases	5,234	5,795	6,172	6,157	6,511	7,077	7,358	40.6	4.0
Federal question	3,697	4,053	4,483	4,521	4,676	5,267	5,589	51.2	6.1
Contract actions	91	132	113	163	126	143	137	50.5	-4.2

Tort actions	191	262	381	319	310	341	349	82.7	2.3
Civil rights	804	991	953	1,118	1,126	1,297	1,334	65.9	2.9
Antitrust	227	131	190	256	233	251	261	15.0	4.0
Habeas corpus	1,261	1,319	1,301	1,084	871	866	837	-33.6	-33.5
Prisoner civil rights	311	349	478	472	633	619	774	148.9	25.0
Other prisoner petitions	71	56	49	46	48	54	39	-45.1	-27.8
Labor laws	236	226	260	235	284	279	287	21.6	2.9
Patent	134	117	144	114	149	150	95	-29.1	-36.7
All other	371	470	614	714	896	1,267	1,476	297.8	16.5
Diversity of citizenship	1,286	1,499	1,468	1,527	1,745	1,714	1,713	33.2	-0.1
									5.7
Contract actions	665	789	779	864	1,004	942	996	49.8	-12.3
Tort actions	562	610	620	605	619	709	622	10.7	50.8
All other	59	100	69	58	122	63	95	61.0	
General local jurisdiction	251	243	221	109	90	96	56	-77.7	-41.7
Contract actions	77	25	119	73	47	46	33	-57.1	-28.3
Tort actions	54	65	74	22	22	25	14	-74.1	-44.0
Prisoner petitions	22	7	5	11	6	11	9	-	-
All other	98	146	23	13	15	14	-	-	-
Total criminal cases	3,197	3,980	4,453	4,067	4,187	4,650	4,738	48.2	1.9
Homicide	66	76	97	46	63	48	39	-40.9	-18.8
Robbery and burglary	500	515	518	435	420	484	396	-20.8	-18.2
Larceny and theft	248	261	268	223	276	303	251	1.2	-17.2
Embezzlement and fraud	285	288	369	392	424	482	650	128.1	34.9
Auto theft	180	178	178	164	143	139	116	-35.6	-16.5
Narcotics	565	820	1,271	1,328	1,332	1,388	1,381	144.4	-0.5
Extortion, racketeering and threats	78	162	165	145	111	184	176	125.6	-4.3
Firearms	173	246	215	258	265	301	276	59.5	-8.3
Selective Service Act	261	324	214	95	56	14	5	-98.1	-64.3
All other	841	1,110	1,158	981	1,097	1,307	1,448	72.2	10.8

Percent not calculated where base is 25 or less.

Source: *Administrative Office of the United States Courts.*

ber, over 60 percent came from four major administrative agencies of the federal government: National Labor Relations Board (661), Immigration and Naturalization Service (387), Internal Revenue Service (269), and the Interstate Commerce Commission (229). (See Table 3-5).

The Jurisdiction of the Special Three-Judge District Courts

These special district courts, much maligned by jurists such as Chief Justice Warren Burger,[62] were convened 208 times during 1976. This figure is a decline of 22 percent in one year and is the lowest number of hearings since 1968. Two obvious reasons account for this drop: passage of 1975 legislation that took away three-judge district court jurisdiction over Interstate Commerce Commission orders (and gave this responsibility to the courts of appeals), and 1976 legislation that abolished the general jurisdictions of these special courts as enumerated in 28 USC Section 2281–2282.

Under 28 USC Sections 2281–2282, prior to the 1976 changes, any suit for a permanent injunction[63] against the enforcement of an Act of Congress or a state statute on the grounds that it conflicted with the United States Constitution (and was therefore unconstitutional) must be heard by a three-judge district court. These three-judge courts are *ad hoc* creations and are convened in the following manner: (1) A party files a suit in a district court. (2) The district court judge who receives the application immediately notifies the chief judge of the court of appeals in that district. (3) The chief judge then appoints two other judges to sit with the district court judge who received the application. (4) At least one of the two judges appointed by the chief judge must be a member of the court of appeals of that circuit. (5) All three members of this temporary panel must put aside their ongoing legal activity and hear the case.

Five days notice of the hearing must be given by the clerk of the district court to the appropriate governmental agents. With the cases that involve federal statutes, the Attorney General of the United States and the U.S. attorney in the federal district are notified. In cases involving state statutes, the governor and the attorney general of the state are given the notification by the district court clerk. All appeals from final orders and interlocutory orders[64] of these three-judge district

---

[62]See Burger, "Reducing the Load."

[63]An injunction is a court order requiring a party to refrain from carrying out a particular activity.

[64]An interlocutory order is an order of the three-judge district court (and other trial courts in both state and federal judicial systems) that is provisional and temporary

TABLE 3-5   ADMINISTRATIVE AGENCY CASES FILED IN THE U.S. COURTS OF APPEALS, FISCAL YEAR 1976

AGENCY	TOTAL	D.C.	FIRST	SECOND	THIRD	FOURTH	FIFTH	SIXTH	SEVENTH	EIGHTH	NINTH	TENTH
Total	*2,515*	*563*	*62*	*313*	*212*	*108*	*318*	*216*	*131*	*81*	*440*	*71*
Civil Aeronautics Board	36	30	—	2	—	—	—	—	—	1	3	—
Commissioner of Internal Revenue	269	5	10	54	23	14	48	21	14	7	65	8
Department of Labor	87	7	2	10	20	12	16	5	4	3	8	—
Environmental Protection	209	54	3	9	38	8	11	24	7	7	29	19
Federal Communications Commission	158	132	2	9	2	8	1	—	1	2	—	1
Federal Power Commission	218	101	1	5	1	—	71	—	2	4	24	9
Immigration and Naturalization Service	387	2	11	99	47	2	42	15	10	4	154	1
Interstate Commerce Commission	229	124	2	5	9	5	28	24	9	10	11	2
National Labor Relations Board	661	38	22	99	53	46	74	103	63	26	118	19
Occupational Safety and Health	73	9	3	10	9	2	7	5	6	5	13	4
Other	188	61	6	11	10	11	20	19	15	12	15	8

Source: *Administrative Office of the United States Courts.*

TABLE 3-6   THREE-JUDGE COURT HEARINGS BY NATURE OF SUIT, STATISTICAL YEARS 1963-1977

FISCAL YEAR	TOTAL	REVIEW OF ICC ORDERS	CIVIL RIGHTS	REAPPOR-TIONMENT	ALL OTHER
1963	129	67	19	16	27
1964	119	50	21	18	30
1965	147	60	35	17	35
1966	162	72	40	28	22
1967	171	64	55	10	42
1968	179	51	55	6	67
1969	215	64	81	1	69
1970	291	42	162	8	79
1971	318	41	176	2	99
1972	310	52	166	32	60
1973	320	52	183	7	78
1974	249	51	171	8	19
1975	267	47	192	9	19
1976	208	25	161	5	17
1977	112	2	59	6	45
Percent Change 1977 over 1976	-46.2	-92.0	-63.4	20.0	164.7

Source: *Administrative Office of the United States Courts.*

courts are appealed directly to the United States Supreme Court. Table 3-6 illustrates the kinds of hearings that were convened in 1976.

Along with the abolition of the sections in 28 USC that gave the three-judge district courts jurisdiction to hear suits calling for permanent injunctions by the 1976 legislation, the Congress amended the conditions under which a three-judge district court could be convened (as written in Section 2284 of 28 USC):

1. in existing statutes calling for three-judge provisions such as the 1964 Civil Rights Act and the 1965 Voting Rights Act;
2. an action that challenges the constitutionality of apportionment of congressional districts; or,
3. suits filed challenging the constitutionality of the apportionment of any statewide legislative body.[65]

As the most recent statistics indicate, the greatest number of three-judge district court hearings involve civil rights disputes (see Table 3-7). One hundred sixty-one (or 77 percent) of the 208 three-judge hearings in 1976 involved civil rights suits.

---

in nature. It is an order that calls for additional proceedings that would lead to a final order or decree. See 28 USC Sections 1291–1293.

[65]*Annual Report of the Director,* p. 209.

TABLE 3-7   THREE-JUDGE CIVIL RIGHTS CASES BY NATURE OF SUIT, STATISTICAL YEARS 1974-1977

NATURE OF CIVIL RIGHTS SUITS	1974	1975	1976	1977
Total	*171*	*192*	*161*	*67*
Abortion laws	2	10	3	3
Assistance to nonpublic schools	5	1	3	2
Attachment, seizure without hearing	16	15	17	2
Education for handicapped	2	1	1	1
Employment	13	12	14	5
Expelling or suspending students	2	—	—	—
Housing	5	—	—	—
Jury selection procedures	2	—	—	—
Licensing procedures	11	14	10	5
Mental patients, commitment	7	4	6	1
Obscenity	11	5	3	1
Penal codes and prisoner petitions	3	9	7	3
Prescription drug advertising	2	3	—	—
Racial discrimination	2	2	—	—
Residency requirements	2	8	2	1
Sobriety tests	—	—	—	1
Taxes	1	4	5	—
Voting and election laws	20	32	19	13
Welfare, social security, unemployment benefits	17	18	23	9
Constitutionality of other state statutes	29	30	27	9
Other (not specified, or otherwise unclassifiable)	18	24	21	11

Source: *Administrative Office of the United States Courts.*

Given the judicial politics and pressures against the continuation these special district courts, and given the fact that the Congress in 1975 and 1976 did radically change the jurisdiction of these courts, the future of three-judge district courts is not clear. The probability is that these courts will be abolished in the near future.

The Jurisdiction of the United States Supreme Court

The United States Supreme Court is the highest court of justice in America. Given the description of judicial power in Article III and the grants of jurisdiction by the Congress in 28 USC, this tribunal has the power to hear, if the justices so determine, cases and controversies from the lower federal courts and from final judgments of the highest courts of individual states—so long as there were *federal questions of substance* raised in the state cases.

As will be illustrated in the chapter that discusses access, justiciability, and standing to sue, the justices of the Supreme Court are in almost total control of the cases they will hear during a given term of the Court. Their jurisdiction is both original and appellate; however, the workload of the Supreme Court is primarily appellate as the figures in Table 3-8 clearly indicate.

TABLE 3-8   FINAL DISPOSITION OF CASES

	DISPOSED OF	REMAINING ON DOCKET
Original Docket	2	6
On Merits	2	
Leave to File Complaint Denied	0	
Appellate Docket[a]	1929	395
On Merits	309[b]	
Appeals and Petitions for Review		
Denied or Dismissed[c]	1620	
(Review Granted: 147 (8.3%))[d]		
Miscellaneous Docket[a]	2075	323
On Merits	62[b]	
Appeals and Petitions for Review		
Denied or Dismissed[c]	2013	
(Review Granted: 22 (1.1%))[d]		
Total	4006	724

Method of Disposition			
By Written Opinion	170[e]	By Denial or Dismissal of Appeals or Petitions for Review[c]	3633
(Number of Written Opinions: 142)[f]			
By Per Curiam Decision	203	By Denial of Leave to File Complaint—Original Cases	0
Total			4006

Disposition of Cases Reviewed on Writ of Certiorari			
	Reversed[g]	Vacated[h]	Affirmed	Total
Full Opinions	58 (50.9%)	18 (15.8%)	38 (33.3%)	114
Memorandum Orders	5 (4.3%)	108 (93.9%)	2 (1.7%)	115
Total	63 (27.5%)	126 (55.0%)	40 (17.5%)	229

[a]The appellate docket consists of all paid cases. The miscellaneous docket consists of all cases filed in forma pauperis.

[b]Including cases summarily affirmed, reversed, or vacated.

[c]This category primarily includes dismissals of appeals and denials of petitions for certiorari. It also includes denials of other applications for review, such as petitions for writs of habeas corpus or writs of mandamus.

[d]In computing the percentage of cases granted review last Term, the divisor is obtained by adding the number of cases denied or dismissed to the number of cases granted review. Petitions remaining on the docket on which no action has been taken are not included.

[e]Including 16 cases disposed of in 16 per curiam opinions containing sufficient legal reasoning to be considered "written opinions" and not included in the per curiam decision figures.

[f]Including 16 per curiam opinions containing substantial legal reasoning.

[g]Including five cases reversed in part and affirmed in part.

[h]Including one case affirmed in part and vacated in part.

Source: *91* Harvard Law Review, *November 1977, p. 298.*

Original Jurisdiction

As enumerated in Article III and clarified by congressional statutes, the original jurisdiction of the United States Supreme Court falls into two categories: original and exclusive, and original but not exclusive. Original and exclusive jurisdiction of the Supreme Court extends to cases and controversies involving (1) two or more states, and (2) all legal actions *against* ambassadors or other public ministers of foreign states.

Original but concurrent jurisdiction of the Supreme Court extends to (1) actions brought to the Court *by* ambassadors or other public ministers of foreign states or actions to which consuls are parties to the dispute (this type of legal dispute can, at the option of litigants, be brought into the U.S. district courts); (2) controversies between the United States and a state; and (3) proceedings by a state against citizens of another state or against aliens.

These clusters of original jurisdiction areas do not clog the calendar of the Supreme Court. In the entire 1976 term of the U.S. Supreme Court, as seen in Table 3-8, there was a total of just two original jurisdiction cases disposed of on the merits, with but another six remaining on the docket of the Supreme Court. These were 2 of the 4,006 cases that were disposed of during this particular term of the Supreme Court. It is obvious that the Supreme Court is not really a court of original jurisdiction! (A question that will be raised in the next segment is whether or not the Supreme Court can be considered a typical appellate court.)

Appellate Jurisdiction

As already noted the Supreme Court controls both its original and its appellate dockets. It was given this general discretion indirectly when the Congress reorganized the federal judicial system in 1891. At that time the creation of the federal courts of appeals with jurisdiction to hear appeals from the district courts took away the burdensome mundane appellate responsibilities that the Supreme Court had shouldered since 1789.[66] At that time, 1891, the Supreme Court became essentially a major policy maker in the federal system of government. It was freed to use its jurisdictional powers in a selective manner so that its opinions would have an even greater impact on the politics and economics of American society.[67]

The passage of the Judges Bill in 1925—a piece of legislation whose major lobbyist was the Chief Justice of the United States, William H. Taft—"culminated a calculated effort by the Congress to transform the

[66]Richardson and Vines, *Federal Courts,* p. 30.
[67]Ibid.

Supreme Court from a workaday appellate tribunal to a more selective policy role."[68] The 1925 legislation gave the Supreme Court the power to determine its docket, especially control of the granting of the writ of certiorari. Essentially, as will be noted in the following segments and in the upcoming chapters, the justices of the Supreme Court carefully select a very small percentage of petitions to the Court for review on the merits. In order for the Court to take the case, it must—in the estimation of the sitting justices—be a controversy of major proportions.

The justices, however, have this discretion within the confines of their appellate jurisdiction. This appellate jurisdiction is clustered about three kinds of appeals: direct appeals from three-judge district courts, appeals from courts of appeals and other specialized federal courts, and state court appeals. (See Table 3-9 for a detailed examination of the workload of the Supreme Court at the end of the 1976 term.)

APPEALS FROM THREE-JUDGE DISTRICT COURTS   The Supreme Court's power to hear cases extends to judgments of these special district courts. Section 1253 of 28 USC allows any party to appeal directly to the Supreme Court from any order granting or denying an interlocutory or final decree.

TABLE 3-9   SUBJECT MATTER OF DISPOSITIONS WITH FULL OPINIONS[a]

| | PRINCIPAL ISSUE | | DECISION | | |
	CONSTITU-TIONAL	OTHER	FOR GOV'T[b]	AGAINST GOV'T	TOTAL
ORIGINAL JURISDICTION	0	0	0	0	0
CIVIL ACTIONS FROM INFERIOR FEDERAL COURTS	43	41	49	24	84
FEDERAL GOVERNMENT LITIGATION	11	18	23	6	29
Taxation	*0*	*3*	*2*	*1*	*3*
Review of Administrative Action	*2*	*8*	*10*	*0*	*10*
Administrative Procedure	0	1	1	0	1
Benefits Review Board	0	1	1	0	1
Dep't of Agriculture	0	1	1	0	1
Environmental Protection Agency	0	1	1	0	1
Health, Education, and Welfare	1	1	2	0	2
Nat'l Labor Relations Board	0	2	2	0	2
Occupational Safety and Health Review Commission	1	0	1	0	1
Securities and Exchange Commission	0	1	1	0	1

[68]Ibid., p. 32.

TABLE 3-9   SUBJECT MATTER OF DISPOSITIONS WITH FULL OPINIONS[a] *(continued)*

	PRINCIPAL ISSUE		DECISION		
	CONSTITU-TIONAL	OTHER	FOR GOV'T[b]	AGAINST GOV'T	TOTAL
Other Actions by or Against the United States or Its Officers	*9*	*7*	*11*	*5*	*16*
Armed Forces	1	1	1	1	2
Civil Rights Act of 1964	0	3	1	2	3
Due Process	1	0	1	0	1
Federal Tort Claims Act	0	1	1	0	1
Immigration and Nationality Act	1	0	1	0	1
Internal Revenue Code	0	1	1	0	1
Labor Relations	0	1	1	0	1
Presidential Recording and Materials Preservation Act	1	0	1	0	1
Search and Seizure	1	0	0	1	1
Social Security	2	0	2	0	2
Voting Rights Act of 1965	2	0	1	1	2
STATE OR LOCAL GOVERNMENT LITIGATION	28	8	28	8	36
Abortion	2	1	3	0	3
Abstention	1	0	1	0	1
Civil Rights	3	1	4	0	4
Commerce Clause	3	0	2	1	3
Due Process	4	0	4	0	4
Equal Protection	7	1	5	3	8
Establishment of Religion	1	0	1	0	1
Freedom of Speech and Press	3	0	1	2	3
Indian Affairs	0	1	1	0	1
Intervention in State Proceedings	0	1	1	0	1
Mootness	1	0	1	0	1
Privacy	1	0	0	1	1
Procedure	0	1	1	0	1
Self-Incrimination	1	0	0	1	1
Voting Rights Act of 1965	1	1	2	0	2
Welfare Rights	0	1	1	0	1
PRIVATE LITIGATION	4	15	—	—	19
Federal Question Jurisdiction	*3*	*15*	—	—	*18*
Antitrust	0	5	—	—	5
Civil Rights	3	3	—	—	6
Labor Management Relations Act	0	2	—	—	2
Military Selective Service Act	0	1	—	—	1
Procedure	0	2	—	—	2
Securities Acts	0	2	—	—	2
Diversity Jurisdiction	*1*	*0*	—	—	*1*
Conflict of Laws	1	0	—	—	1
FEDERAL CRIMINAL CASES	**11**	**6**	**12**	**5**	**17**
Construction of Statute	0	5	4	1	5
Double Jeopardy	5	1	4	1	5
Due Process	3	0	2	1	3

TABLE 3-9   SUBJECT MATTER OF DISPOSITIONS WITH FULL OPINIONS[a] *(continued)*

	PRINCIPAL ISSUE		DECISION		
	CONSTITU-TIONAL	OTHER	FOR GOV'T[b]	AGAINST GOV'T	TOTAL
Search and Seizure	2	0	1	1	2
Self-Incrimination	1	0	1	0	1
FEDERAL HABEAS CORPUS	9	1	6	4	10
FEDERAL PRISONERS	1	0	1	0	1
Due Process	1	0	1	0	1
STATE PRISONERS	8	1	5	4	9
Due Process	4	0	2	2	4
Equal Protection	1	0	0	1	1
Federal Habeas Procedure	1	1	1	1	2
Self-Incrimination	2	0	2	0	2
CIVIL ACTIONS FROM STATE COURTS					
STATE OR LOCAL GOVERNMENT	**14**	**3**	**4**	**7**	**17**
LITIGATION	10	1	5	6	11
Commerce Clause	1	0	0	1	1
Constitutional State Sovereignty	1	0	1	0	1
Contract Clause	1	0	0	1	1
Due Process	1	0	0	1	1
Freedom of Speech and Press	2	0	0	2	2
Indian Affairs	0	1	1	0	1
Labor Relations	1	0	1	0	1
State Taxation	3	0	2	1	3
PRIVATE LITIGATION	4	2	—	—	6
Construction of Statute	0	1	—	—	1
Equal Protection	2	0	—	—	2
Freedom of Speech and Press	2	0	—	—	2
Labor Relations	0	1	—	—	1
STATE CRIMINAL CASES	**14**	**0**	**6**	**8**	**14**
Capital Punishment	4	0	0	4	4
Double Jeopardy	1	0	0	1	1
Due Process	3	0	1	2	3
Ex Post Facto	1	0	1	0	1
Freedom of Speech and Press	2	0	2	0	2
Search and Seizure	1	0	0	1	1
Self-Incrimination	2	0	2	0	2
TOTAL	**91**	**51**	**77**	**48**	**142**

[a]This table deals only with full opinions of the Court that disposed of cases on the merits. 16 per curiam decisions containing substantial legal reasoning have been treated as full opinions for purposes of this table.

[b]"Government" refers to federal, state, or local government or an agency thereof, or to an individual participating in the suit in an official capacity. A case is counted "for the government" if the government as a party prevails substantially on the principal issue. When the federal government opposes a state or local government, a decision is counted "for the government" if the federal government prevails.

Source: *91* Harvard Law Review, *November 1977, pp. 299–301.*

DIRECT APPEALS FROM DISTRICT COURTS   In a legal dispute where any court in the federal district court system, including the territorial courts, invalidates an act of the Congress or where the United States (and any officers or employees of the government) is a party to the dispute, the Supreme Court has jurisdiction to take the case directly from that trial court (see Section 1252).

APPEALS FROM THE COURTS OF APPEALS   Section 1254 of 28 USC gives the Supreme Court jurisdiction to review judgments of the 11 courts of appeals—if the Supreme Court justices so decide to hear these petitions—using three methods:

1. writ of certiorari
2. appeal as of right
3. certification.

The *writ of certiorari,* originally an extraordinary writ of equity,[69] is a means of gaining appellate review by a litigant. If the writ is granted by the higher court, the lower court sends the complete record up to the Supreme Court for review and judgment. With respect to the Supreme Court, *certiorari* is a totally discretionary writ. Supreme Court Rule 19, governing considerations regarding the review on certiorari, states in part that "a review on writ of certiorari is not a matter of right, but of sound judicial discretion, and will be granted only where there are special and important reasons therefor."[70] If four of the justices, as will be discussed in the chapter on Supreme Court decision making, agree that a controversy is of sufficient public importance, certiorari will be granted. As the information of Table 3-8 indicates, few petitions for certiorari are granted; most requests are denied by the court.

The *appeal "as of right"* is a method that is not used by litigants very often due to the parameters that the Congress established in Section 1254. If there is a final order of a court of appeals in which the federal judges ruled that a state statute was invalid because it conflicted with the U.S. Constitution, laws, or treaties of the national government, the losing party may appeal as of right to the Supreme Court. (If the party does use this method, he or she cannot later on use the certiorari method

[69]Writ of equity: In the development of the English legal system, demands for justice due to the inability of the common law to cover all kinds of legal disputes led the monarch to create a Court of Chancery. The judges were commanded to provide justice to parties involved in disputes that were not covered in the statutory and common laws of England. Today, in America, there is no distinction between law and equity.
[70]*U.S. Supreme Court Rule 19 Considerations Governing Review on Certiorari,* in Murphy and Pritchett, *Courts, Judges,* p. 81.

if the Supreme Court dismisses the appeal.) The justices of the Supreme Court use discretion with respect to appeals; the mandatory characteristic of this method is muted by the fact that the Court can dismiss the appeal "for *want* of a *substantial* federal question." They can do this because the statute states that the justices can take these cases for review but that the review is limited to the federal question issue alone. Therefore, if there is a federal question raised in the litigation, but if it is not a "substantial" federal dispute, the justices of the Supreme Court will not hear the case.

Certification is a method originated by the federal court of appeal itself. The lower federal appeals court, if the panel of judges so desires, can ask the Supreme Court for instructions regarding a *question of law*. This process is seldom used in contemporary times. Very infrequently is a question certified by a court of appeals to the Supreme Court for review. The justices of the Supreme Court, according to Section 1254 of 28 USC, may either give the court of appeals binding instructions or they may require that the entire record be sent up to the Supreme Court for review and final disposition.

APPEALS FROM SPECIALIZED FEDERAL COURTS   Section 1255 of 28 USC gives the Supreme Court jurisdiction to hear, through either certiorari or certification, appeals from decisions of the lower specialized federal courts such as the Court of Claims or the Court of Customs and Patent Appeals (Section 1256). This is not a major source of appeals to the United States Supreme Court.

APPEALS FROM STATE COURTS   The Congress has given the Supreme Court jurisdiction to hear certain kinds of appeals from the final judgments of the highest state courts. Review may be requested by using the *certiorari* or the *appeal as of right* methods. The basic stipulation in the statute is that a *federal question* be present in the appeal to the Supreme Court and that it be presented in state courts from the very inception of the legal process—the trial itself in the local court that retained jurisdiction to hear that particular case. The claimant must have exhausted all his state remedies and must have been reviewed by the state supreme court (which must have rendered a final judgment or decree in the case) before the person can approach the U.S. Supreme Court.

If there is an appeal as of right, the petitioner must show one of two things: either that the state courts invalidated a federal statute or that a petitioner challenged the constitutionality of a state statute (with respect to being in conflict with the U.S. Constitution) and the state courts validated the legitimacy of the state statute. The petition for the writ of certiorari must clearly raise the federal issue; the briefs presented by counsel must present substantive reasons for the necessity of Supreme

Court review of the case. In both instances, the Supreme Court has the discretion to take or not to take these petitions and appeals. As the figures in Table 3-8 indicate, the justices of the Supreme Court choose not to hear most of these appeals and petitions.

These five areas enumerated above constitute the scope of appellate review possessed by the United States Supreme Court. As the statistics indicate, less than six percent of these thousands of petitions are examined on the merits by the Supreme Court. To that extent this highest tribunal in the federal judicial system is not a traditional appellate court. The justices use their powers to hear and resolve disputes with a great deal of discretion; they take only those cases and controversies which, in their reasoned judgment, need to be heard by the highest court in America. A later chapter will discuss this decision-making process.

FEDERAL AND STATE COURT INTERACTION AND THE PRINCIPLE OF COMITY

The segments in this chapter have described the difficulties that nationalists had in developing a viable federal judicial system that would function alongside the existing state judicial systems. A very critical junction took place in 1789 when the Congress passed the Judiciary Act which, in part, created the inferior federal courts. Although it was almost a century later that these federal courts received broad jurisdiction, their creation in 1789 was very important.

There are certain issues that, when they are substantively present in state legal trials, can lead to removal of these cases from state courts into the federal courts. The very nature of the issues suggests the reasons for this removal: federal questions, diversity of citizenship. Although the federal district courts can remove certain cases that had commenced in the state courts when the *defendant* petitions for this action, they do so only when serious federal questions are raised by these defendants. Chapter 89 of 28 USC lists the four basic reasons for removal:

1. where district courts have original jurisdiction and plaintiff had claimed a federal right, defendant may remove the case;
2. when a defendant, in a diversity suit, asks for removal;
3. when federal officers, acting under authority of federal law, are sued civilly or prosecuted criminally;
4. when, in civil rights litigation in state court, a defendant seeks relief from local prejudice that denies him "equal civil rights of citizens."

The Congress has given jurisdiction to these federal trial courts only when there is a legal clash that centers around the concept of federalism. Short of that basic foundation for removal, the federal courts will respect the autonomy and jurisdiction of state courts.

Although the Supreme Court has the jurisdictional power to hear appeals from final judgments of the various state supreme courts, the jurisdiction is clearly limited to the federal question factor. If the state supreme court invalidates federal rights and statutes or if it upholds state statutes against challenges that the state law violated the Constitution, then the Supreme Court *may* review the action of the state court and it may be reversed or affirmed by the justices of the United States Supreme Court.

This is as it should be for the judiciary, national and state, is part of the federal system. It is a federal system that is based, in the final analysis, on the substance of Article VI of the United States Constitution: the Supremacy Clause. In any dispute between federal laws, treaties, and the Constitution versus state statutes, the federal orders, treaties, and the U.S. Constitution are "the Supreme Law of the Land." The national legislature has wisely given the national courts limited supervisory power (discretionary with respect to the United States Supreme Court) in that one very critical area: federalism.

Although the federal courts have some power to hear cases from the state courts, the federal judges are bound by the general principle of comity in most instances. Comity is a general rule of legal courtesy whereby one court defers (or equitably abstains) to the jurisdiction of another court that has already begun proceedings in that case.

The history of the federal court system emphasizes slow, ad hoc growth of the judiciary. It is a history replete with political, economic, and sectional concerns and pressures for and against the development of the federal judicial system. However, after almost 200 years of growth and expansion, there exists—alongside still viable state judicial systems— a strong, overcrowded, and overarching federal judicial system. To fully understand the dynamics of the federal judicial system, it is necessary to go beyond organization and jurisdiction and examine the dynamics of getting the cases and controversies into the federal courts. Chapter 4, "Gaining Access to the Federal Courts," examines that dimension.

gaining access to the federal courts

4

The functions, organization, and the jurisdiction of the federal courts have already been discussed. This chapter focuses on "the conditions that are necessary to activate" the federal courts.[1] Once jurisdiction is established, certain characteristics must be manifested in the litigation that comes to the courts before the judges will *hear* and *decide* these legal issues. Although the federal judges have the responsibility to do justice to rich and to poor alike, these jurists—through the judicial creation of certain mechanisms which will be discussed and illustrated in this chapter—"make sure they do not handle controversies that the judges feel it imprudent to handle."[2] The justices of the United States Supreme Court play an especially critical role in developing and operationalizing these judicial mechanisms that operate as a form of self-restraint on the federal judges.

The United States Supreme Court operates as a legal gatekeeper for the federal courts. Through its judgments the lower federal judges are given cues regarding the kinds of legal cases and controversies they can hear in their courts—given that the jurisdiction to hear such cases exists in the first instance. This gatekeeping function of the courts, especially the Supreme Court, is an aspect of the separation of powers

---

[1]David W. Rhode and Harold J. Spaeth, *Supreme Court Decision Making* (San Francisco: Freeman, 1976), p. 9.
[2]Murphy and Pritchett, *Courts, Judges, & Politics* (New York: Random House, 1975), p. 260.

discussion that began in our constitutional era and continues to this day.

"The problem of access to the federal courts is a problem in the separation of powers."[3] A federal judicial system that allows all kinds of social, political, and economic conflicts to be argued and litigated in its courts—and resolved by the federal judges—affects the sensitive political equilibrium of the federal system. To the extent that the judges debate and reach substantive judgments on these important social issues, the role of more traditional political agencies (legislators, executives, bureaucrats) is lessened. What kinds of disputes should the federal judges be hearing? What should be left to the democratically elected political actors?

To answer these questions is to get to the essence of the issue of access. If the federal judges *narrow* the circumstances under which lower federal courts"[4] and the Supreme Court itself can properly hear cases coming into these courts, then these disputes are either resolved in the political system or they are not: In either case the federal judges are not deciding the social or political issue. This judicial deference to the political processes in a democracy is an important characteristic of judicial behavior that emerges very early in our republic. Throughout our history many federal judges have urged such *judicial restraint.* The propriety of the federal courts to act as political decision makers is eschewed by these federal judges.[5]

However, if the federal judges *broaden* the circumstances under which cases can be heard in the federal courts, then these judges are in effect stating that it is proper for the federal judiciary to hear a wide range of social and political issues that have emerged as legal controversies in our political system. This perception, commonly called *judicial activism,* is a characteristic held by judges and courts ever since Chief Justice John Marshall wrote in the 1803 case of *Marbury v. Madison* that it was "emphatically the province and the duty of the courts to say what the law is."

As will be pointed out in the chapter, throughout our history there have been both kinds of majorities on the federal courts—especially the United States Supreme Court. If the Court acts as a gatekeeper, it can either open the legal gate wide to let in many interesting political questions or it can just barely crack open the door to the federal courts. By so narrowly holding open the door to the federal courts, these Supreme

---

[3]Wallace Mendelson, "Mr. Justice Douglas and Government by the Judiciary," *Journal of Politics,* vol. 38 no. 4 (November 1976), p. 937.
[4]Rhode and Spaeth, *Supreme Court,* p. 4.
[5]Ibid., p. 3. See also Justice Felix Frankfurter's classic statement in *West Virginia Board of Education v. Barnette* 319 US 624 (1943).

Court strictures keep out many social and political issues that had not been resolved in the political system.

GATEKEEPING AS RULES OF JUDICIAL ABSTENTION

A person believes that a legal right he possesses has been violated by someone else. He then proceeds to complain about his loss of rights. If the person is really serious he initiates a lawsuit. When this occurs, the person who complains is referred to as the *plaintiff* and the person against whom the action is brought is called the *defendant*. The jurisdiction concept suggests that the plaintiff can go into a court only if that legal tribunal has been given the authority to hear that particular kind of dispute.[6]

Let's assume that the plaintiff chooses to litigate his claim in a federal district court. The plaintiff must get the defendant into the court and he must (in the complaint for relief) state what he wants the court to do about providing him or her with relief. Assume, also, that the federal district court has been given the power—by Congress—to hear that kind of claim. Before the case is disposed of in the federal district court, the judge has to determine whether or not certain conditions are present in the case brought to the court by the plaintiff.

If these conditions are not present, the federal court will not hear the case. Jurisdiction therefore is the *beginning point* for the plaintiff and for the judge. Without jurisdiction the courts cannot even begin to adjudicate disputes. However, jurisdiction alone is not enough. If that were all that was necessary to get the federal judges to decide problems, the gates to the judicial system would have been torn down by the heavy traffic many years ago.

Beyond the jurisdiction issue is a general consideration by the judges as to *whether or not the complaint is a true dispute* and *whether* or not, if it is a true dispute, *the court can provide a legal remedy.* Although the "federal judges cannot apply their power until someone brings a case before them,"[7] they *will not* apply their power if they believe that a dispute brought before them does not merit judicial examination. As United States Supreme Court Justice Louis Brandeis once said: "The

---

[6]See, generally, Carl Auerbach et al., *The Legal Process* (San Francisco: Chandler, 1961).
[7]Rhode and Spaeth, *Supreme Court*, p. 5. See also Murphy and Pritchett, *Courts, Judges*, p. 260.

most important thing we do is not doing."[8] In a society that is as litigation-oriented as ours, this judicial *discretion* of the federal judges, based on rules created by the judges themselves, has a major impact on the making and modification of public policies. The segments that follow discuss and illustrate some of these judicially created rules of access that determine the kind of role the federal courts will play in the political process.

Standing To Sue

Assuming jurisdiction of the federal courts to hear certain kinds of legal disputes, the plaintiff entering the court must have *standing to sue* in the federal court in order for the federal judge to hear and resolve the dispute. This involves a "court's determination of whether a person's dispute with another party is deserving of judicial resolution."[9] The American legal system is an adversarial one which means, in most instances, that there must be a real dispute between the plaintiff and the defendant. For a case to be adjudicated in the federal courts, this kind of situation must be clearly perceived for the case to proceed.

Since "generalizations about standing to sue are largely worthless as such,"[10] it is imperative that certain basic components of the concept be reviewed. By examining these judicial constructs (which *in toto* give to those in the legal process an understanding of the dimensions of standing) greater clarity will be given to the notion of standing to sue.

Cases and Controversies

Article III of the United States Constitution (and 28 USC) extends to the federal courts the judicial power to hear certain kinds of cases and controversies. This language of the Constitution and statutes has been interpreted by federal judges so as to require *real* and *substantial* disputes, affecting the legal rights and obligations of plaintiffs and defendants.[11] Federal judges do not hand down advisory opinions—i.e., friendly, nonadversary, legal questions will not be heard by federal judges.

There must also be presented to the court by the plaintiff arguments that spell out the kind of relief the federal court can provide him

---

[8]Quoted in Mendelson, "Mr. Justice Douglas," p. 918.
[9]Rhode and Spaeth, *Supreme Court,* p. 13.
[10]*Association of Data Processors Service Organization v. Camp,* 397 *US* 150 (1970).
[11]*Aetna Life Insurance Company v. Haworth,* 300 *US* 227 (1937); "One must show a direct relationship between injury and claim sought to be adjudicated." *Linda R. S. v. Richard D.,* 410 *US* 614 (1973).

through the issuance of a judicial order. If these conditions are met, among others to be discussed below, then there is a case or controversy that can be adjudicated by the federal judges.

Furthermore, if the real, substantial dispute involves a question that raises the meaning of the Constitution itself, there are additional restrictions or limitations that have been developed by the federal judges. These have come to be called the *Ashwander* rules because, in a 1936 opinion, *Ashwander v. TVA*, a concurring opinion of the Supreme Court enumerated some judicially created restraints on the federal courts.

For example, a court will only decide those constitutional questions that are actually raised in the litigation and only if there are no other ways the judges can resolve the legal dispute.[12] "Courts," as one English jurist said centuries ago, "will not stoop to pick up a pin."[13] A plaintiff brings suit in a federal court challenging the legality of an action of the Congress. If the plaintiff does not challenge the action on constitutional grounds in the federal district court, he or she cannot later on raise the constitutional question. Furthermore, even if the plaintiff raises the constitutional issue in the proper fashion, the appeal court will do all it can to reach a judgment in a manner that evades discussion of the constitutional question. "It is a cardinal principle that this Court will first ascertain whether a construction of a statute is fairly possible by which the (constitutional) questions may be avoided."[14]

Courts generally attempt to avoid constitutional interpretation for a basic reason. If they can resolve the legal dispute through interpretation of the statute and if their interpretation of the legislation is incorrect, the Congress can fairly easily rectify that problem by passing amending legislation. If, however, the federal judges reach out and interpret the Constitution when resolving a legal dispute, it is fairly difficult to rectify that judicial action if it is not consistent with the essential meaning of the document itself.[15] (Here is one example of how an issue involving the question of access raises basic questions about such constitutional principles as checks and balances and separation of powers.)

Direct, Legal Injury

The plaintiff must suffer a *direct, personal* impairment of *his own* constitutionally or statutorally *protected rights* in order for the federal

---

[12]See Murphy and Pritchett, p. 257.
[13]Quoted in Mendelson, "Mr. Justice Douglas," p. 921.
[14]*Ashwander v. T.V.A.*, 297 *US* 288 (1936).
[15]See, generally, Howard Ball, *Judicial Craftsmenship or Fiat? Direct Overturn by the U.S. Supreme Court* (Westport, Conn.: Greenwood Press, 1978).

courts to hear the legal dispute. The injury suffered (and the case/controversy criterion demands that there be such a real injury) must be one that is *legally protected* by statute or Constitution and it must be suffered by the party bringing suit in federal court in order for the judge to hear the case. A third party who has not suffered such a direct injury cannot bring suit in a federal court.[16] (A segment to come discusses the class action suit in federal courts. Class action, as will be seen, involves someone who has suffered a direct injury and is seeking a remedy from the federal judge for himself "and others similarly situated.")

Finality of Action

A person lacks standing to sue if, in the estimate of the federal judge, that plaintiff has not exhausted all the available remedies open to him *before* coming to the federal court. For example, if the plaintiff comes to the federal court challenging an action of the Interstate Commerce Commission, that party must have exhausted all administrative appeals or else he or she does not have the necessary standing to bring the case to the federal court. If the plaintiff proceeds in federal court prior to exhausting all these legal steps, the case is not "ripe" for adjudication in the federal courts: It has come to the courts "too soon."[17]

Mootness of an Issue

If ripeness involves the problem of a premature claim by a plaintiff in a federal court, mootness is where a plaintiff comes too late to the federal courts for relief. Courts do not "sit to decide arguments after events have put them to rest."[18] There are exceptions, however, to the mootness concept. These involve situations where the issue is "capable of repetition, yet evading review."[19] For example, an event of limited duration, such as pregnancy, might raise a legal issue in which a person does have standing to sue but for the fact that she has given birth before the appeal court has heard her argument. Such a case can be heard by the federal courts if two conditions are met: if (1) the challenged action was too short to be fully litigated while it existed, and if (2) the judges feel that there is a "reasonable expectation" that the plaintiff—or others similarly situated—will be subjected to the same action again.[20] Abortion cases also serve as an example of this kind of exception to mootness. In the 1973 cases, pregnant women challenged the constitutionality of the

[16]*Tileston v. Ullman*, 318 US 44 (1943).
[17]Mendelson, "Mr. Justice Douglas," p. 923.
[18]*Doremus v. Board of Education*, 342 US 429 (1952).
[19]*Sosna v. Iowa*, 42 LED 532 (1975).
[20]*Dunn v. Blumstein*, 405 US 330 (1972).

state abortion laws. The fact that the plaintiff was not pregnant at the time the Supreme Court heard the arguments did not make the case moot. The case was treated as a class action and the federal judges adjudicated the issue.[21]

These various criteria of *standing* in sum state that, all other considerations aside, a plaintiff will be able to have his problem adjudicated if he or she:

1. has personally suffered a real injury,
2. where a right or obligation allegedly deprived or denied has been protected by statute or constitution,
3. for which the federal courts can provide a remedy,
4. and that the plaintiff has followed the appropriate channels in his or her pursuit of justice, and, finally,
5. where the issue has not resolved itself prior to judicial examination.

The Class Action Suit in Federal Courts

A class action suit in a federal court is where the plaintiff, who has actually suffered direct injury, is allowed to bring the suit on behalf of other persons who have similarly been injured. For example, in the civil rights struggles of the 1950s and 1960s, many cases were brought to the federal courts by the NAACP on behalf of specific individuals who had been subjected to racially discriminatory policies as well as other blacks who were similarly subjected to the same direct injury.[22]

In order to have standing to sue in such a class action, there must be an identification of all members of a class who can be identified. The class must be a specific one rather than the abstract "public interest," if there is to be a valid class action in the federal courts. For example, in the case of the *Sierra Club v. Morton* (1972), an environmentalist group wanted to challenge a state action that involved alleged exploitation of a national park; in order to do so, the group had to show harm to members of the organization. Mere interest in the problem of alleged despoliation of a natural resource was not enough to get the Sierra Club case to the federal courts on the merits. The Sierra Club, wrote Justice Potter Stewart for the Supreme Court majority, "failed to allege that it or its members would be affected in any of their activities or pastimes by the . . . development."

[21]*Roe v. Wade,* 410 *US* 113 (1973).
[22]See, generally, Richard Kluger, *Simple Justice* (New York: Random House, 1977) for an excellent study of civil rights class action strategies and struggles during the 1950s.

TAXPAYER SUITS AGAINST THE UNITED STATES: THE SUPREME COURT'S EVOLVING DEFINITION OF THE CONCEPT OF STANDING TO SUE

Standing to sue "is a relatively new doctrine, unheard of at the time the Constitution was drafted, which developed independently of English law."[23] Prior to 1923 the Supreme Court had not specifically called for standing as a prerequisite to federal jurisdiction.[24] In 1923, however, in the case of *Frothingham v. Mellon*, the justices of the Court, although not using the term "standing," developed the concept.

Frothingham v. Mellon, 1923

In 1921 the Congress passed the Maternity Act. This legislation provided grants for states on condition that they agreed to establish, consistent with the statute's provisions, programs for the care of infants and mothers-to-be in order to reduce infant mortality. Mrs. Frothingham, a private citizen and taxpayer, herself not pregnant, brought suit in federal court as a federal taxpayer, alleging that the federal expenditure of federal funds violated the Tenth Amendment of the Constitution and deprived her of her economic liberty without due process guaranteed by the Fifth Amendment.

Mrs. Frothingham's contention "seems to be that the effect of the appropriations complained of will be to increase the burden of future taxation and thereby take her property without due process of law." After noting that the question of whether a federal taxpayer can seek to enjoin the execution of a federal appropriation on the ground that it is invalid "has never been passed upon by this court," the justices then proceeded to enunciate the concept of standing.

> We have no power *per se* to review and annul acts of Congress on the ground that they are unconstitutional. That question may be considered only when the justification for some direct injury suffered or threatened, presenting a justiciable issue, is made to rest upon such an act. The party must be able to show, not only that the statute is invalid, but that he has sustained or is immediately in danger of sustaining some direct injury as a result of its enforcement, and not merely that he suffers in some indefinite way in common with people generally.

[23]William Smith, "Standing in Taxpayer Suits," *Mississippi Law Journal*, 46 (1975), 360.
[24]See Raoul Berger, "Standing to Sue in Public Actions," *Yale Law Review*, 78 (1969), 818.

As Mrs. Frothingham did not show direct injury—personal or economic—the Supreme Court dismissed the suit because it did not have a basis in law to hear it. The justices believed that the relation of the federal taxpayer to the federal expenditures was so minute that a court could simply not determine the extent of the taxpayer's interest in the expenditure. For the justices to act otherwise and hear the case would be "to assume a position of authority over the governmental acts of another and coequal department, an authority which plainly we do not possess."

The Supreme Court's *Frothingham* ruling established a precedent that would last more than 45 years. *Frothingham* "declared a rule of judicial self-restraint rather than a jurisdictional limitation based on the Article III 'case or controversy' clause."[25] *Frothingham* was the beginning of the law of standing. From 1923 to the 1968 *Flast* case, it "stood as an absolute bar to federal taxpayer suits."[26] In 1968, however, another federal taxpayer suit came to the United States Supreme Court. Given the changing times and the new personnel on the Court, an important modification was made in the standing principle that had existed since 1923.

Flast v. Cohen, 1968

Mrs. Flast filed suit in a federal district court to enjoin the enforcement of the Elementary and Secondary Education Act of 1965. Under the act federal funds would be spent to finance instruction in secular subjects (English, arithmetic) in religious schools. Her argument was that this expenditure of funds by the federal government ran into conflict with the First Amendment: These expenditures promoted and financed religious activities in violation of the "establishment of religion" constitutional prohibition. The lower federal court, acting as norm enforcer (the norm enforced was the *Frothingham* precedent) ruled that Mrs. Flast lacked standing to sue. The federal taxpayer then took her argument to the Supreme Court.

The Supreme Court, in response to her petition, distinguished *Frothingham* from the case before the justices. Mrs. Frothingham's case reflected the self-restraint philosophy of the justices of the Supreme Court majority in 1923; it was, however, not an iron-clad constitutional rule, said Chief Justice Earl Warren for the majority. The "gist of the question of standing is whether the party seeking relief has alleged such a personal stake in the outcome of the controversy as to assure that

[25]Smith, "Standing in Taxpayer Suits," p. 361.
[26]Ibid.

concrete adverseness which sharpens the presentation of issues upon which the court so largely depends for illumination of difficult constitutional questions."

Then, consistent with this view, Chief Justice Warren stated that a "taxpayer may or may not have the requisite personal stake in the outcome, depending upon the circumstances of the particular case." Therefore no absolute bar exists to federal taxpayer suits. The question the court majority had next to answer was this: When does a federal taxpayer have standing to challenge an appropriation of money by the national legislature?

In order for a federal taxpayer to have the requisite standing to sue in a federal court, a certain connection or nexus must exist between the taxpayer and the program he or she is challenging. First of all, said the court, there must be established "a logical link between (the taxpayer) and the type of legislative enactment attacked." For example, a federal taxpayer can properly challenge "only exercises of congressional power under the taxing and spending power of Article 1, Section 8 of the Constitution." In addition, the federal taxpayer "must establish a nexus between that status and the precise nature of the constitutional infringement alleged. . . . When both nexuses are established, the litigant will have shown a taxpayer's stake in the outcome of the controversy and will be a proper and appropriate party to invoke a federal court's jurisdiction."

The *Flast* case in 1968 produced the *nexus* rule. The Supreme Court was telling lower court judges in the federal system that standing to sue in a federal taxpayer case depended on whether the interest asserted by the taxpayer fell within the zone of interests protected by the right claimed. If the question involves congressional actions under its spending and taxing authority and, further, if the federal taxpayer alleged that a specific constitutional prohibition on such activity was ignored, then the federal courts can hear the case.

The nexus concept is a judicially created extension of the "case and controversy" stipulation in Article III of the Constitution. "Nexus is not constitutionally required, but is instead the product of a number of policy considerations bearing on the sound administration of the federal courts."[27] *Flast* was written in a period of time when the Warren Court majority was restructuring procedural rules as "part of a general trend toward recognizing the right of litigants to bring 'public actions' seeking to vindicate public rights."[28] Indeed, Justice John M. Harlan II

---

[27]Laurence Tribe, *American Constitutional Law* (New York: Foundation Press, 1978), p. 99.
[28]*Flast v. Cohen*, 392 *US* 83 (1968).

dissented in the *Flast* case due in part to his concern about the consequences of this restructuring effort:

> There is every reason to fear that unrestricted popular actions (federal taxpayer suits) might well alter the allocation of authority among the three branches of the federal government.[29]

Harlan's concern was the concern of the Supreme Court majority in 1923: judicial usurpation of the congressional responsibilities through review of congressional expenditures challenged by federal taxpayers who are "private attorneys-general."[30] Moreover, Harlan's fear was shared by critics of the Warren Court, among them the man who would replace Warren as chief justice within the next two years, Warren Earl Burger. With the arrival of Burger and three other Nixon appointees, there developed renewed interest in the impact of the *Flast* opinion. With respect to federal taxpayer standing to sue, the new Court majority reexamined *Flast* in the 1974 cases of *United States v. Richardson* and *Schlesinger v. Reservists Committee to Stop the War*. The pendulum, which had swung away from *Frothingham* in *Flast*, seemed to be moving back to the self-restraint views of the 1923 opinion.

United States v. Richardson, 1974

Mr. Richardson, a federal taxpayer, brought suit in federal district court in order to have the Central Intelligence Act ruled unconstitutional. The Act permits the CIA to account for its expenditures "solely on the certificate of the director." Arguing that he suffered personal injury due to his inability to obtain documents setting forth the expenditures and receipts of CIA spending, Richardson urged that the statute passed by the Congress—which did not provide for a detailed postaudit of the intelligence agency's expenditures—be declared unconstitutional.

He brought suit in the federal court because Richardson believed that the *Flast* ruling gave him standing to sue in that tribunal. Richardson was trying to find out how the CIA spent federal funds; he was not charging that the funds were spent in violation of a specific constitutional limitation on the spending and taxing power of the Congress. He argued, instead, that Article 1, Section 9, which requires that "a regular statement and account of the receipts and expenditures of all public money shall be published from time to time," had been ignored when

[29]Ibid.
[30]Ibid.

the Congress passed the Central Intelligence Act. His argument: The Constitution calls for a public accounting of receipts and expenditures of all public money; as a taxpayer he had standing to sue in a situation where there was, due to congressional statute, no public accounting by an agency of the federal government.

The federal district court judge dismissed Richardson's complaint because of lack of standing: The facts in *Richardson* were not like those in the 1968 *Flast* precedent. However, the U.S. Court of Appeals overturned the district court ruling, holding that *Richardson* met the two-pronged test of *Flast*. The United States appealed to the Supreme Court and, in the 1974 ruling, the Court majority reversed the ruling of the court of appeals.

The question of law raised in the *Richardson* opinions was whether there was sufficient personal injury caused by the CIA Act to give the litigant standing to sue. In a close vote, 5 to 4, the Supreme Court concluded that there was no standing to sue. In an opinion, written by Chief Justice Warren Burger, the justices argued that Richardson was merely challenging the statutes regulating the CIA. There was no claim made that funds were being spent in violation of "a specific constitutional limitation upon the taxing and spending power. . . . Rather, he asks the courts to compel the Government to give him information on precisely how the CIA spends its funds."

Richardson's appeal was a sort of "generalized grievance," concluded the chief justice. It did not rise to the level of a *justiciable* controversy. The citizen was demanding detailed information on how the CIA used the congressional appropriation; the judicial opinion's implication was that he must seek this information elsewhere for the federal courts would not provide him access to that data.

The fifth vote was in the form of a concurring opinion written by another of the Nixon appointees, Lewis Powell. His concern about consequences if the Court allowed Richardson's suit to be heard reflected the 1923 majority opinion and the 1968 dissent of Justice Harlan. Relaxing requirements for standing in federal court by federal taxpayers meant the expansion of judicial power. "Allowing unrestricted taxpayer or citizen standing would significantly alter the allocation of power at the national level, with a shift away from a democratic form of government."

Justices William Douglas, Potter Stewart, William Brennan, and Thurgood Marshall (all of whom had voted with Chief Justice Warren in the expansive *Flast* opinion of 1968) dissented. Douglas' dissent argued that *Flast* gave Richardson standing to sue. Article 1, Section 9, the *receipt and expenditure* clause, was designed to give citizens information about how public monies were being spent. "No one has a greater 'personal stake' in policing this protective measure than a tax-payer. Indeed, if a taxpayer may not raise the question, who may do so?"

Justice Stewart's dissenting opinion argued that there was, in the Constitution's Article 1, Section 9, an affirmative obligation on the part of the Congress to provide information about expenditures and that Richardson had standing to sue. "When a party is seeking a judicial determination that a defendant owes him an affirmative duty, it seems clear to me that he has standing to litigate the issue."

The dissenter's position was consistent with the broad terms of the *Flast* opinion: Courts must provide an arena for grievances if the person shows some nexus between his status and a right present in the Constitution. However, the five-man Burger majority prevailed in *Richardson* as they prevailed in the companion case of *Schlesinger v. Reservists Committee to Stop the War*.

Schlesinger v. Reservists Committee to Stop the War, 1974

In the second companion case involving federal taxpayer suits announced the same decision day in 1974, the Court majority reemphasized the points made in *Richardson* about standing to sue in federal courts. The litigants in this suit, members of an association composed of members of the armed forces reserves, challenged the membership in the military reserves of more than 100 members of the United States Congress. The arguments: (1) Congressional membership in the reserves conflicts with Article 1, Section 6, Clause 2 of the Constitution (which states that "no person holding any office under the United States shall be a member of either house during his continuance in office"), and (2) such membership places these legislators in a potentially dangerous "conflict of interest" environment due to the fact that a great deal of legislation involves military appropriations.

The legal action attempted to force the Secretary of Defense (James Schlesinger) to strike from the military rolls of the reserves all those members who were congressmen or senators. The U.S. district court judge in the District of Columbia, held that (1) the litigants had standing to sue as U.S. citizens but not as taxpayers, (2) a commission in the reserve forces is an "office under the United States" within the meaning of Article 1, Section 6, and (3) members of Congress were ineligible to hold reserve commissions during their stay in office.

The Court of Appeals in the District of Columbia affirmed the judgment of the federal district judge. The United States government immediately appealed the adverse judgment to the United States Supreme Court. In a six to three vote, the Supreme Court reversed the judgments of the lower federal courts. Chief Justice Burger again delivered the opinion for the Court majority. The basic question for the justices was this: Did the litigants have standing to sue either as federal taxpayers or as citizens of the United States?

The Chief Justice noted that the issue really was a challenge by an antiwar organization of an administrative decision within the executive branch to permit members of Congress to maintain their reserve status; there was no challenge to the manner in which the Congress carried out its taxing and spending powers.

> The very language of the complaint . . . reveals that it is nothing more than a matter of speculation whether the claimed nonobservance of (the incompatibility) clause deprives citizens of the faithful discharge of the legislative duties of reservist members of Congress. . . . To permit a complainant who has no concrete injury to require a court to rule on important constitutional issues in the abstract would create the potential for abuse of the judicial process, distort the role of the judiciary in its relationship to the Executive and the Legislature, and open the judiciary to an arguable charge of providing "government by judiciary."

Justice Douglas dissented, joined by Justice Marshall. He believed that there was standing to sue because there was an obvious nonobedience to the affirmative constitutional command in Article 1, Section 6. "The interest of citizens in guarantees written in the Constitution seems obvious. Who other than citizens have a better right to have the Incompatibility Clause enforced?"

Justice Brennan argued that the allegations raised by the litigants in the case were sufficient to give them standing to sue in the federal courts. However, the argument of the dissenters—that is, that federal courts ought to hear *and* decide citizen grievances regarding alleged constitutional violations and that *Flast* enabled them to have standing in federal courts—was rejected by the Burger Court majority.

By the mid-1970s, the pendulum was swinging in the direction of *Frothingham v. Mellon.* The majority refused to see and resolve the broad constitutional issues posed in these cases. Instead, the view presented in *Richardson* and in *Schlesinger* was that the cases did not have adverseness and that there was not the "personal stake in the outcome" factor present.

Both opinions "rest on (judicial) reluctance to transform the federal judiciary into an ombudsman for generalized citizen grievances."[31] The

---

[31]Tribe, *American Constitutional Law,* p. 92.

majority was unwilling to go beyond *Flast* and allow such general grievances—absent the *Flast* nexus requirement—into the federal courts. "The Court recognized (by its actions in these cases) that its decisions may leave only the political processes to remedy certain constitutional violations."[32] This self-restraint view was given a further airing in the following case.

Simon v. Eastern Kentucky Welfare Rights Organization, 1976

This case involved litigants who had challenged actions of the United States Secretary of the Treasury and the Commissioner of Internal Revenue. An IRS policy had been modified by the Nixon administration that, in the eyes of the litigants, adversely affected poor and indigent citizens. Prior to the change, the IRS definition of a "nonprofit hospital"—which received favorable treatment from the federal government—was this: one which operates exclusively for charitable purposes and must serve indigents without cost or at reduced rates.

In 1969, the IRS ruling changed the direction of hospital care: Emergency care for indigents had to remain without cost for a hospital to be considered a "nonprofit" institution. However, for all other services the patient (regardless of ability to pay) will be charged the cost of hospitalization. Patients who cannot "meet the financial requirements for admission are normally referred to another hospital."

The suit was instituted because the 1969 ruling, according to the plaintiffs who were suing the government, "encouraged" hospitals to deny services other than emergency service to indigent patients. They argued that the government was encouraging these hospitals to deny services to the poor by extending tax benefits to them.

The federal district court judge, sitting on the District of Columbia bench, agreed that the litigants had standing to sue and voided the 1969 ruling. The United States Court of Appeals in the District of Columbia also found standing to sue but upheld the revenue ruling of 1969. The government brought suit before the Supreme Court. The argument made by government lawyers was that no court had the capacity to decide the issue on the merits because the litigants did not have standing to sue in the federal courts.

Justice Lewis Powell wrote the decision for a unanimous Court (Brennan and Marshall concurred). The constitutional question was whether or not these litigants, a group of indigents who had received

---

[32]Bruce E. Fein, *Significant Decisions of the Supreme Court, 1973-1974 Term* (Washington, D.C.: American Enterprise Institute, 1975), p. 91.

medical treatment in the past, had sufficient standing for the case to be considered on its merits. The Supreme Court instructed the federal district court to dismiss the complaint because the litigants lacked standing to sue.

"The test of standing," wrote Powell, was "whether the plaintiff has shown an injury to himself that is likely to be redressed by a favorable decision. Absent such a showing, exercise of its power by a federal court would be gratuitous and thus inconsistent with Article III of the Constitution."

Furthermore, if there were actual injury suffered or alleged by the litigant, the fact that the hospitals were not the defendants (federal government officials were) in the litigation meant that standing was not present. Standing requires "that a federal court act only to redress injury that fairly can be traced to the challenged action of the defendant, and not injury that results from the independent action of some third party not before the court."

The fact that the litigants were challenging the alleged impropriety of federal officials with regard to the 1969 decision by the IRS was irrelevant. Since there was no direct injury, the Court would not examine the case on the merits. To do so, stated the Court majority, would be to dramatically broaden the standing concept.

What this segment has tried to illustrate is the fact that standing to sue is "an area of tremendous complexity."[33] Federal judges have always been aware of their place in the larger political and social system and of their sensitive relationship with the other two coordinate branches of the federal government. However, throughout our history there has been the basic judicial activism versus judicial restraint dichotomy that is well illustrated in these taxpayer suits in the federal courts.

In 1923, a self-restraint majority on the Supreme Court blocked the gates of the federal courts from federal taxpayers trying to get in an order to allege that the government was spending public monies in violation of constitutional prohibitions. In the 1960s a more active Supreme Court majority, while aware of the potential consequences of opening up the judicial gates with respect to federal taxpayer suits, nevertheless felt compelled to act in a way that gave those citizens who showed a certain nexus access to the federal courts.

The lone 1968 dissenter, Justice John Harlan, argued vigorously against this action. He feared that an opening of the gates would embroil the federal courts in conflicts with the coordinate branches. He believed that federal courts were not the panacea for all the social and political ills that existed in our society. Federal judges ought to restrain them-

[33]Note, "Federal Jurisdiction and Procedure," *Harvard Law Review*, 90 (1976), 205.

selves from the temptation to offer citizens entrance to the federal courts in order to resolve problems that are rightfully settled in the political processes.[34]

The Harlan dissent in *Flast,* reflecting his self-restraint, jurisprudential views, became the view of the new Supreme Court majority in the mid-1970s. *Richardson, Schlesinger,* and *Simon* illustrate the Supreme Court's reluctance in recent years to open the judicial gates to citizens who allege a general complaint about governmental action.

The basic response of the justices in the mid-1970s has been the 1923 response and the Harlan dissent response. Generalized grievances against the CIA, the Treasury Department, or the Internal Revenue Service, although real, ought not to be debated in the federal courts. Instead, the forum for these discussions is the political process itself. The problem, of course, is that these groups went to the courts because they were not given an opportunity to make their cases in the political processes or, if they did make the attempt, they had failed miserably. Acting as gatekeeper, the Supreme Court majority in recent years has effectively frustrated efforts by federal taxpayers to get into the federal courts unless they meet the two-tier *Flast* test. Any broadening of the *Flast* standard must await the arrival of new personnel on the Supreme Court. But this is the way it has been since the beginning of our republic in 1789: New judges to the federal courts will eventually lead to modification of legal policies and judicial procedures.

There are occasions, however, where a suit is dismissed even though there is jurisdiction and the litigant does have standing to sue. If standing "is but one aspect of justiciability,"[35] then the "political question" doctrine is another very important aspect. In the *Richardson* case the Supreme Court

> explained that a person could have standing and the case could still be dismissed under Article III because the issue in controversy was a political question, and therefore not fit for judicial determination. The political question aspect of justiciability, unlike standing, focuses on the substantive issue to be adjudicated and not the parties themselves. . . . The doctrine's basic premise is that the courts should not hear a case involving an issue that is constitutionally committed to a coequal branch of government.[36]

As indicated by the Court in *Richardson,* if the judges believe that the *issue* presented to them for adjudication is inappropriate for judicial resolution—regardless of the presence of actual injury—then it is a "political question" and the judges will dismiss the case. As will be shown

[34]*Baker v. Carr,* 369 *US* 186 (1962), dissenting opinion.
[35]Smith, "Standing in Taxpayer's Suits," p. 362.
[36]Ibid., footnote 32, p. 362.

in the next segment, what is or is not a "political question" depends upon the perceptions of the federal judges who are sitting at the time the case or controversy comes into the federal judicial system. "Political questions are those which judges choose not to decide and a question becomes political by the judge's refusal to decide it."[37]

POLITICAL QUESTIONS AND ACCESS TO THE FEDERAL COURTS

The preceding characteristics, when present in a particular legal dispute, will generally make that matter a *justiciable* one. An issue is justiciable if the case or controversy is one that is proper and feasible for the federal courts to decide. If the court believes that the case is one that is properly before the judges and, furthermore, there are appropriate judicial remedies available, then the matter is a justiciable one. On the other hand, a nonjusticiable matter is a case or a controversy that a court decides it would be imprudent to adjudicate. Jurisdiction exists but, for reasons discussed below, the federal judges decide not to hear the dispute.

Chief Justice Earl Warren said, in *Flast v. Cohen*, that:

> Justiciability is itself a concept of uncertain meaning and scope. . . . Justiciability is not a legal concept with a fixed content or susceptible of scientific verification. Its utilization is the resultant of many subtle pressures.

One can best define justiciability by examining what the courts have held to be nonjusticiable. For example, asking for an advisory opinion from a court is a nonjusticiable matter. So too is the situation where "the question sought to be adjudicated has been mooted by subsequent developments, and when there is no standing to maintain the action.[38] Perhaps the most interesting and discretionary kind of nonjusticiable issue is one where the parties "seek adjudication of [what is referred to as] a political question."[39]

What precisely does the Supreme Court mean by "political question?" There are some basic questions that arise in a legal context that ought not to be resolved by the courts at all due to the nature of the subject matter. As suggested by Chief Justice Warren, rules or guidelines

---

[37]Jack Peltason, *Federal Courts in the Political Process* (New York: Random House, 1955), p. 10.
[38]Mendelson, "Mr. Justice Douglas," p. 927.
[39]Ibid., p. 929.

on what these *political questions* are that courts cannot adjudicate have not been defined with any degree of precision. As a matter of fact these rules are quite soft and malleable. Indeed, what has been referred to by one federal court as a *political question* turns out to be a very justiciable issue in the eyes of another court majority.

Professor A. M. Bickel came closest to the essence of the political question phenomenon when he wrote, in *The Least Dangerous Branch*, that a political question is identified by the court when the judges "sense a lack of capacity" to resolve the issue before them. It may be that the judges are not comfortable with the issue or believe that another branch of government should deal with the problem. It may very well be the "sheer momentousness" of the dispute, or judicial anxiety over the impact of judicial scrutiny and judgment. It may also be the judges' perceived vulnerability to political processes in a democracy should the courts adjudicate that particular issue.[40]

A political question might be, as the U.S. Supreme Court said, a situation where there is a lack of adequate standards for judicial resolution of the issue or a lack of adequate judicial remedies. A political question is also the sort of dispute that involves a "textually demonstrable commitment" of the issue by the Constitution to either the Congress or to the president of the United States.[41]

For example, the Supreme Court has stated that determining the meaning of a "republican form of government" (guaranteed the states in the U.S. Constitution, Article IV, Section 4), is a *political question* and, therefore, the matter was determined to be a nonjusticiable one. The matter of how the national guard was trained and equipped was also deemed a political question by the Supreme Court: The Congress and the president have the responsibility to handle national security matters in accordance with Article I, Section 8, Clause 16.[42] Other specific examples of political questions would include:

1. *Coleman v. Miller* (1939) where the Court ruled that the question of when or whether a constitutional amendment had been duly ratified was a political question;

2. *Oetjen v. Central Leather* (1918) where the Court majority stated that questions involving the cessation of hostile action was a political question best left to resolution in the political processes;[43]

[40]Alexander M. Bickel, *The Least Dangerous Branch* (Indianapolis: Bobbs-Merrill), 1972.
[41]See, generally, Philippa Strum, *The Supreme Court and "Political Questions"* (University: University of Alabama Press, 1974).
[42]*Gilligan v. Morgan*, 413 *US* 1 (1973).
[43]See, however, the 1948 case of *Woods v. Miller*, 333 *US* 138, where the Supreme Court validated, on the merits, a postwar piece of legislation, enacted under the war power of the legislature.

3. *O'Brien v. Brown* (1972) where the Court voiced its "grave doubts" regarding the question of whether the federal judges had the power and authority to review actions of political parties at national conventions.

The Political Question Doctrine and Reapportionment: The Supreme Court Changes Direction

The most dramatic example of the contraction and expansion of the "political question" doctrine in the twentieth century would have to be the Supreme Court's response to the reapportionment controversy. In 1946 the Supreme Court believed that the question of reapportionment—legislative redistricting—was a "political question" and that the federal courts were not capable of dealing with such a volatile political issue. That case was *Colgrove v. Green* and the author of the majority opinion was Justice Felix Frankfurter, a champion of judicial self-restraint.[44]

Colegrove v. Green, 1946

Apportionment determines the distribution of political power in a democratic society by dividing seats in a particular legislature according to an established procedure. Generally, this apportionment and reapportionment of legislative seats takes place after the dicennial census. People ought to be represented fairly and routinized reapportionments, reflecting the shifts within a particular state, operationalize this manifestation of democratic theory.

However, if those responsible for reapportioning fail to rearrange legislative representation after the census figures are published and, over a period of 50 to 60 years, repeatedly fail to change the seating arrangements, a certain imbalance occurs. Representatives who in 1900 might have had a district of 50,000 people were in the 1940s representing districts of either many, many more people (900,000) or, due to the vagaries of population shifts over half a century, many fewer citizens (6,000). Voters in these very large districts felt that they ought to have more representatives than they had in the legislature and so demanded that reapportionment take place to rearrange the seating in the assembly. However, they ran into serious difficulty implementing this position for legislators had to do the reapportionment and, for many

[44]*Colegrove v. Green*, 328 *US* 549 (1946), but see *Baker v. Carr*, 369 *US* 186 (1962).

reasons, the entrenched legislators simply refused to reapportion. In some cases this refusal went directly against both state and federal constitutions that called for such reapportionment after the census figures were published.

In 1946 Kenneth Colegrove, a political science professor at Northwestern University, along with two associates, filed suit as three qualified Illinois voters. They challenged, in federal district court, the legitimacy of the congressional districts in the state because the Illinois legislature had failed to reapportion these seats since 1901. At the time they filed suit in federal court, the population in the various Illinois congressional districts ran from 112,116 to 914,053.

Their constitutional argument was that, as citizens of the overpopulated congressional district, they were denied the Article I protection of fair representation in the national legislature. They were asking the federal courts to restrain the officers of the state from taking action to hold the congressional elections in 1946 unless there was a redistricting or at-large elections. State officials had done nothing for over 40 years, they argued. Therefore, the elections ought not to take place under these allegedly unconstitutional conditions.

Their argument, that "their vote is much less effective than the vote of those living in a district under which the 1901 Act is also allowed to choose one congressman, although its population is sometimes only one-ninth that of the heavily populated districts," was an abstract one in one sense. These people were *voting;* the *weight* of their votes was the issue. (Their argument, then, was unlike the argument made by black citizens who could not vote at all and who used the courts to gain that fundamental right of democratic citizens.)

The federal district court dismissed the complaint and Colegrove took the case to the United States Supreme Court. In a four to three vote, the Supreme Court employed the "political question" doctrine to affirm the judgment of the lower court. Justice Frankfurter wrote the opinion for the Court. "For want of equity we are of the opinion that the appellants ask of this Court what is beyond its competence to grant."

"It is hostile to a democratic system," stated the self-restraint justice, "to involve the judiciary in the politics of the people. And it is not less pernicious if such judicial intervention in an essentially political contest be dressed up in the abstract phrases of the law." If evils exist in the reapportionment policy area, it is for appropriate agencies in the political process to rectify them. Urging the people to go to the Congress for a redress of grievances because of the fact that the national legislature guarantees to every state a republican form of government (Article IV and Article I, Section 4), Frankfurter reemphasized the point that courts "ought not to enter this political thicket." The remedy, if there is one, "ultimately lies with the people."

Justice Black wrote the dissenting opinion. He believed that the issue was a justiciable one and that the federal courts ought to provide a remedy to a situation that had gone remedyless for almost half a century. Black maintained that if Colegrove's allegations were correct, then he had been denied "the full right to vote and equal protection of the laws. . . . Under these circumstances and since there is no adequate legal remedy for depriving a citizen of his right to vote, equity can and should grant relief."

Arguing that the Constitution guarantees the right to vote and to have that vote counted fairly, Black reasoned that the Illinois reapportionment Act of 1901 was unconstitutional. It was the Court's duty to invalidate the law and supply a remedy until the state properly reapportioned itself. Although the issue itself was an electoral and therefore a political issue, Black concluded that it was "a mere play on words to refer to a controversy such as this as 'political' in the sense that courts have nothing to do with protecting and vindicating the right of a voter to cast an effective ballot." Black's remedy would have been to order at-large congressional elections for Illinois in 1946 and afterwards until the state leaders came up with a constitutionally permissible reapportionment plan.

It was, however, the Frankfurter position that became the precedent for the federal courts for the next two decades. It was not until the 1960s that the Supreme Court would examine the issue of reapportionment again. However, when the Supreme Court in the 1960s heard the Tennessee case, *Baker v. Carr*, it was a Court with different personnel and under the leadership of a Chief Justice, Earl Warren, who repeatedly would ask a brief but profound question to attorneys arguing cases before the Supreme Court: "Was that action/inaction, etc., *fair?*"

Baker v. Carr, 1961

The Tennessee case, *Baker v. Carr*, was a classic situation that reflected the malaise that existed with respect to reapportionment of state and national legislatures. The state had not reapportioned since 1901. More than 60 years had passed and the seat distribution in this midsouth state had remained as it had been structured at the turn of the century. There had been efforts by urban leaders to get the legislature to reapportion itself but these proved to be fruitless attempts. In 1959 a suit was initiated in federal district court, middle district-Tennessee, by citizens and political leaders from the city of Memphis, Tennessee. They asked for a declaration that the 1901 Tennessee Reapportionment Act was unconstitutional and that an injunction be issued restraining the state from holding any elections under the 1901 plan. In February 1960 a three-judge district court dismissed the complaint for want of jurisdiction and because it was a "political question." Baker and others then took the case to the United States Supreme Court. In a watershed case, the Court majority set aside the *Colegrove* view and concluded that if the allegations made by the litigants were correct, then the courts are bound to formulate an appropriate remedy.

The majority opinion was written by Justice William J. Brennan. "If it develops at trial that the facts support the allegations, "then the malapportionment that existed in Tennessee constituted a deprivation of the Fourteenth Amendment's equal protection guarantees. Such a situation would then be held to be a "cognizable federal constitutional cause of action." In short, the majority of the Court was saying that if the facts were born out in the trial court, then federal courts were empowered to provide a remedy.

Federal courts will "not stand impotent before an obvious instance of a manifestly unauthorized exercise of power." Furthermore, said Brennan, there are "judicially manageable standards, well developed and familiar" to judges that should be employed if there is the factual case of diluted voting because of malapportioned legislatures.

While the issue was certainly a political issue, Brennan noted that it was not a "political question," that is, the type of controversy that courts ought not to hear because they lack remedies or because it is best handled by some other agency of government. "The mere fact that the suit seeks protection of a political right does not mean that it presents a political question." With that statement, the Court sent the case back to the district court. Federal courts could hear such cases if the traditional standing requirements were met and if the case fell within the jurisdiction of the federal courts. Reapportionment was not, however, to be considered a "political question."

Justices Felix Frankfurter and John M. Harlan II dissented in this important case that redirected the law with respect to reapportionment. Both argued that federal courts, especially the United States Supreme Court, ought not to be embroiled in such political issues. Reapportionment was a basic political question and federal judges did not have the power under the Constitution to involve themselves in such naked political disputes. The federal courts, using the language of the Harlan dissent, are not "the last refuge for the correction of all inequality or injustice, no matter what its nature or its source."

For federal judges to function in this manner goes against all the legal and political traditions of the society. "The court's authority," stated Frankfurter in dissent, "possessed of neither the purse nor the sword ultimately rests on sustained public confidence in its moral sanction." By involving the federal courts in what was a basic political conflict, the Supreme Court decision will force judges into these political thickets thereby destroying the image of "complete (judicial) detachment from political entanglements."

This view was, however, the dissenting view; *Baker v. Carr,* by redirecting the law of the land with respect to reapportionment and political questions, instructed federal courts to hear and resolve these kinds of disputes when they came to the federal courts. Why the shift in the interpretation of the "political question" doctrine? The change can be accounted for by virtue of the fact that questions of access are answered by the judge by reaching into his perception of judicial role and responsibility in a democratic system. "Historically the court has made up the rules (concerning standing to sue and political questions) on the *ad hoc* basis and the use of the political question doctrine has depended upon the particular configuration of the political context of the cases and the dominant values of the justices."[45]

By determining the meaning and extent of standing to sue and of political questions, court majorities determine how wide or how narrow the judicial gates will be thrown open to litigant demands for remedying injustices and inequities. If *Colegrove* closed the gates to reapportionment suits in 1946, *Baker* opened them wide in 1961.

The political question issue completes the circle for that concept and dramatically highlights the gatekeeping function of the U.S. Supreme Court. There are essentially three basic judicial perceptions of the judicial gatekeeping function: administrative, legal, and political.[46] The "administrative" perception, held by some of the federal judges, suggests the necessity of careful control of access in order to control the docket of the federal courts and minimize overcrowded dockets. Some justices of the U.S. Supreme Court, Chief Justice Burger among them, have urged such administrative control because it would regulate the time the judges have to hear and adjudicate cases and controversies. If the gate is opened narrowly by virtue of judicial narrowing of the parameters of standing, class action, justiciability and nonjusticiability, po-

---

[45]Sheldon Goldman, "In Defense of Justice," *Journal of Politics,* vol. 39 no. 1 (February 1977), p. 155. For a critical analysis of the U.S. Supreme Court's reapportionment opinions, see Howard Ball, *The Warren Court's Perception of Democracy* (Rutherford, N.J.: Fairleigh Dickinson University Press, 1972).
[46]Rhode and Spaeth, *Supreme Court,* p. 4.

litical questions, etc., then the lower federal court judges begin to handle certain kinds of cases in a certain way and various legal pressure groups are wary of instituting legal questions for fear of these suits being labeled, ultimately, as nonjusticiable.

The "legal" perception suggests either judicial self-restraint or judicial activism.[47] A federal judge employing self-restraint can narrow the gates by arguing that certain questions ought not to be heard by the judiciary because of the character of the issue raised in the dispute. This jurisprudential response employs the political question doctrine to prevent the judiciary from interfering with national or state policy makers. On the other hand, the gatekeeping function, as perceived by another judge, can involve the federal judiciary in all major social and political issues of the society. In the hands of the judicial activist, the political question doctrine is defined in such a manner as to enable the court to hear a host of issues that involve political rights and obligations.[48]

The "political" perception of the gatekeeping function and the uses of *political question* doctrine get to the substance of the laws and public policies involved in the case before the judges. This last perception is what Chief Justice Earl Warren had in mind when he wrote in the *Flast* case that the utilization of these mechanisms has "the resultant of many subtle pressures." Simply put, a federal judge will determine that a dispute before him or her is nonjusticiable based upon the judge's perceptions of the public policy involved.

If the federal judge is inclined to adjudicate, the judicial response may well be the recitation of the words of Marshall in *Marbury:* It is emphatically the province and the duty of the judiciary to say what the law is. If the judge is not so inclined to review and adjudicate, then the matter may be settled by declaring that the case is nonjusticiable because of the "political question" character of the dispute.[49]

What is important to note is that all three perceptions—administrative, legal, political—turn on the dominant values of the federal judges. Judicial *discretion* is the indispensable element in this discussion of access. Given the mechanics and the tools that can be employed, the federal judges can lean in various ways in deciding a legal question as well as in deciding whether they will even begin to hear the question.[50]

---

[47]Ibid.

[48]See *Baker v. Carr,* 369 *US* 186 (1962).

[49]See, generally, Strum, *The Supreme Court.*

[50]See Gregory Rathjen and Harold Spaeth, "Access Policy Making on the United States Supreme Court," paper presented at the Southern Political Science Association meeting, New Orleans, La. (November 1977), pp. 6–8.

The remaining segments of the chapter present examples of the use of judicial discretion in cases involving questions of access to the federal courts.

FEDERAL DISTRICT COURT JUDGES AND THE QUESTION OF ACCESS

The federal district court judges are the trial judges of the federal judicial system. These "working judges"[51] must have rudimentary knowledge of the rules of criminal and civil procedure, rules of evidence, as well as knowledge of the existing common law, i.e., those rulings handed down by the appellate court with jurisdiction over his court actions as well as the United States Supreme Court's rulings with respect to substantive law and procedures.

The spectrum of activities of these trial judges of the federal system, to be discussed at length in chapter six, covers three types of litigation: (1) the private case (involving questions that deal with personal property losses, personal injury, torts, etc.); (2) the criminal case (involving criminal prosecutions of individuals charged with violating statutes); and (3) a small number of policy-setting cases of major importance.

The following segments will illustrate the dynamics of gaining access by viewing the Buffalo Creek disaster of 1972 and the litigation that led to the resignation of President Richard M. Nixon. These sections will also illustrate two types of lawyers at work in the federal judicial system: the private attorney and the government lawyer.

The Buffalo Creek Disaster

The Dam Breaks

On a rainy Saturday morning in late February 1972 in the state of West Virginia a "massive dam used by a coal company to filter the black waste water from its coal cleaning plant . . . collapsed, and a seventeen-mile valley of small coal-mining towns lay in ruins."[52] More than 125 men, women, and children were killed as the rampaging torrents of black water swept down the valley. Thousands more were left home-

---

[51]Stephen T. Early, *Constitutional Courts of the U.S.* (Totowa, N.J.: Littlefield, Adams, 1977), p. 50.
[52]Facts and quotes about the Buffalo Creek litigation found in Gerald Stern, *The Buffalo Creek Disaster* (New York: Random House, 1976).

less in the aftermath of the wild river of black terror that had torn up and destroyed everything in its path.

What had caused the dam to burst and cause this death and destruction? Answering this question, lawyers for hundreds of plaintiffs won a major victory in court over the coal mining company that owned the dam. As determined during the preliminary legal preparation, in 1947 the Buffalo Mining Company had built a large burning refuse pile as part of its coal cleaning operation. The operation proceeded as follows: Coal came from the mine and was washed and cleaned. The clean coal was dropped into railroad cars and shipped to customers. The waste products—solid and liquid—had to be disposed of by the coal company. This was initially accomplished by dumping the liquid waste (the water used to clean the coal) directly into the Buffalo Creek and by hauling the solid waste—slate, rocks, coal waste—to a hollow above the Buffalo Creek Valley and dumping the waste along the side of the Middle Fork hollow.

By the time the disaster took place in 1972, that solid refuse dump "was a smoldering mass of 3 million cubic yards, ... over 2,000 feet long and over 400 feet wide. It burned constantly because of the waste coal compressed within it." In the 1950s West Virginia had prohibited the coal industry from dumping the liquid wastes directly into rivers and the Buffalo Mining Company built a dam across the Middle Fork hollow by having the trucks deposit the solid waste across instead of along the side of the hollow. For a time this procedure worked well and Dam 1 held the liquid waste and allowed the waters to filter down to the creek below. (Dam 1 was about 8 feet high, 20 feet long, and 100 feet wide across the hollow.)

By 1967 Dam 1 had silted up[53] and a second dam was built upstream. It too was built the same way: solid smoldering refuse dumped across the hollow. Dam 2 was larger: 20 feet high, 25 feet long, and 450 feet wide. It too soon silted up and a third dam was built further upstream. This structure, Dam 3, built in 1968, was 60 feet high, 500 feet long, and 600 feet across the hollow. "The water in this dam towered almost 250 feet above the town of Saunders at the mouth of the Middle Fork below. It was the failure of Dam 3 which caused the Buffalo Creek disaster on February 26, 1972."

There had been a considerable amount of rainfall in the days preceding the tragedy. Water had built up behind Dam 3 and, the night before the disaster, it had crested. Many of the residents in the 16

[53]Silt up: This occurred when the minute deposits in the liquid waste—coal deposits in this situation—built up behind the dam so that the liquid itself could not be filtered through the solid waste dam and down into the creek itself.

communities located in the valley below the dam voiced concern to the local authorities and some had moved to safer shelters because they feared some flooding. Unfortunately, their fear was a well-founded one. On the morning of February 26, 1972, Dam 3—weakened over the years because of the constant smoldering of the solid waste and because there were no spillways to relieve pressure on the structure—broke and sent a "wall of black water" down the hollow and into the Buffalo Creek Valley. In two hours, the powerful black waters inundated and destroyed the 16 communities situated in the 17-mile valley.

Lawyer for the Plaintiffs

Hundreds of people who lived in the valley joined together after the disaster and, through a spokesman, contacted the Washington, D.C., law firm of Arnold and Porter for legal assistance. The firm assigned their *pro bono publico*[54] attorney for that year to look into the incident. The lawyer chosen was Gerald M. Stern. He was one of close to 500,000 attorneys practicing law in 1973 in the private and public sectors (almost 20,000 attorneys were employed by the federal government alone in that year).

The immediate technical problem for Stern was getting the case into the federal judicial system. He wanted to get the case into federal court rather than into the West Virginia state court system because the attorney believed that the chances of winning the case were better in the federal courts. "The local citizens, the survivors, preferred the federal court. The reason was obvious—coal companies had more influence with the local West Virginia courts than they do with the less political federal courts. . . . (Their) lawyers could pull tricks they could not get away with in federal court."

The procedural difficulty was due to the nature of federal court jurisdiction: If no federal question is raised then there has to be a diversity of citizenship element to get into the system. The mine and dams were owned by the Buffalo Mining Company, a West Virginia corporation. However, the sole stockholder of the local company was the Pittston Corporation, a New York-based holding company involved in various kinds of commercial ventures.

Stern had to convince the federal judge that the parties to the dispute were the local miners (plaintiff) and the New York-based corporation (defendant). The defendant had to be Pittston or else the case

[54]Pro bono publico: This term, translated from Latin, means for the public good or welfare. This occurs when attorneys take on cases without compensation for the public good.

would have to be heard in the West Virginia state courts. The initial response of the Pittston Corporation was expected by Stern: The tragedy was an act of God; there was neither negligence nor recklessness shown by the mining company. For Stern, the plaintiffs' strategy was simple: "Blame Pittston and ignore the Buffalo Mining Company. If a man worked for the Buffalo Mining Company, he was still a 'Pittston employee' to us."

Jurisdiction: Piercing the Corporate Veil

Stern initiated the process when he filed a complaint with the clerk in the United States District Court, Southern District, Charleston division. He had researched the backgrounds of the various federal judges sitting in West Virginia and had found what he thought was a "favorable" judge in the person of Sidney Christie.

Judge Christie had written an opinion that, Stern believed, would have a favorable impact on the Buffalo Creek case if the earlier ruling were to be followed. Christie had once permitted an injured person to sue a corporation's sole stockholder for injuries caused by the corporation itself. This kind of ruling, very rare in American law, is called *piercing the corporate veil.*

Piercing the corporate veil was critical for Stern's case if they wanted to remain in federal court. In order for Stern to argue his case for monetary damages for victims of the flood he had to get a favorable ruling on the procedural issue of jurisdiction. The plaintiffs had to be allowed to pierce the Buffalo Mining corporate veil to be able to sue Pittston, the sole shareholder of Buffalo Mining. If the judge rejected the piercing the veil argument, there was no diversity and therefore no jurisdiction. "It would be critical to have a judge, like Judge Christie, who understood the necessity for piercing a corporation's veil in certain cases." In response to the complaint, the attorney for the Pittston Corporation, a colorful West Virginia attorney named Zane Grey Staker, moved in federal court to dismiss the complaint filed by Stern on the ground that Pittston was "not a proper party to this action." The New York-based corporation did not own the dam; it was merely a stockholder in the Buffalo Mining Company. The brief for the defendant closed with these words:

> The short of the matter is that because plaintiffs regard Pittston as a more desirable defendant than Buffalo Mining for their purposes here, they seek in a manner wholly defiant of the facts to fabricate a wrongful domination of Buffalo Mining by Pittston that has never in truth existed, and without which, in light of the principles of law . . . , vicarious liability for the acts of Buffalo Mining cannot be laid to the door of Pittston.

Stern had one month to respond. "Our entire legal strategy," he later recalled, "was riding on this narrow, technical procedural question." He had to show that the Buffalo Mining Company was not a separate, independent corporation and he had to have the federal judge accept that information for the case to continue in the federal court.

Stern, using his *discovery*[55] rights, uncovered enough information to respond to the motion to dismiss. His rejoinder emphasized three sets of facts:

1.   Discovered documents indicated that Buffalo Mining was a "division" of the Pittston Corporation and not a separate corporate subsidiary. For example, the president of Pittston had written that the vice president of Buffalo Mining was acting as the Pittston Corporation "agent."

2.   Pittston had failed to follow normal corporate formalities in holding Buffalo Mining Company shareholders and directors meetings.

3.   It was unjust to require the plaintiffs to sue Buffalo Mining Company since that small company did not have the assets to pay any damages that might arise from the suit. (Stern had asked, in his initial complaint, for a $52 million dollar judgment against the Pittston Company.)

A few days after Stern's response, the plaintiffs' strategy "was in shambles. We had made a major mistake," he recalled. Judge Christie had removed himself from the case because the president of Pittston Company was an old and dear friend of the judge! After planning a response that would strike a warm chord in the judge's heart and mind, Stern found himself without his judge. Christie immediately sent the case to Judge Knapp, the next senior judge in the district. But Judge Knapp, a recent Nixon appointee, decided not to take the case and turned it over to the last of the federal judges that sat in the Charleston division, southern district, Judge K. K. Hall.

It takes luck as well as preparation to win cases in court. It turned out that Judge Hall "had risen from poverty to judgeship, and had an understanding of the little people's problems. He was a solid 'let's get the work done' kind of person, a very practical man with a great deal of common sense." The judge immediately set a hearing date for Pittston's motion to dismiss the complaint.

[55]Discovery is a pretrial procedure whereby one party acquires information concerning the litigation held by the adverse party. Facts, deeds, documents, statements, etc., which are in one party's possession and which are necessary to the other party's defense are revealed. The purpose of discovery is simple: to lay out all the facts before the actual trial so as to encourage settlement and/or speed up the ensuing stages of the litigation.

Almost six months after the initial complaint was filed by Stern, the parties to the dispute finally appeared before the judge in federal court. Stern and Stakes were to argue their case orally before the judge. Judge Hall had by now read the original complaint, the Pittston response, the Stern response to the motion to dismiss, and the Pittston response to Stern's response. Just before the oral arguments began with respect to dismissal of the suit, Stern knew he had won the issue. Judge Hall, greeting the lawyers from out of state, said to Stern: "You are welcome to appear before this Court in this case, on this matter, and on all other matters that might arise in connection with this case."

"My heart leaped," wrote Stern. "We'd won. There would be no need to permit us to appear before him on all matters that might arise in the future if he was about to dismiss our case." The oral arguments proceeded and, after the formalities, Judge Hall ruled from the bench that Pittston's motion to dismiss the case would be denied for the time being. The plaintiffs had to receive full discovery on all the issues of the case before final judgment on the Pittston motion.

Stern believed that the judge would not have the plaintiffs go through the discovery process—time-consuming and costly—only to dismiss the suit later on. He was right. The suit was not dismissed from federal court. Jurisdiction was there and "we had a judge who was willing to listen to the sympathetic concerns of our plaintiffs." As Stern noted: "A plaintiff's lawyer often is only as good as the judge he gets." Prepared for Christie, they received Hall. Their strategy turned out to be equally valid because of the quality of the federal judge.

The Plaintiff's Case: Reckless Disregard and Psychic Impairment

Once the federal judge noted jurisdiction (by denying Pittston's motion to dismiss), the plaintiff's attorney was then able to present the more substantive case against the Pittston Corporation that had been in preparation for over six months. Stern's civil suit revolved primarily around the notion of mental suffering of the survivors of the flood. The compensatory damages, i.e., monetary awards for loss of homes, cars, etc. was a minor aspect of the civil suit.

Stern believed that the coal company had acted recklessly and in utter disregard for the safety of the people living in the valley below the dam. As a consequence, his suit asked for punitive damages to compensate those survivors of the disaster. The figure Stern presented in the complaint was $52 million ($11 million in personal property losses; $20 million in mental suffering (psychic impairment); and $21 million in punitive damages).

At this point in the litigation, which was typified by negotiations between the lawyers for both sides which would end without Judge Hall's further participation, two basic issues emerged: (1) Did the Pittston Company act recklessly and in utter disregard for the safety of the coal mining villages? (2) Would a court accept the psychic impairment argument on behalf of survivors, even those survivors who had not been in the waters, or even in the immediate area of the flood at the time the dam broke?

RECKLESS DISREGARD   All civil cases tried in federal district courts must follow the appropriate state statutes. Application of the relevant state law in the federal court is one example of the principle of *comity* in a federal system. West Virginia law, with respect to damages, states that if conduct of a defendant is more than merely careless or negligent, if it is willful, wanton, or reckless, the plaintiff can conceivably recover his own losses (compensatory damages) but can also claim and recover "punitive damages." Punitive damages are awarded to punish the defendant for his reckless and wanton actions and to deter the defendant from again harming the plaintiff and others.

In this case, the Pittston Corporation argued that the dam that had burst had been built according to traditional coal mining "customs and usage." The president of the New York company had stated that:

> the embankment had been constructed by experienced coal mining men in accordance with methods and techniques for years characteristic of the manner in which water impoundments have been constructed throughout West Virginia and elsewhere.

Stern responded to this argument by pointing out that, in a 1926 U.S. district court case, from West Virginia, the federal judge found that custom and usage was no defense in a negligence suit against a coal mining company. Due to negligence, a disaster occurred involving a dam that flooded and killed a family of seven. (The district court judgment was upheld by the Fourth Circuit Court of Appeals.) But this was not enough for Stern; he had to show *recklessness* in order to collect punitive damages against the Pittston Corporation.

Working from written depositions taken from defendants during the discovery process, Stern soon found a number of facts that in his mind, taken together, added up to recklessness and wantonness on the part of the coal company:

1. Pittston purchased the Buffalo Mining Company in 1970 because the West Virginia Company did not have enough capital to comply with new federal safety regulations promulgated in the Coal Mine Health

and Safety Act of 1970. After purchasing the mine and dams, Pittston did nothing to comply with the federal regulation although the company knew that Buffalo Mining Company had been in violation of the Act. The "agent" for the parent company had written Pittston's legal counsel regarding Section 77.215 of the Act which prohibited the use of refuse piles to impede drainage or impound water. He had asked the company lawyer the following:

> Lorado plant pumps plant water in Middle Fork Hollow. This hollow is blocked by a refuse constructed dam to allow the solids to settle out. The clean water percolates or is decanted. What about the existing dams?

An answer was never sent by the legal counsel to the Pittston Corporation.

2. Just two days before the disaster, Pittston officials were in an automobile above the dam watching the rain pour down and the waters behind the dam rise. One of them asked about the emergency overflow system required by the federal law and was told there was none.

3. Pittston officials admitted that Dam 3 did not follow custom and usage as practiced in the Pittston Company itself in four significant ways:

a. there was no emergency spillway, even though there were both federal regulations and warnings by state inspectors that Dam 3 lacked such an emergency spillway;

b. the dam, unlike all others built by Pittston, blocked a stream;

c. the dam was much larger than any others built by the company;

d. there was, unlike all other Pittston dams, haphazard construction. The site for these dams overlooking the Buffalo Creek Valley had been *picked by the truck drivers who had dumped the solid waste!* "There were no engineering calculations whatsoever on Middle Fork (Dam 3)," stated the vice president of the Buffalo Mining Company.

Stern believed that, given these items, the case could be made for reckless disregard on the part of the mine company. He believed that a jury would award punitive damages to the plaintiffs given these and other facts that clearly illustrated a pattern, over the years, of recklessness on the part of the New York company.

MENTAL SUFFERING   There was no doubt in Stern's mind that the plaintiffs would collect compensatory damages; he was concerned about one aspect of that phrase: the mental suffering of the survivors of the tragedy. There were no precedents[56] for Stern and his associates to follow in this area. He was maintaining that the mental tortures the survivors would

---

[56]Precedent: earlier judicial opinions that are used to control decisions in later cases that are factually similar.

have for the rest of their lives must be compensated for by the company just as the company had to compensate for loss of limbs or loss of life. However, the question was: What was the dollar value on this kind of psychic or mental injury? Would a jury accept this kind of characteristic as a loss covered under the compensatory damages category?

For Stern, the mental suffering of the survivors (referred to as the survival syndrome) became the "most significant element of the compensatory damages claims." Through his discussions with both the survivors themselves and the psychiatric experts, Stern "was beginning to understand the emotional problems which are typical for survivors of disasters." Stern concluded that almost all of the over 600 plaintiffs showed manifestations of the survivor syndrome. As one expert stated in his report to Stern:

> The psychological and psychosomatic effects of this disaster resemble those encountered in Hiroshima. Though a flood experience cannot be equated with exposure to an atomic bomb, the survivors of both had much in common, which itself is an indication of the extraordinary human destructiveness of the Buffalo Creek disaster.

The Pittston Corporation responded to this survival syndrome claim with disdain. The proof of mental suffering, argued their lawyer in a meeting with Stern, "requires more than mere puff and blow." (Their doctors did note the mental anguish of survivors but believed that it would soon wear off, much like shell shock.) Stern was satisfied that he had sufficient material to make the case for mental suffering and began to push for a trial date.

The Settlement

It had taken Stern and his associates from the Arnold and Porter firm almost two years and over 40,000 man-hours (value: over $1 million) to collect all this information through the discovery process. The Pittston attorneys had continually acted to slow down the process, to wear out the plaintiffs in the hope of an easy settlement. The defendants had not yet finished with their discovery process by the time the second anniversary of the disaster came around. Stern asked Judge Hall in February 1974 to set a trial date. Stern had cried out in the brief to the judge: Enough! Pittston asked for a delay but the judge set the trial date for July 15, 1974.

It is at this time in civil proceedings in federal court—when the judge sets the trial date—that both sides seriously consider an out-of-court settlement. (Almost all civil cases are settled between the setting of the trial date and the trial itself.) Discovery had ended; both sides knew the information they and their adversary had collected and would use in the jury trial. Settlement discussions, both in writing and orally, began, while both sides prepared for the jury trial if that proved necessary. In March of 1974 Stern wrote a settlement note asking for $32.5 million. The Pittston response was to offer the plaintiffs $3 million. Preparation for the trial went on. However, May 1974 was the "showdown with Pittston."

In May, Judge Hall made another dramatic ruling. He ruled that, if recklessness were shown, then (as he interpreted the law) West Virginia law would permit recovery for mental suffering without physical impact or physical injury. This was, along with the jurisdictional issue (piercing the corporate veil) a major victory for the plaintiffs and a severe setback for Pittston's case.

Stern had told the attorneys for the defendant that any settlement had to be worked out by June 15 at the latest so he could go over the settlement figures with each of the plaintiffs. After a series of legal chess moves, in late June 1974, the Pittston Company offered Stern $13.5 million as a settlement figure for the plaintiffs. Stern accepted the offer. After almost 29 months, the legal battles involving the Buffalo Creek Valley disaster were over. Coal miners had beaten a large coal company that had wantonly ignored mine safety. It was a significant victory for the lawyers. As lawyer Stern noted:

> (The litigation effort) is the story of our legal system's ability to respond, to create new precedents, to fashion a remedy which may permit any one of us to recover for the mental suffering which normally follows when we survive another's reckless act, physically unharmed but mentally scarred.

In the Buffalo Creek case, known formally as *Prince et al. v. Pittston Corporation,* the federal judge played a very significant part although there was no trial and most of the drama unfolded outside the courtroom. However, Judge Hall did make two significant rulings at key points in the litigation process that swung the case to the plaintiffs.

Hall ruled that the federal court had jurisdiction when he decided that the corporate veil argument of Pittston was invalid. By allowing Stern to pierce the veil, Hall's court took jurisdiction over the civil suit. When Judge Hall ruled that psychic impairment was, if recklessness could be shown, a legally protected injury that fell under compensatory damages, Stern had another legal victory. Standing to sue was noted by Judge Hall in these two critical rulings.

Quite simply, the judicial discretion of Judge Hall made all the difference in the world to the case for the Buffalo Creek survivors. Ironically, the very day Judge Hall announced the date for the trial, Judge Christie suffered a massive heart attack and died. Had Christie been on the bench instead of Hall, there would have been a lengthy delay in the litigation proceedings and no one would have been able to determine the outcome. Judicial discretion played an important role in the Buffalo Creek case. By interpreting federal and state statutes and precedents, Judge Hall made the case for the plaintiffs. Who knows how another federal judge would have responded to these same facts and rules of law.

The Resignation of a President

Gerald Stern's litigation experiences in the West Virginia federal district court occur daily in the federal judicial system. Judicial discretion is a fact of life for lawyers. (Another chapter will have more to say about lower federal court decision making.) This segment focuses on a very atypical fact situation, yet it also illustrates the dynamics of gaining access to the federal judicial system. The lawyers involved in this case were counsel for President Richard Nixon and lawyers chosen to act as special prosecutors. Their concerns, much like the counsel for both parties in the Buffalo Creek litigation, involved questions of jurisdiction and justiciability.

Impeachment or Resignation of a President

The Watergate break-in occurred shortly before the election of 1972. Two years later, in August of 1974, President Richard M. Nixon resigned. The resignation was one of the most dramatic political events in our nation's history. Never before had a president been forced to resign or face the certainty of impeachment in the United States House of Representatives and conviction in the United States Senate for various "high crimes and misdemeanors."[57]

His resignation came in the wake of a series of judicial orders that commanded the president to turn over to the special prosecutor, investigating the possibility of criminality, a series of tape recordings Nixon had in his possession.[58] Shortly after the United States Supreme Court upheld a lower court order that commanded Nixon to release a number of tapes, the president resigned. One of the tapes he handed over had clearly implicated Nixon in the Watergate coverup effort.

The litigation began when the public found out that President Nixon had secretly been taping conversations in his office since he be-

---

[57]U.S. Constitution, Article II, Section 4.
[58]Facts and quotes about Watergate tapes litigation found in Howard Ball, *No Pledge of Privacy: The Watergate Tapes Litigation* (New York: Kennikat Press, 1977).

came president in 1969. Given the fact that the president had been forced into appointing a special prosecutor to look into the Watergate break-in and possible coverup, the existence of these tapes became a matter of concern for the lawyers investigating possible criminality in the White House itself.

The lawyer appointed by Nixon was Archibald Cox, a well-known legal scholar. Cox began his legal work in the spring of 1973. Charged by the Congress and the president to get to the bottom of the Watergate break-in, Cox had great difficulty getting information from the White House. When the tapes' existence became known, Cox asked the president for the tapes. When he was refused permission to use them, Cox asked the federal court to issue a subpoena to the president, ordering the chief executive to give the tapes up. The president refused to obey the subpoena and litigation commenced in the federal district court.

From the start of the litigation proceedings in August of 1973 in the federal courts, President Nixon and his counsel repeatedly argued two major themes: (1) Presidential confidentiality was an absolute aspect of presidential powers and only the president himself could determine whether and when any private conversations would be released—regardless of the need for these conversations. (2) Nixon and his counsel also argued (unsuccessfully) that the federal courts did not have jurisdiction to hear the case and that, furthermore, the relationship between the chief executive and one of his subordinates (the special prosecutor) was an intraagency dispute and therefore nonjusticiable because of the *political question* doctrine.

The Jurisdiction Question in the Lower Federal Courts

THE U.S. DISTRICT COURT OPINION   Cox had to go to court to get the tapes. He had to show the federal judge in the district court that the matter fell within the jurisdiction of the federal court and that it was a justiciable issue, that is, the court could construct an appropriate, manageable remedy for the special prosecutor. Nixon's attorneys argued that no president could be compelled by the judiciary to produce information that, in the president's mind, would not be in the public interest to disclose. Given the notion of the separation of powers concept inherent in the federal system itself, the president's attorneys argued that the president could interpose and refuse to obey a court order and that the matter was simply outside the jurisdiction of the courts. To subject the president to the ordinary processes of the law would mean that the 400 judges in the federal district courts could, potentially, handcuff the chief executive and rob the president of his substantive powers.

A second legal argument developed by the counsel for the president grew out of the unique circumstances of the Watergate drama. Nixon argued that since the special prosecutor was a subordinate employee of the president, there was no need for the president to supply him with the tapes. Furthermore, since it was an intrabranch problem, the courts lacked the jurisdiction to enter the controversy. Cox rejected the superior-inferior relationship and when he was refused permission to take the tapes, he went to the federal court for a subpoena.

When the president refused to obey the subpoena, both sides prepared legal arguments to determine whether or not Nixon had *shown cause*[59] for not handing over the subpoenaed material. Before Judge John Sirica, lawyers for the president, in response to the show cause order, maintained that the matter was a nonjusticiable question involving the president and one of his subordinates and was none of the courts business. The problem was, they inferred, a "political question" that federal judges typically leave for resolution through the political processes.

Archibald Cox argued otherwise. He argued that everyone, including the president of the United States, is subject to the compulsory processes of law. "Even the highest officials are subject to the Rule of Law, which it is emphatically the province and the duty of the Courts to declare. . . . The president is bound by legal duties in appropriate cases just like other citizens—in this case by the duty to supply documentary evidence of crime."

Sirica listened to the arguments and framed the important questions in his mind. There were two that were critically important to both sides: (1) Did the federal court have jurisdiction to decide the question of presidential privilege? (2) Could the court enforce a subpoena by ordering the production of the presidential tapes for inspection in Judge Sirica's chambers?

Judge Sirica spent a week examining these questions. (Sirica was the judge who had presided over the first trial of the Watergate Seven— the men who had actually broken into the Democratic party headquarters located in the Watergate building. His probing during the trial and his posttrial sentencing of the men to 35-year indeterminate sentences led some of them to confess that there had been planning by members of the White House staff. This discretion by Judge Sirica in the first case proved to be a pivotal factor in the unfolding of the Watergate coverup.) He handed down his judgment on August 29, 1973.

[59]Show cause order: an order of a court requiring a party to a dispute to appear in court and argue why a certain thing should not be done by that party. In this case, Nixon's attorneys were arguing why the president need not submit the tapes to the judge or to the special prosecutor—unless the president wanted to turn them over.

Sirica ordered Nixon to turn over the tapes to the federal judge for examination. Assuming jurisdiction of the matter, Sirica concluded that judicial examination of the evidence would protect those privileged portions of the tapes. The other nonprivileged tapes would be handed over to the special prosecutor for use in preparing indictments against those who might have been involved in an obstruction of justice.

Contrary to the arguments of the president's lawyers, Sirica stated that "the court cannot agree with respondent that it is the Executive that finally determines whether its privilege is properly invoked. The availability of evidence, including the validity and scope of privileges, is a judicial decision." Sirica commented that for the federal judiciary "to abdicate this role to presidents or anyone else (would be) to make each officer the judge of his own privilege (and) would dishonor the genius of our constitutional system and breed unbearable abuse." Noting that federal courts had passed judgment in numerous litigations where claims of executive privilege have been interposed, Sirica concluded that the federal court had jurisdiction to hear and to decide the questions raised by Cox.

Presidential privilege was not an enumerated power of the executive branch. If the concept has developed over the centuries, it certainly is not an absolute privilege of the presidency. Confidentiality cannot be interposed by the president without a judicial examination of the justification for that interposition. The right of the grand jury to all papers and documents and other testimony that throws light on its investigations into alleged criminal activity cannot be negated by the claim of presidential privilege. He concluded that the federal courts can create a remedy and that the court "has authority to order a president to obey a command of a grand jury subpoena as it relates to the unprivileged evidence in his possession." The propriety of "introducing any paper into a case as testimony must depend on the character of the paper, not on the character of the person who holds it," stated the federal judge.

Cox's arguments generally prevailed. The federal judge had noted federal jurisdiction over this dispute and had ruled that the matter was justiciable. President Nixon did not comply with the order; instead, he chose to appeal the ruling to the United States Court of Appeals in the District of Columbia.

THE U.S. COURT OF APPEALS OPINION   When the case came to the court of appeals, sitting *en banc* (all the appeals court judges sat together for this important case), the federal appeals court did an unusual thing. It sent a message to the parties, urging them to work out an accommodation without proceeding down the legal appeal road.

This attempt failed and the federal appellate court then examined the issue on the merits. After oral arguments and time for deliberation the judges ruled that they had the constitutional power and the constitutional responsibility to examine presidential claims of privilege.

In the opinion, handed down on October 12, 1973, the federal judges concluded that the president was not above the commands of the law. It was for the judiciary and not for the president to determine whether or not privilege could be invoked. "The [Sirica] order represents an unusual and limited requirement that the president produce material evidence. We think this is required by law, and by the Rule that even the Chief Executive is subject to the mandate of the law when he has no valid claim of privilege." The federal appeals court upheld the Sirica order of August 29, 1973.

The presidential response was the spectacle now referred to as the "Saturday Night Massacre." In a vain effort to circumvent the order, the president concocted a plan that would give Cox a transcript of the tapes—prepared by the White House—rather than the actual tapes themselves. When Cox refused to accept this plan, he was fired. Prior to the firing of the special prosecutor, Attorney General Elliot Richardson and his second in command at the Department of Justice, William Ruckleshaus resigned. They resigned because they felt that the firing of Cox was improper. (Robert Bork, Solicitor General of the United States who was hastily appointed Attorney General, did the actual firing of Cox.)

When the story broke Saturday evening, the American people were stunned and the national outcry was so great that Nixon was forced to capitulate. When his lawyers appeared before Judge Sirica the following Monday, they announced that the president would turn over the subpoenaed tapes to the federal court for examination and transmittal to the new special prosecutor. (The newly appointed special prosecutor was Leon Jaworski, a Texas attorney who had been approached by President Nixon's lawyers in the spring and had turned the job down when it was offered at that time.)

The Supreme Court Reviews the Question of Jurisdiction

With the material found on the released tapes, the grand jury guided by the second special prosecutor, Leon Jaworski, handed down indictments against seven men in March of 1974. Included among the seven charged with obstruction of justice and perjury were key White House figures such as John Mitchell, John Ehrlichmann, and H. R. Haldeman. The prosecutor, Jaworski, now had the difficult task of getting ready to go to trial in the federal district court in the District of Columbia in the fall of 1974.

Preparing for the trial, Jaworski requested an additional 60-odd tapes that were in President Nixon's possession. The prosecutor argued that they were needed for inculpatory or exculpatory[60] reasons. Jaworski was charged with doing justice in the Watergate matter: All evidence that threw light on the question of guilt or innocence was relevant to the prosecutor. His request, however, was turned down by the attorneys for the president. They claimed that the prosecutor had sufficient information to take the case to trial.

Jaworski went to the U.S. district court in April 1974. He asked Judge Sirica to issue a trial subpoena directing the president to produce tapes and documents relating to specified conversations held between Nixon and the defendants Haldeman, Ehrlichmann, Mitchell, et al. Sirica signed the order which meant that the president had to hand over the tapes or appeal the issuance of the legal instructions.

President Nixon's attorneys again argued the points debated earlier in the tapes litigation: executive privilege and lack of jurisdiction. Attorneys for the president insisted that this was an intraagency dispute that was essentially a political question and therefore outside the scope of federal jurisdiction. Jaworski argued, as Cox did in the earlier litigation before Sirica, that the possession of the tapes was necessary for a fair trial and due process of law.

In late May 1974, Sirica issued his order in the case of *United States v. Nixon*. He ruled that Jaworski's status was that of an independent prosecutor; the dispute was not a typical intraagency controversy between a superior and a subordinate. The Congress and the president had given Jaworski, in written and oral statements, complete freedom to investigate the matter of Watergate. Nixon's "attempt to abridge the special prosecutor's independence is a nullity and does not defeat the court's jurisdiction."

Further, the subpoena would not be quashed[61] by the federal court because it was based on a "good cause" showing—that is, the material sought was solely in the possession of the president and it was necessary for the proper preparation of the trial. Since it was not a hunt for information but a request for information whose existence was known, Sirica ruled that the president had to obey the commands of the subpoena.

The Nixon attorneys immediately went to the U.S. Court of Appeals in the District of Columbia to appeal the Sirica opinion. Jaworski,

[60]Inculpatory: that evidence which would tend to incriminate or bring about a criminal conviction. Exculpatory: that evidence which would clear or excuse a defendant from fault or guilt.
[61]Quash: when a judge overthrows or annuls an unreasonable subpoena, injunction, etc.

however, took the unusual step of appealing directly to the United States Supreme Court. According to 28 USC Sections 1254 and 2102 and Rule 20 of the Supreme Court guidelines, this unusual procedure is available in order to "promote judicial efficiency and hasten the ultimate termination of litigation." The justices of the Supreme Court, on May 31, 1974, agreed to hear the case of *United States v. Nixon* in this expeditious manner.

The Supreme Court heard the arguments in early July (the written briefs had arrived at the Court in early June). The arguments made before the Supreme Court were the same ones raised in the lower federal courts: executive privilege, jurisdiction, justiciability. The justices were told quite bluntly by Nixon's counsel not to "interfere, impair, or otherwise participate" in this intraagency dispute between Nixon and Jaworski. Jaworski argued that his office had sufficient independence to negate the presidential argument.

The opinion of the Supreme Court was announced on July 24, 1974. In a unanimous judgment, the highest Court in America ruled that Nixon had to turn over the tapes to the special prosecutor. With respect to the issue of jurisdiction and justiciability, the Court stated that "justiciability does not depend on . . . surface inquiry. . . . Courts must look behind names that symbolize the parties to determine whether a justiciable case or controversy is presented."

Going behind the names Nixon and Jaworski, the Court found jurisdiction and justiciability. Jaworski was an independent investigator conducting a criminal investigation: He was responsible for "a judicial proceeding in a federal court alleging violation of federal laws and . . . brought in the name of the United States of America as sovereign." Given the special provisions that were drawn up between the attorney general and Jaworski that gave the Texas lawyer "unique authority and tenure," and given the fact that this arrangement had not been terminated, the Court concluded that the special prosecutor was independent of ordinary presidential controls:

> The demands of and the resistance to the subpoena present an obvious controversy in the ordinary sense, but that alone is not enough to meet constitutional standards. In the constitutional sense, controversy means more than disagreement and conflict; rather it means the kind of controversy courts traditionally resolve. . . . This issue (presented in *United States v. Nixon*) is one of a type which are traditionally justiciable. . . . There is concrete adverseness which sharpens the presentation of issues upon which the court so largely depends for illumination of difficult, constitutional questions. . . . The fact that both parties are officers of the Executive Branch cannot be viewed as a barrier to justiciability. . . . The Special Prosecutor has standing to bring this action and [there is] a justiciable controversy presented for decision.

With this opinion the Nixon presidency rapidly drew to a close. Written by a chief justice appointed by Nixon himself four years earlier, the order of the Supreme Court forced the president to turn over the tapes to the federal district court for transmittal to Jaworski. Within weeks of the July 24, 1974, opinion of the Court, the United States lost the president through resignation. For the first time in history, both the president and the vice president were forced to resign from office under clouds of mischief and possible criminal activity. In both cases, the federal judiciary and government lawyers played critical roles.

SUMMARY

United States district courts "do damnably important business in our nation," wrote an observer of the federal judicial system. "They are the shock troops of the judiciary. As courts of first resort they have initial contact with the cases that so frequently evolve into momentous decisions by the Supreme Court."[62] This chapter focused on the way in which procedures can be used by the judges in cases and controversies before their courts. Hall and Sirica played pivotal roles in the civil and criminal cases they supervised. The gatekeeping functions of these two judges led to the determination of jurisdiction and standing and justiciability in the Buffalo Creek and in the Watergate litigation cases.

It has been pointed out that luck is an essential part of the litigation process in the federal and state judicial systems. As one lawyer stated: "Sure, the federal judiciary is good; I'll go federal rather than state any day. But so much of it is the luck of the draw. You get a lazy judge, or a dumb judge, and you'd be better off trying the case before a justice of the peace in rural Kentucky."[63] The rules of abstention discussed in this chapter are applied by men and women. Some of them are quite intelligent; others are senile. Some are racist; others fair and impartial. The dynamics of gaining access is based on the skill of the lawyer and on the facts of the case. Gaining access also is determined by luck: Who did the lawyer draw as the sitting judge in the case?

Discretion of judges is an overriding consideration in an attempt to understand the nature of the federal judicial system and the decision-making process within that judicial system. So far the chapters have discussed discretion as it relates to the judicial functions, jurisdiction, and justiciability. Case studies have been presented that illustrate the

[62]Joseph C. Goulden, *The Benchwarmers* (New York: Weybright and Talley, 1974), pp. 2–3.
[63]Ibid., p. 12.

uses of judicial discretion. The next chapter examines the dynamics of selecting these federal judges, magistrates, and United States attorneys. The selection process determines in large measure the kind of discretionary actions one sees on the federal bench. To fully understand why a judge acts the way he does, one has to understand the dynamics of judicial socialization and judicial selection.

It is important to remember that jurisdiction and justiciability are not mechanical terms that can be programmed into a computer so that decisions could be forthcoming in that manner. Judges are not computers; they are not robots or automatons. They are thinking, feeling, human beings who employ these concepts—standing, mootness, justiciability, etc.—according to the dictates of their hearts and their legal minds. They are also politically oriented people. Chapter 5 illustrates this dimension clearly.

staffing
the federal judicial
system

5

He is our kind of Democrat.

Letter from a federal judge to
Attorney General Robert Kennedy (D), 1962.

*My political loyalty to the Republican
party is well-established.*

Letter from a seeker of a federal
judgship to Attorney General Richard
Kleindienst (R), 1972.

*If federal judges (were) appointed solely on the basis of merit
that would be the millennium.*

Chief Judge Edward Devitt,
U.S. District Court, Minnesota.

We have seen how important a factor judicial discretion is in the exercise of judicial power. Had lawyer Stern faced another judge in West Virginia, the Buffalo Creek case might well have been thrown out of the U.S. district court. If lawyer Jaworski did not have Judge John Sirica hear the Watergate tape arguments, that case may have taken a different turn. This chapter focuses on the factors that account for the selection of these and other federal judicial officers who often make major policy decisions from the bench. Essentially, the chapter will illustrate Professor Jack Peltason's truism that "the decision as to *who* will make the decisions affects *what* decisions will be made."[1]

Who hears the case often determines the outcome of the case; the turn of mind of the judge is often the decisive factor in the outcome of the litigation. This fact has not escaped the notice of the president, the political agent charged with the constitutional responsibility to nominate and, with the advice and consent of the Senate, to appoint federal judges to the bench. President George Washington began the process of politicization of the judicial branch. In a defense of his judicial appointees, he stated that the judges were "the keystone of our political fabric."[2] President Abraham Lincoln said the following: "We wish for a Chief Justice [a man] who will sustain what has been done in regard to emancipation and the legal tenders. We cannot ask a man what he will do . . . we must take a man whose opinions are well known."[3] President Theodore Roosevelt once commented that "a judge of the Supreme Court is not fitted for the position unless he is a party man, a constructive statesman, . . . keeping in mind his relations with his fellow statesmen who in other branches of the government are striving to cooperate with him to advance the ends of government."[4] Table 5-1 clearly illustrates the politicization of the federal judiciary.

The selection of judges to the federal courts is "frankly and entirely a political process."[5] United States Attorney General Griffin Bell, appointed to that position in 1977 by President Jimmy Carter, had been a judge on the United States Court of Appeals (Fifth Circuit) during the 1960s. Of that appointment, Bell stated quite frankly:

> Becoming a federal judge wasn't very difficult. I managed John F. Kennedy's presidential campaign in Georgia. Two of my oldest and closest friends were the two Senators from Georgia. And I was campaign manager and special, unpaid counsel for the Governor of Georgia.[6]

One other example of this politicization of the federal judiciary will set the tone for the segments that follow: In August 1973, the chief judge of the United States Court of Appeals, Fourth Circuit, Clement

[1]Jack Peltason, *Federal Courts in the Political Process* (New York: Random House, 1955), p. 29.

[2]James F. Simon, *In His Own Image: The Supreme Court In Richard Nixon's America* (New York: David McKay, 1972), p. 9.

[3]Ibid., p. 12.

[4]President Theodore Roosevelt to Henry Cabot Lodge, June 2, 1902, quoted in Murphy and Pritchett, *Courts, Judges, and Politics,* (New York: Random House, 1975).

[5]C. Herman Pritchett, *The American Constitution* (New York: McGraw-Hill, 1977), p. 101.

[6]James Goodman, "The Politics of Picking Federal Judges," *Juris Doctor,* vol. 7, no. 6 (June 1977), p. 20.

TABLE 5-1   **PERCENTAGES OF FEDERAL JUDICIAL APPOINTMENTS ADHERING TO THE SAME POLITICAL PARTY AS THE PRESIDENT, 1888–1977**

PRESIDENT	PARTY	PERCENTAGE
Cleveland	Democrat	97.3
B. Harrison	Republican	87.9
McKinley	Republican	95.7
T. Roosevelt	Republican	95.8
Taft	Republican	82.2
Wilson	Democrat	98.6
Harding	Republican	97.7
Coolidge	Republican	94.1
Hoover	Republican	85.7
F. D. Roosevelt	Democrat	96.4
Truman	Democrat	90.1
Eisenhower	Republican	94.1
Kennedy	Democrat	90.9
L. B. Johnson	Democrat	93.2
Nixon	Republican	93.7
Ford	Republican	79.0
Carter	Democrat	94.7

Haynesworth (who will be discussed in another context later in this chapter), had to appoint U.S. District Court Judge Walter Hoffman, who sat on the district court in Norfolk, Virginia, to hear the government's case against Vice President Spiro Agnew (who eventually resigned the vice presidency due to the charges brought against him by the U.S. attorneys in Baltimore). The reason the chief judge had to appoint a Virginian to hear the case in Maryland was simple yet profound: "All nine of the federal judges sitting in Maryland had disqualified themselves, citing some past association with Agnew."[7]

(This legal politicization extends to the United States attorneys, the 94 lawyers "directly responsible for the enforcement of federal criminal law via prosecution."[8] As the chapter will illustrate, these are basically political appointments by the president and his attorney general. One recent study of differences between U.S. attorneys appointed by President Lyndon Johnson (a Democrat) and by President Richard Nixon (a Republican) concluded that there was considerable variation among the federal prosecutors "along partisan lines. Nixon appointees do not subscribe to the thesis that crime is largely a product of such social ills

[7]Richard M. Cohen and Jules Whitcover, *A Heartbeat Away: The Investigation and Resignation of Vice President Spiro Agnew* (New York: Viking Press, 1974), p. 260.
[8]Gregory J. Rathjen and Thomas D. Ungs, "United States Attorneys and The Lower Federal Courts: Some Effects on Law and Order," paper delivered at the Midwest Political Science Association Meeting, Chicago, April 1978, pp. 2–3.

as poverty, unemployment, poor education, and unequal opportunities, while Johnson appointees do hold such a view."[9] Here, too, these appointments are based on the fact that the appointing agents seek out "their kind" of attorney to prosecute cases in the federal courts.)

A recent study of President Jimmy Carter's appointments to the lower federal courts clearly indicates that he too has appointed men and women who come from his political party and who have had partisan political experiences. What has been strikingly different about Carter's appointments is the fact that he has appointed a "significantly larger proportion of black Americans and women."[10] (See Tables 5-2 and 5-3 for comparisons between President Carter and the three presidents who preceded him into the White House.)

The segments that follow will illustrate the political character of the selection process. Judges are policy makers; they are seen as partners in the political process. From the very beginning of the selection process to the firing and retirement of judges and attorneys in the federal structure, there is the ubiquitous political dimension. For all know that *who* the policy makers select to sit on the federal courts will determine *what kinds* of cases they *hear* and what kinds of policy decisions they will *make* from the federal bench.

THE APPOINTMENT POWER: CONSTITUTIONAL LANGUAGE, CUSTOM, AND CONTROVERSY

The Constitutional Debates, 1787

The appointment of federal judges was the subject of extensive debate and compromise in 1787. One of many compromises worked out during the debates at the 1787 Constitutional Convention in that Philadelphia summer was the issue of who shall make federal judicial appointments. The Virginia delegation, led by John Randolph, initiated the dialogue when the group introduced a series of proposals (the Randolph Plan) for modifying the Articles of Confederation system in May 1787. One of these, proposal nine, called for the creation of a national judiciary (there wasn't a national judiciary in the Articles of Confederation political system), with one or more supreme tribunals whose

---

[9]Ibid., p. 9.
[10]Sheldon Goldman, "A Profile of Carter's Judicial Nominees," *Judicature,* 62 no. 5 (November 1978,) p. 249.

TABLE 5-2   HOW CARTER'S NOMINEES TO THE DISTRICT COURTS COMPARE TO THE APPOINTEES OF FORD, NIXON AND JOHNSON

CHARACTERISTIC	CARTER NOMINEES	FORD APPOINTEES	NIXON APPOINTEES	JOHNSON APPOINTEES
Occupation:				
Politics/gov't	4.4%	21.2%	10.7%	21.3
Judiciary	42.2	34.6	28.5	31.1
Large law firm	40.0	34.6	39.7	21.3
Moderate size firm	2.2	5.8	11.7	4.9
Solo or small firm	8.9	3.9	6.7	18.0
Other	2.2	—	2.8	3.3
Undergraduate education:				
Public-supported	46.7	48.1	41.3	38.5
Private (not Ivy)	33.3	34.6	38.5	31.1
Ivy League	17.8	17.3	19.5	16.4
None indicated	2.2	—	0.6	13.9
Law school education:				
Public-supported	37.8	44.2	41.9	40.2
Private (not Ivy)	33.3	38.5	36.9	36.9
Ivy League	28.9	17.3	21.2	21.3
Experience:				
Judicial	46.7	42.3	35.1	34.3
Prosecutorial	33.3	50.0	41.9	45.8
Neither one	33.3	30.8	36.3	33.6
Party:				
Democrat	95.6	21.2	7.8	94.8
Republican	4.4	78.8	92.2	5.2
Party activism:	53.3	50.0	48.6	48.4
Religion:				
Protestant	57.8	73.1	72.1	57.4
Catholic	31.1	17.3	18.9	31.9
Jewish	11.1	9.6	8.9	10.7
Race:				
White	91.1	90.4	97.2	96.7
Black	8.9	5.8	2.8	3.3
Asian-American	—	3.9	—	—
Sex:				
Male	86.7	98.1	99.4	98.4
Female	13.3	1.9	0.6	1.6
TOTAL nominees or appointees	45	52	179	122

Source: *S. Goldman, "A Profile of Carter's Nominees,"* Judicature, *vol. 62, no. 5 (November 1978) p. 248.*

TABLE 5-3   HOW CARTER'S NOMINEES TO THE COURTS OF APPEALS COMPARE TO THE NOMINEES OF FORD, NIXON AND JOHNSON

CHARACTERISTIC	CARTER NOMINEES	FORD APPOINTEES	NIXON APPOINTEES	JOHNSON APPOINTEES
Occupation:				
Politics/government				
Judiciary	—	8.3%	4.4%	10.0%
Large law firm	41.7	75.0	53.3	57.5
Moderate size firm	25.0	16.7	24.4	20.0
Solo or small firm	16.7	—	6.7	2.5
Other	—	—	2.2	7.5
	16.7	—	8.9	2.5
Undergraduate education:				
Public-supported	41.7	50.0	40.0	32.5
Private (not Ivy)	41.7	41.7	35.6	40.0
Ivy League	16.7	8.3	20.0	17.5
None indicated	—	—	4.4	10.0
Law school education:				
Public-supported	41.7	50.0	37.8	40.0
Private (not Ivy)	33.3	25.0	26.7	32.5
Ivy League	25.0	25.0	35.6	27.5
Experience:				
Judicial	58.3	75.0	57.8	65.0
Prosecutorial	41.7	25.0	46.7	47.5
Neither one	25.0	25.0	17.8	20.0
Party:				
Democrat	91.7	8.3	6.7	95.0
Republican	—	91.7	93.3	5.0
None	8.3	—	—	—
Party activism:	75.0	58.3	60.0	57.5
Religion:				
Protestant	83.3	58.3	75.6	60.0
Catholic	8.3	33.3	15.6	25.0
Jewish	8.3	8.3	8.9	15.0
Race:				
White	66.7	100.0	97.8	95.0
Black	25.0	—	—	5.0
Asian-American	8.3	—	2.2	—
Sex:				
Male	100.0	100.0	100.0	97.5
Female	—	—	—	2.5
TOTAL nominees or appointees	12	12	45	40

Source: S. Goldman, "A Profile of Carter's Nominees," Judicature, vol. 62, no. 5, (November 1978) p. 251.

judges would be chosen by the national legislature and who would serve for life, assuming good behavior on their part.[11]

In support of the Randolph proposal were such leading political leaders as Benjamin Franklin and Roger Sherman. However, others were not pleased with such an arrangement. These opponents, men such as James Madison and Alexander Hamilton, feared that such an arrangement would make the judiciary dependent upon the national legislature. An alternative series of proposals was introduced by the New Jersey delegation. This counter set of ideas, known as the William Patterson Plan, included a fifth proposal that focused on the creation of a national judiciary. That particular proposal called for the creation of a single federal judicial agency, a "supreme tribunal," whose judges would be appointed by the chief executive alone and who would hold office, after appointment, for life during good behavior.[12]

Matters remained deadlocked with respect to the appointment of the judges of the federal judiciary until July 18, 1787. On that day, one of the delegates, Nathaniel Gorham from the state of Massachusetts, the chairman of the convention's committee of the whole, offered a compromise: Let the judges of the federal court be appointed by the chief executive with the advice and consent of the second branch of the legislature (the Senate) "in the mode prescribed by the Constitution of Massachusetts."[13] This compromise, like the others struck toward the end of the Constitutional Convention, reflected the concept that dominated the proceedings: checks and balances. And the compromise, like the others, was accepted by most of the delegates; it was tolerable to most of them. It found its way into the Constitution and, as worded in Article II, Section 2 (and 3) reads as follows:

Section 2: (The President) shall nominate, and, by and with the advice and consent of the Senate, shall appoint . . . judges of the Supreme Court. . . .

Section 3: The President shall have power to fill up all vacancies that may happen during the recess of the Senate, by granting commissions which shall expire at the end of their next session.

Two questions arose almost immediately and are even today still interesting political queries: (1) Precisely what kind of role was the Senate to play in the appointment process? (2) To what extent did the president have power to creatively expand on the meaning of recess appointments

---

[11]Saul K. Padover, *To Secure These Blessings* (New York: Ridge Press, 1962), p. 53.
[12]Ibid., p. 84.
[13]Ibid., p. 401.

to the Supreme Court and other federal courts? It is also necessary to point out that the Constitution is silent on the question of appointment of inferior federal judges. As will be seen in an upcoming segment in this chapter, soon after 1789 there developed the fundamentally politicalized customs and traditions of appointing lower federal judges. It was not until 1948 (when the Congress took on the task of recodification of federal statutes) that the Congress enacted legislation which specified that the Senate would "advise and consent" on inferior federal judicial appointments.[14]

The Uneasy Constitutional Partnership between the President and the Senate

What did the Constitution makers mean by the phrase "advice and consent"? As already noted, presidents since George Washington have held to a politicized view of judgeships. They have attempted to appoint certain kinds of persons to the federal judiciary and have viewed this power as a presidential prerogative—with senatorial advice and consent being mere window dressing. During the G. Harrold Carswell nomination fight (January through April 1970), President Richard M. Nixon sent a letter to one of the U.S. senators. In that note, Nixon argued the presidential prerogative position:

> What is centrally at issue in this nomination is the constitutional responsibility of the President to appoint members of the Court—and whether this responsibility can be frustrated by those (in the Senate) who wish to substitute their own philosophy or their own subjective judgement for that of the one person entrusted by the Constitution with the power of appointment. . . . The fact remains, under the Constitution, it is the duty of the President to appoint and of the Senate to advise and consent. But if the Senate attempts to substitute its judgement as to who should be appointed, the traditional constitutional balance is in jeopardy and the duty of the President under the Constitution impaired. . . . What is at stake is the preservation of the traditional constitutional relationships of the President and the Congress.[15]

This position has not gone without criticism. Indeed, the history of presidential appointments to the Supreme Court (see Table 5-4), replete with examples of senatorial rejection of presidential nominees, is proof of the contrary position. Senators and scholars have repeatedly

[14]Harold W. Chase, *Federal Judges: The Appointing Process* (Minneapolis, University of Minnesota Press, 1972), p. 5.
[15]Letter from Richard M. Nixon to Senator William B. Saxbe, U.S. Senate, March 31, 1970.

TABLE 5-4   ONE IN FIVE SUPREME COURT NOMINATIONS HAS FAILED

Through and including the nomination and appointment of Justice John Paul Stevens (nominated by President Gerald Ford, 1976), 28 of the 136 presidential nominations for positions on the Supreme Court (more than one in five) failed to obtain Senate confirmation. The list of those who failed to achieve confirmation follows:

NOMINEE	YEAR	PRESIDENT	ACTION
Wm. Patterson	1793	Washington	Withdrawn
John Rutledge	1795	Washington	Rejected
Alex. Wolcott	1811	Madison	Rejected
John Crittenden	1828	John Adams	Postponed
Roger B. Taney	1835	Jackson	Postponed
John Spancer	1844	Tyler	Rejected
R. Halworth	1844	Tyler	Withdrawn
Edward King	1844	Tyler	Withdrawn
R. Halworth	1844	Tyler	Withdrawn
Edward King	1844	Tyler	Withdrawn
John Read	1845	Tyler	Postponed
G. Woodward	1846	Polk	Rejected
Ed. Bradford	1852	Fillmore	Postponed
George Badger	1853	Fillmore	Postponed
William Micou	1853	Fillmore	Postponed
Jeremiah Black	1861	Buchanan	Rejected
Henry Stanbery	1866	Johnson	Postponed
Ebenezer Hoar	1870	Grant	Rejected
George Williams	1874	Grant	Withdrawn
Caleb Cushing	1874	Grant	Withdrawn
Stanley Matteys	1881	Hayes	Postponed
W. B. Hornblower	1894	Cleveland	Rejected
W. H. Peckham	1894	Cleveland	Rejected
John J. Parker	1930	Hoover	Rejected
Abe Fortas	1968	L. Johnson	Withdrawn (associate justice nominated for chief justice)
Homer Thornberry	1968	L. Johnson	Withdrawn
C. Haynsworth	1969	Nixon	Rejected
G. H. Carswell	1970	Nixon	Rejected

insisted that the Senate "had the right and the obligation to decide in its own wisdom whether it wishes to confirm or not to confirm a Supreme Court nominee."[16] Charles Black, noted constitutional scholar, has argued that in effect the Article II, Section 2 constitutional appointment procedure involves two separate sets of opinions: The first opinion is the president's nomination, while the Senate's duty to advise and consent "constitutes the taking of the second opinion."[17]

[16]Senator Birch Bayh quoting Republican Michigan Senator William Griffin, April 3, 1970.
[17]Charles L. Black Jr., "A Note On Senatorial Consideration of Supreme Court Nominees," *Yale Law Journal*, 79 (1970), p. 659.

The fundamental reason for senatorial interposition has been stated by Black. If the U.S. Senate believes, and offers justification for the belief, that a nominee's views on the major issues confronting society would be harmful to the country, then it can and should reject the nominee. The words of the Constitution in Article II, Section 2 "do not suggest a rubber stamp function."[18]

The best response to the Nixon perception is found in one of the earliest explanations of the constitutional processes: the *Federalist Papers* of 1787–1788. Alexander Hamilton (who had opted for a process whereby the executive alone appointed the federal judges) wrote *Federalist Paper* No. 76, "The Appointing Power of the Executive." In that essay, Hamilton wrote of the senatorial power of advice and consent:

> In the act of nomination, the presidential judgement alone would be exercised. . . . To what purpose then require the cooperation of the Senate? I answer . . . it would be an excellent check upon a spirit of favoritism in the President, and would tend greatly to prevent the appointment of unfit characters from state prejudice, from family connection, from personal attachment, or from a view to popularity. . . . The possibility of rejection would be a strong motive to care in proposing.[19]

An assumption of the founding fathers was that the president would select federal judges from among those men who were most knowledgeable in the law. If the chief executive uses his appointment power to nominate a person who in the eyes of the Senate is not worthy of the high judicial position, then the Senate has the option—acting on its independent (collective) opinion—of rejecting that nominee. As U.S. Senator Birch Bayh (D-Ind.) stated during the Carswell nomination debates in the spring of 1970:

> The Senators who oppose Judge Carswell's nomination are not trying to usurp the President's constitutional function; they are, rather, exercising their constitutional obligation. The President can nominate a man with a racist philosophy to sit on the Court if he wishes to do so. But this Senator will exercise his constitutional and moral responsibility by opposing the nomination of a racist to the highest court of the land.[20]

In sum, presidents since George Washington have on occasion resorted to "common politics" in the selection of federal judges; many senatorial rejections of presidential nominations have likewise been for reasons of political advantage. The Senate's power, however, is a neg-

---

[18]Ibid.
[19]*The Federalist Papers* (New York: Random House Modern Library, 1937), p. 494.
[20]Congressional Record, April 3, 1970.

ative one. As Hamilton said in the *Federalist Papers*, "They (Senate) may defeat one choice of the Executive and oblige him to make another, but they cannot themselves choose—they can only ratify or reject the choice of the President." The basic point, with respect to the constitutional relations between the president and the Senate is this: the Chief Executive does not have freedom of choice—although presidents wish this were so. "The judges are not the President's people."[21] If the presidential choice is an obviously poor choice, then the Senate is constitutionally free to interpose and negate the presidential choice.

Recess Appointments of the President

Article II, Section 3 of the United States Constitution gives the president the power to make recess appointments: "The President shall have power to fill up all vacancies that may happen during the recess of the Senate." President Washington was the first president to use the recess appointment to fill a vacancy on the Supreme Court. He was the first president to run into senatorial objections.

John Rutledge had been an associate justice of the Supreme Court from 1789 to 1791 but left the Court for the chief justiceship of the South Carolina court system. When John Jay resigned the chief justiceship of the U.S. Supreme Court to become governor of New York State, Washington filled the vacancy during the Senate recess by appointing Rutledge. (In all recess appointments, the commission expires at the end of the next Senate session, which means that, if the appointee is to continue on the bench, the Senate has to confirm the recess appointee when it reconvenes.) Rutledge however had made a fateful error. Prior to the Senate approval of his appointment, he made a speech that was highly critical of the recently signed Jay Treaty with Great Britain. The Federalist controlled Senate had just ratified that treaty when Rutledge condemned it. The Senate, when it returned from recess, quickly defeated the appointee by a vote of 14 to 10.[22]

This kind of senatorial response is the major pitfall of the recess appointment. By having a candidate assume the position while the Senate is not in session, the president gains the advantage of having his appointee in place and at work when the Senate returns to business. To defeat the candidate would be to disrupt the judicial business that the judge has gotten involved with during the recess appointment.[23] This

---

[21]Black, "Senatorial Consideration," p. 660.
[22]Simon, *In His Own Image*, p. 100.
[23]Joel V. Grossman, *Lawyers and Judges: The Politics of Judicial Selection* (New York: John Wiley, 1965), p. 31.

potential cost, however, outweighs the benefit because the appointee has to be concerned about the fact that the senators will carefully examine what he has been doing while serving as a recess appointee. He may have acted injudiciously from the bench, decided a case or written an opinion for the majority on the Court that has the potential for angering the senators who have to pass on his qualifications. The obvious reason for defeating the Rutledge appointment in 1797 was because of the jurist's intemperate criticism of the recently concluded piece of foreign policy.

Another recent recess appointment caused some concern on the part of the president and legal scholars. In September of 1953, Chief Justice Fred M. Vinson suddenly died. The Congress was not in session and would not return for many months. Yet the Supreme Court of the United States was to open its 1953 term in a matter of weeks. By October 5, 1953, President Dwight Eisenhower had selected a replacement and made the recess appointment. The man chosen for the task of leading the U.S. Supreme Court was Earl Warren, the former governor of the state of California (and a supporter of Eisenhower at the 1952 Republican convention). Eisenhower, was, however,

> caught up in a constitutional bind. . . . A recess appointment would place the newly designated Chief Justice in the embarrassing position of having to serve for some months before he could be confirmed by the Senate. The necessity of participating in decisions likely to stir the passions of Senators who had not yet voted on the appointment would threaten the delicate balance of power between the judicial and legislative branches.[24]

Given the nature of litigation pending before the Supreme Court—in particular the school segregation cases and the Communist party controversies—there was serious concern that Warren's appointment would be endangered. "The situation was viewed with such gravity by a group of Harvard Law School professors that they urged the President to call the Senate back to Washington to act on the nomination at once."[25] (As it turned out, when the Senate did convene, it took more than seven weeks to clear the nomination due to the senatorial concern about the quality of the nominee.)

There is some danger, therefore, when a president is forced to fill a judicial position under circumstances similar to the Rutledge or Warren recess appointments. Both of these situations arose when the vacancy occurred while the Senate was not in session. Another constitutionally

---

[24]John D. Weaver, *Warren: The Man, The Court, The Era* (Boston: Little, Brown, 1965), p. 191.
[25]Ibid.

based question arises however: Can the president wait *until* the Senate adjourns and then appoint someone to fill a vacancy that had arisen in a federal court prior to the Senate recess?

What does the phrase in Article II, Section 3, "vacancies that may happen during the recess," really mean? Narrowly interpreted, it means that only when a vacancy occurs *during* the Senate recess itself can a president appoint a replacement without prior senatorial approval. The broader interpretation of the phrase suggests that the chief executive can wait for a recess and then fill a vacancy that has developed prior to the senatorial adjournment. Although the Constitution itself is silent on the meaning of Article II (as are the debates surrounding the ratification of the Constitution), presidents have taken the broader definition of recess appointments and this broad definition has been upheld in the federal courts.[26]

In sum, the recess appointment can be filled with danger for it places the judicial nominee in the dangerous and embarrassing position of being forced to justify actions that he or she had taken while serving on the federal bench during the term of the recess appointment. This led to the defeat of John Rutledge in 1795; this threatened the confirmation of Earl Warren in the early months of 1954. A president, however, can hope that such a recess appointment will be accepted by the Senate when it returns because the nominee has shown himself to be a person with the appropriate judicial skills and temperament. In any event, the Senate will carefully examine the credentials of the recess nominee and will advise and consent or reject the nominee in much the same manner—and with much the same political overtones—as the more traditional manner of judicial appointments.

Toward a Merit Selection of Federal Court Judges

After the election of Jimmy Carter to the presidency in 1976, his attorney general, Griffin Bell, introduced a plan for the merit selection of all lower federal court judges. The plan was adopted by the president and Executive Order No 11972, Feb. 14, 1977, was issued establishing U.S. Circuit Judge Nominating Commissions, i.e., "citizen panels for the selection of federal judges to the eleven U.S. Circuit Court of Appeals."[27]

[26]See, for example, *United States v. Allocco*, 305 Fed Supp 2. 704 (1962), at p, 711. Cert Denied, 371 *US* 964 (1963).

[27]Goodman, "Picking Federal Judges," p. 19. See also Susan Carbon, "The U.S. Circuit Judge Nominating Commission: A Comparison of Two of its Panels," *Judicature*, vol. 62, no. 5 (November 1978).

As originally proposed by Bell and accepted by Carter, the plan called for merit selection of *all* lower federal court judges. However, this idea was not favorably received by the chairman of the Senate Judiciary Committee, Senator James Eastland (D-Miss.), "who served notice on the White House that no judge would be approved by his committee without senatorial clearance. As a concession he agreed to accept only Appeals Court judges on merit."[28]

"Under the President's order, one of the 13 citizen panels is 'activated' whenever an opening exists for one of the 97 circuit judgeships."[29] The panels reflect the 11 circuits in the United States (with an additional panel for each of the two geographically large circuits: the fifth—deep south—and the ninth—far west). Made up of citizens chosen by the president and, in Carter's words, "a membership not to be limited to lawyers,"[30] these panels would be activated when a vacancy developed. Within 60 days after being notified of an opening in the U.S. Circuit Court of Appeals, the panel must present the president with a list of five people it feels best qualified to fill the vacancy. Choosing the nominee from this list, the president then sends the name to the Senate for confirmation.

The success of President Carter's merit plan rests ultimately on the willingness of the Senate to accept such a plan (and the nominees the plan produces) and on the nature and composition of each of these panels in the eleven circuits. This merit selection of lower federal judges, if accepted by the Senate as a body, would be a major change from the way federal judges have been chosen since the administration of George Washington. The following segments review the politics and the complexity of the judicial selection process as it has existed since 1789.

THE COMPLEXITY AND UNIQUENESS OF THE SELECTION PROCESS

An Overview of the Selection Process

Although the constitutional language suggests simplicity itself in the selection of federal judges (presidential nomination, senatorial advice and consent, appointment), the process itself is far more complex. (See Figures 5-1 and 5-2 for a graphic illustration of the judicial selection process in general.) There are relevant patterns of behavior followed

---

[28]Jack Anderson, "Merit Selection May Choose Judges," *Mississippi Clarion-Ledger*, June 18, 1978, p. 9.
[29]Goodman, "Picking Federal Judges," p. 19.
[30]Anderson, "Merit Selections."

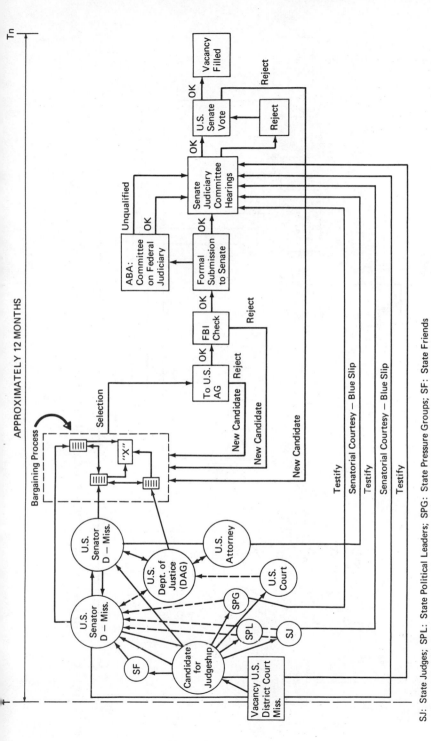

APPROXIMATELY 12 MONTHS

SJ: State Judges; SPL: State Political Leaders; SPG: State Pressure Groups; SF: State Friends

FIG. 5-1   THE JUDICIAL SELECTION PROCESS: LOWER FEDERAL COURTS

173

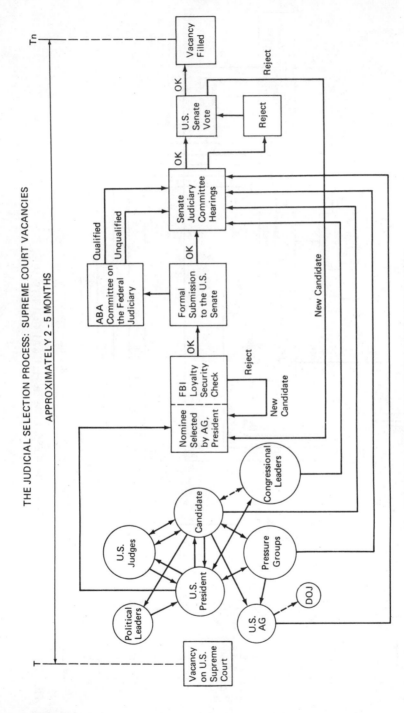

THE JUDICIAL SELECTION PROCESS: SUPREME COURT VACANCIES

APPROXIMATELY 2 - 5 MONTHS

FIG. 5-2   THE JUDICIAL SELECTION PROCESS: SUPREME COURT VACANCIES

by the actors in the selection process; these norms have developed over the years in a slow incremental fashion. The pattern of *senatorial courtesy* is one of these norms that developed very early in our constitutional history. It is, as will be discussed below, a norm that is an institutionalized part of the selection process and suggestions for changing this particular norm—such as the merit proposal suggested by President Carter in 1977—are not met with very positive responses.

In addition to senatorial courtesy, other norms of behavior that have developed over the years would include regional geographical considerations, the role of the Federal Bureau of Investigation in the selection process, the responsibility of the American Bar Association's Committee on the Federal Judiciary, and the impact of pressure groups on the selection process. However, while there is a regularity to the selection process—that is, although various actors transact with each other according to these norms every time there is a vacancy to be filled,[31] each nomination process is different.

Different actors come upon the scene with each new vacancy. Different states (and therefore different U.S. senators) are involved, different candidates from these states are involved, and so forth. The intensity of pressure group participation will vary based upon the candidates being considered or nominated—and the records they have developed prior to their nomination for the federal bench.

"Once it is known that there is or will be a vacancy on the federal bench, the jockeying for position begins in earnest."[32] For many months before the formal notice of vacancy, the position is "pursued by a lineup of individuals who man certain positions. These players interact differently each time a position must be filled. The play involved in each appointment is unique."[33] The president, the attorney general, the deputy attorney general and his staff of Department of Justice lawyers along with their legal/political contacts across the country (senators; state political leaders; pressure groups; judges—federal and state; and the potential nominees as well) all participate—to a greater or lesser extent based upon the judicial vacancy that must be filled—in these judicial transactions.

Some of these actors collect names of possible candidates and information about these potential federal judges. This data is collected from the political actors, from the candidates themselves, from friends of the candidates, and from contacts the collecting actors have in the

[31]See generally David J. Danelski, *A Supreme Justice Is Appointed* (New York: Random House, 1964).
[32]Chase, *Federal Judges*, p. 3.
[33]Quoted in Goodman, "Picking Federal Judges," p. 22.

political, administrative, and legal communities. Other players man screening positions: They evaluate the credentials—legal and political—of potential nominees to the federal bench. Still other actors affirm or reject the person that emerged as the nominee of the president.

The relative power of the many actors in the judicial selection process varies with the type of federal judicial position being filled at that time. The Senate (and "senatorial courtesy") is the dominant actor with respect to the filling of federal district court judgeships. Joe Dolan, assistant attorney general in the John F. Kennedy administration, put it bluntly when he stated that "the Constitution is backwards. Article II, Section 2 should read: 'The senators shall nominate, and by and with the consent of the President, shall appoint.' "[34]

When a vacancy arises at the U.S. court of appeals level, other actors play more prominent roles. "The first reality is that the president's men in the Justice Department, i.e., the Attorney General and the Deputy Attorney General and his assistants, are primarily responsible for the judicial selection. . . . These officials use their vast network of friends, acquaintances, and friends of friends as a source for possible appointees."[35] The president of the United States, along with his attorney general, is the dominant political actor in the selection of Supreme Court justices. Although there are influences upon the chief executive (see Figure 5-2), he "has almost complete discretion in filling a vacancy on the Supreme Court" (subject, of course, to the senatorial advice and consent process).[36]

What follows is a more detailed examination of the various actors that participate in the judicial selection process, and some case studies that illustrate the process at its best and at its worst. The point is that beneath the constitutional language and the customs and traditions that have developed over the years, there is the basic political imprint on the manner in which the system fills these judicial vacancies on the federal bench. The humble apolitical candidate who rests on his laurels will very seldom get the nomination. If a person covets a federal judicial position he had better seek it out and work hard to get to be a federal judge.[37] For the most part, the man seeks the position in the federal judicial selection process and not the reverse.

[34]Harold Chase, "Federal Judges: The Appointing Process," *Minnesota Law Review,* 51 (1966), 185, 211.
[35]Sheldon Goldman, "Judicial Appointments to the United States Court of Appeals," *Wisconsin Law Review,* 1967, (1967), 186–87.
[36]Murphy and Pritchett, *Courts, Judges,* p. 156.
[37]For an interesting commentary on how one judge got to be a federal judge, see Joseph Samuel Perry, "How I got to be a Federal Judge," in Murphy and Pritchett, pp. 168–69.

The Major Participants in the Judicial Selection Process

A contemporary newspaper account of legislative inaction dramatically illustrates the political dynamics and some of the major sets of participants in the federal judicial selection process.

> Arkansas, whose backlog of federal court cases ranks among the highest in the nation, is not likely to get relief from Congress this year through the addition of two federal judges. . . . House and Senate conferees have agreed to postpone the effective date for nominations of 152 new federal judgeships until November 1, assuring senators up for reelection that they won't have to disclose their choices for the patronage in the middle of their campaigns. This means that Senate confirmations of the new federal judges would not occur until sometime in early 1979.[38]

Because of the political sensitivity of the issue, the Congress would not act to fill these needed positions until after the 1978 election. Senators, potential candidates, state political leaders, and pressure groups in the state are but a few of the major participants in the selection process; a process noted for its outright politicization. The segment that follows examines some of these actors and the positions they man in this process. As Table 5-5 indicates, there are three sets of participants in the federal judicial selection process.

Initiators

The major actors in this stage of the selection process include the president and his key advisors: the attorney general and the deputy attorney general, the senators (especially when the appointment is to a federal district court), local and national political leaders, judges, and the candidates themselves.

THE PRESIDENT   The president does not get personally involved in the selection of nominees to fill lower federal court positions. He generally leaves this patronage job for the attorney general and the key staffers in the Department of Justice. The president is, to a large extent, the prisoner of the practice of senatorial courtesy discussed below. Presidents however do get very much involved when a vacancy occurs on the United States Supreme Court. In any event, whether the position that opens up is a federal district court judgeship or a Supreme Court judgeship, the presidential imprint is present in the process to the extent that

---

[38]John Bennett, "Senate Delays Judges Nominations," *Memphis Commercial-Appeal,* June 13, 1978, p. 3.

TABLE 5-5   THE MAJOR PARTICIPANTS IN THE FEDERAL JUDICIAL SELECTION PROCESS

INITIATORS	SCREENERS	AFFIRMERS
President	Senators—to 1840	Senate Judiciary Committee
Attorney general and staff, including deputy atty. general	Senate Judiciary Committee after 1840	U.S. Senate
U.S. senators (president's party)—1840	Department of Justice	
Local party leaders	FBI—1917	
Judges	American Bar Association—1946	
Candidates for position	Pressure groups Media	

the chief executive, very early in his administration, establishes general criteria that are employed in filling these judicial vacancies. These criteria vary from presidency to presidency; the standards reflect the political, ideological, and policy orientations of the incumbent in the White House.

John F. Kennedy's criteria, for example, emphasized the following qualities: "unquestioned ability," "respected professional skill," "incorruptible character," "firm judicial temperament," "the rare inner quality to know when to temper justice with mercy," and "intellectual capacity to protect and illuminate the Constitution and our historic values."[39] In contrast, Kennedy's predecessor, President Dwight Eisenhower, had announced a series of standards, followed by Justice Department officials, that stressed: outstanding legal and community leadership qualities; age and health of the candidate so that "men of vigor" would be chosen capable of performing the "heavy burdens now imposed on federal judges." Also, outstanding judges "should be carefully considered" for positions on the circuit courts or the Supreme Court, with considerable weight placed on the "recognition of the American Bar Association."[40]

The obvious difference in these two sets of criteria is that Kennedy called for "certain qualities of mind and character desired in judges" while the Eisenhower administration emphasized age, health, and the American Bar Association rating. The ABA input was the basic criterion that distinguished these two administrations. The chairman of the ABA's Committee on the Federal Judiciary in that era, Bernard Segal, pointed out in 1961 that, "it is only three years since it has become *firmly established*

[39]Chase, *Federal Judges*, p. 67.
[40]Ibid., pp. 67–68.

that no lawyer 60 years or older should be appointed to a lifetime judgeship for the first time, unless he is regarded by professional opinion as 'Well Qualified' or 'Exceptionally Well Qualified,' and is in excellent health."[41] Needless to say, the Kennedy and Johnson administrations were not as rigidly bound to this Eisenhower judicial policy.

In sum, although the president may not play a major role in the selection of the lower federal court judges, the fact that he establishes general criteria, and his staff acts in accordance with these general principles when filling vacancies that develop, attests to the overall significance of the chief executive. From Washington to Carter, the presidents of the United States have taken great care to respect these norms so that their kinds of judges were chosen to sit on the federal bench.

THE DEPARTMENT OF JUSTICE   The attorney general of the United States and his deputy attorney general, both political appointees of the president, have the responsibility for locating potential candidates for federal judicial vacancies who (1) meet the general criteria established by the president and, in the case of lower federal judges, (2) meet with senatorial approval. Along with other initiators, the staff of the deputy attorney general seeks out information about potential federal judges. They canvass their friends in the Department of Justice about, for example, "Kennedy" type persons who have the appropriate political and legal background called for in the presidential criteria. They will contact federal officials in the state where the vacancy has developed or officials in Washington, D.C., who might know of potential candidates in that state. They will also be in contact with state political leaders and pressure groups who have supported the administration in the attempt to develop a list of viable candidates for the vacancy on the lower federal court.

These initiators, attorneys in the Department of Justice—some political appointees—work up lists of possible candidates. This workup of the list is not done in isolation. Justice officials work with the criteria developed, explicit and implicit (i.e., party affiliation, attitude on major policy issues, etc.), by the president. They maintain close communications with the senators from the state that has the vacancy (assuming that the legislators are members of the president's political party) and, more directly, with the staff associates of the U.S. senators. They do the research on the candidates—political background as well as legal history of the potential nominee. (On occasion, the Justice lawyers may do a poor or downright bad job of researching the background of the candidate and consequently are publicly embarrassed when opponents of the candidate present the "skeletons" to the Senate Judiciary Committee,

[41]Ibid.

to the national press and, ultimately, to the public. The G. Harrold Carswell nomination in 1970 is a classic case of poor preparation by the Department of Justice. The defeat of Carswell will be discussed in a subsequent segment of this chapter.) To conclude, the Department of Justice staff attorneys do the basic leg work for the attorney general and his deputy, "acquiring data on prospective nominees and negotiating with senators."[42]

The Department of Justice is active in filling vacancies that occur at the court of appeals level. Whereas the president and attorney general play an important role in the selection of Supreme Court justices, and the impact of senatorial courtesy is felt most directly when federal district court vacancies arise, the Department of Justice's impact is greatest with regard to the filling of the federal court of appeals vacancies. "If power shifts markedly to the administration" in this selection of court of appeal judges, it is repeated when a vacancy develops in the federal courts that are staffed by judges chosen without regard to state boundaries: the U.S. district court and the court of appeals located in the District of Columbia, the specialized federal courts such as the Court of Claims, the Court of Customs and Patent Appeals, and the U.S. Customs Court.[43]

UNITED STATES SENATE   The role of the Senate in the judicial selection process has already been discussed. Nowhere is the legislature's influence more profoundly felt than in the selection of federal district court judges. It has already been pointed out that, in creating the district courts in such a manner as to keep them within state lines, the 1789 Congress in effect created the environment for selecting federal judges whose political and legal roots are in these judicial boundaries. Parochialism, localism, and conservatism are words that have often been used to categorize the selection of federal district court judges; "senatorial courtesy" is the appropriate title given to this "law of politics."[44] As one study concluded:

> A persistent factor in the molding of lower court organization has been the preservation of state and regional boundaries. The feeling that the judiciary should reflect the local features of the federal system has often been expressed by local officials most explicitly. Mississippi Congressman John S. Williams declared that he was "frankly opposed to a perambulatory judiciary, to carpetbagging Nebraska with a Louisianian, certainly to carpetbagging Mississippi or Louisiana with somebody north of Mason and Dixon's line."[45]

[42]Ibid., p. 17.
[43]Ibid., pp. 43–45.
[44]Henry J. Abraham, *The Supreme Court in the Governmental Process* (Boston: Allyn and Bacon, 1975).
[45]Richardson and Vines, *The Politics of Federal Courts* (Boston: Little, Brown, 1970), p. 71.

The senator's input begins as soon as a vacancy is announced. The senator and his staff assistants, working at times with staff attorneys from the Department of Justice, collect information about possible candidates whose names have been referred to the legislator by state political leaders, state judges, friends of the senator, and by the candidate himself. When the president's men and the senator's staff agree on the name of a candidate to fill a vacancy on the district court in the senator's home state, the "nomination usually goes through without delay or obstruction."[46]

The process is such that the senator's nominee—if the senator is emphatic about that person—will be the person the president formally submits to the Senate for their advice and consent. Without that informal cooperation and bargaining *and agreement* between the senator and the president, the nominee put forward by the president would have little chance of receiving Senate confirmation.

Assuming that there has been bargaining and accommodation between the senators and the presidential staffers, when the name is formally submitted to the Senate for confirmation, there is very little that can jeopardize the nomination.

A recent example of senatorial-presidential cooperation illustrates the essential nature of the relationship between these two agents. A federal district court judge, Terry Shell, who sat on Arkansas' eastern district court, died in late June 1978. Within days of his death, both (Democratic) senators had selected a replacement—the legislative assistant to one of these senators, Dale Bumpers (D-Arkansas). The report stated that "Governor David Pryor will be consulted" but the name "won't be submitted to [Democratic President] Carter until next week after a discreet period of time following Shell's death. . . . Arnold (the legislative assistant chosen for the federal judgeship) has been with Bumpers since his election in 1974 and served as legislative assistant when Bumpers was governor of Arkansas."[47]

In this brief news article there is revealed the essential relationship between senators and the president. So long as the senators can agree on a candidate to fill the position, the presidential input is slight. However, if a conflict or impasse emerges between the two senators (who are of the president's party), then the president's men in the Department of Justice would move in to fill gaps and work out a settlement. If there is no accommodation between the senators and then between the legislators and the presidential agents: (1) the vacancy will remain open indefinitely, (2) a presidential nominee presented to the Senate without senatorial approval will probably be defeated, or (3) the president will

[46]Ibid., p. 62.
[47]John Bennett, "Arnold Seen As Nominee for Judgeship," *Memphis Commercial Appeal,* June 28, 1978, p. 1.

make a recess appointment.[48] Generally this kind of impasse does not develop. If the two senators are at odds with each other for whatever the reason—political jealousies, ideological estrangement, etc.—there will be a procedure worked out between their staff assistants so that the bottleneck does not develop.

In the Supreme Court selection process, as indicated in an earlier section (and to be illustrated in a subsequent segment of this chapter), the U.S. Senate plays the role of second opinion giver. The president nominates the candidate but the Senate constitutionally must give its advice and consent. Senatorial courtesy does not substantively enter into the process of selecting a justice to the United States Supreme Court, although the president as a courtesy will speak with the senators of the candidate's home state. One or both of these legislators will then formally introduce the candidate to the members of the Senate Judiciary Committee at the first session of the formal hearings on the nomination in the Senate.

The Senate has often rejected candidates for judicial office that have been presented to that body by the president. With regard to nominees for lower federal judicial positions, the essential process is the tactic referred to as "blue slip." This is the basic control associated with the tradition of senatorial courtesy.

If the senator or senators of the president's party have been involved in the judicial selection process with attorneys from the Department of Justice, when the nominee is formally presented to the Senate a standard form, printed on a blue paper, is *not* returned to the Chairman of the Senate Judiciary Committee. This nonreturn of the form indicates that the senator has no objections to the candidate (he has, informally, helped to choose). If the senator of the president's party has not been consulted in the informal proceedings prior to formal nomination or if the name of the candidate is not in accord with his prior judgment, the blue slip is returned (within the week) and the nomination is dead.

The form, which is the basic tool epitomizing "the institutionalization of senatorial patronage,"[49] reads as follows:

Dear Senator:

Will you kindly give me, for use by the Senate Judiciary Committee, your opinion and information concerning the nomination of (name, district, name of former judge).

Under a rule of the Committee, unless a reply is received from you within

---

[48]Chase, *Federal Judges,* p. 41.
[49]Goodman, "Picking Federal Judges," p. 19.

a week from this date, it will be assumed that you have no objection to this nomination.

Respectfully,
(Signature)
Chairman, Senate Judiciary
Committee[50]

Although both senators from the state that has the vacancy receive this form, very little attention is paid to the response (or nonresponse) from the senator or senators who are not members of the president's party. In effect, in the hands of a senator who is of the president's party, the blue slip process "amounts to a 'one person veto,' ending the nominee's chances," stated one congressional aide familiar with the process.[51]

When a vacancy arises on the court of appeals level, there exists the modified process of senatorial courtesy. (As discussed earlier, the Carter administration in 1977 introduced a plan which called for the merit selection of nominees by select citizen committees to these intermediate federal courts of appeal. It is too early to judge the success of the Carter plan, which is a sharp break with tradition.) Given senatorial courtesy, the vacancy on the appeals court is filled by a person from the former judge's home state.

As with all other procedures involving the Senate in the selection process, this is an informal custom that emerged after the courts of appeals were created in 1891. In effect, if a judge, who came to the federal bench from a career in Mississippi politics and Mississippi legal experiences, retires, dies, or resigns (or is impeached and convicted in the Senate), the president is generally bound to choose a successor from the state of Mississippi.

The custom, followed by presidents since the 1890s, allows each state in the federal circuit to keep a seat or seats on that regional appeals court. If there are no consultations between the Department of Justice and the senators (as well as state political leaders), then a president runs the risk of having his candidate defeated via the "blue slip" method. The Carter plan retains the custom of holding the vacant seat for the particular state the retiree came from but changes the process of selecting the new judge.

Rejection of a nominee for a Supreme Court vacancy goes beyond the senatorial courtesy rationale used for rejection of lower court judges. Since the Senate rejection of William Rutledge in 1795, 28 of 136 nominees to the Supreme Court have been rejected by the Senate.[52] There

[50]Found in Richardson and Vines, *Politics*, p. 61.
[51]Goodman, "Picking Federal Judges," p. 211.
[52]Abraham, *Justices and Presidents* (New York: Oxford University Press, 1975), p. 51.

are essentially three factors that are important to the success or failure of the president's efforts to fill a vacancy on the Supreme Court: (1) partisanship, (2) timing of appointment, and (3) personal policy preferences of the candidate.[53]

Partisanship refers to the fact that periodically in American politics the president has been the leader of the party not in the majority in the Senate. Political opposition to the president has led, on occasion, to the defeat of his nominees. For example, poor relationships existed between President John Tyler and the Senate prior to the Civil War, and strained the relations between President Grant and the Senate after the Civil War. This animosity led to the defeat or withdrawal of presidential nominees to the Supreme Court (see Table 5-4).

Timing is another manifestation of the partisan politics surrounding the appointment process and refers to the point in time in the president's tenure of office when the nomination is announced. For example, after President Lyndon B. Johnson announced, in the spring of his last year of his first full term as president, that he would not seek a second term, he became a "lame duck" president. Shortly thereafter, Chief Justice Earl Warren submitted his resignation to the president. Johnson then nominated Associate Justice Abe Fortas to be chief justice of the United States.

A major battle developed in the Senate after Fortas' name was formally presented to the legislative body. The intense, two-month long Senate criticism of the nomination led President Johnson to withdraw the names of his nominees to the Supreme Court (in addition to Fortas, Johnson nominated Judge Homer Thornberry, a federal district court judge from Texas, to fill the vacant seat). One of the arguments made by Republican senators, beyond substantive criticism of the Fortas—and the Warren Court—record on major policy issues, was the fact that a president who was shortly to leave the Executive Office ought not to be allowed to make such a major decision. Instead, argued Republicans, it should be the prerogative of the incoming president (they hoped it would be Richard M. Nixon, a Republican) to make the selection.

Often, the personal policy preferences and ability of the nominee himself will lead to the rejection by the Senate. The very first senatorial rejection, Rutledge in 1795, is a classic example of the Senate responding negatively to a candidate for a federal judgeship after the nominee had openly disagreed with a policy developed by the confirming body. In the twentieth century, Supreme Court nominees have been rejected because of senatorial antipathy toward the candidate's views on labor

[53]David Rohde and Harold Spaeth, *Supreme Court Decision Making* (San Francisco: Freeman Publishing Co., 1975), p. 104.

and right to work laws (John Parker, 1930; Clement Haynesworth, 1969); race relations between blacks and whites (Parker, Haynesworth, and G. Harrold Carswell, 1970); and the candidate's general incapacity to do the job well (Carswell, 1970).

Some other men who were ultimately chosen to sit on the Supreme Court saw the vote to confirm them dragged on and/or become very close due to senatorial criticism of the candidate's ability, his position on issues, and, in some cases, because of the religion of the nominee (e.g., Louis Brandeis who was Jewish). The Senate delay of four months over the Brandeis nomination in 1916 is still a record for Senate procrastination over Supreme Court nominations. Although branded as an economic and political radical by the Senate, "there is no question that much of the anti-Brandeis campaign was anti-Semitic in origin."[54]

Whatever the reason—partisanship, timing, senatorial perceptions of the nominee's ability or lack of ability—the Senate has often played a major role in the selection and rejection of nominees to the Supreme Court. It is, however, a senatorial negative (veto power) role which gives the president another opportunity to fill the vacancy.

LOCAL AND STATE PARTY LEADERS   A fact of life in the selection process is the custom of senatorial courtesy. Senatorial courtesy is rooted in the very creation of the district court system in 1789, a creation that followed the boundaries of the states. As such, since the development of party politics in the early decades of the nineteenth century, the state political machinery, and state political leaders, have had a strong voice in the development of those lists of nominees by legislative assistants of the U.S. senator from that state. "Federal judgeships, with their high prestige, life tenures, and relatively high salaries, are the most desirable political appointments that can be made from the states and for this reason are politically important to the Senator and his supporting party organization."[55] When there are no senators of the president's party in the state that has a vacancy on the federal bench, the president's men often seek out the advice and views of state political leaders of the president's party. Directly or indirectly, the state political organization has a role to play in the selection of federal judges.

FRIENDS OF THE CANDIDATES FOR THE POSITION   Still another input in the process of selecting federal judges comes from persons, including federal judges, who know of and support potential nominees for the federal judgeship. William Howard Taft, while the chief justice of the United States, actively and successfully campaigned to get some of his colleagues

[54]Abraham, *Justices and Presidents*, pp. 171–72.
[55]Richardson and Vines, *Politics*, p. 62.

onto the Supreme Court.[56] More recently, Chief Justice Warren Burger played a role in the selection of federal appeals judge Harry Blackmun to be associate justice of the United States Supreme Court. (Blackmun replaced Justice Abe Fortas who resigned under pressure. After Nixon's first two nominees for the vacancy, Haynesworth and Carswell, were rejected by the Senate in November 1969 and April 1970, Blackmun was selected by Nixon and was easily confirmed by the Senate.)

THE CANDIDATE   "[I]f I wanted that appointment, I had better get back into politics—which I did," stated federal district court judge Joseph Perry to a meeting of the Chicago Bar Association.[57] A great number of lawyers covet the position of federal district court judge. When a position opens up due to death, resignation, or retirement, these lawyers seek out the job and "fight like tigers for the position of federal district court judge."[58]

They have prepared for this moment by joining the appropriate party organization, by working tirelessly for the party, by supporting the party organization candidates, by contributing time and money to the party, and by befriending men who ultimately become senators, congressmen, governors, etc. Given their prior political activities, along with their intellectual ability and legal temperament, there is the opportunity to become a federal judge provided the candidate seeks it vigorously and is of the president's party. Therefore, another quite active participant in the initiator phase of the selection process is the candidate himself.

Through letters, telephone conversations, and personal contacts he makes his name known to the White House, Department of Justice, and the United States Senate. It is quite common for senators to be bombarded by dozens of potential candidates as soon as a vacancy develops in the federal district court within their state.

As a consequence, on occasion, these judgments will be made after elections are over so as to prevent an incumbent senator from suffering political estrangement and possible defeat in that election due to the anger on the part of rejected candidates. Politically, it is expedient to make a decision after the election or to appear to allow the Department of Justice to make the selection.

Screeners

INITIATORS AS SCREENERS   Screening the potential nominee is a responsibility of some of the initiators. In particular, the staff of the senators

[56]William Goulden, *The Benchwarmers* (New York: Weybright & Talley, 1974),p. 31.
[63]Ibid., pp. 150–52.
[64]Ibid., p. 153.

has the responsibility of examining carefully the backgrounds of the nominees the senators will ultimately present to the Department of Justice. In addition, the staff of the deputy attorney general is responsible for both initiating and screening those names that have been generated by the Department of Justice. However, there are four other actors who play a major role in the screening of potential candidates for federal judgeships: the Federal Bureau of Investigation, the American Bar Association's Committee on the Federal Judiciary, the Senate, and various national pressure groups who screen and then support or contest particular nominees put forward by the president.

THE FEDERAL BUREAU OF INVESTIGATION (FBI)   Shortly after World War I, presidents began sending the names of potential candidates for judicial positions to the FBI for a security/loyalty check. These FBI reports, essentially raw data, i.e., information that has not been evaluated by the FBI, are then presented to the Department of Justice. The raw data contains information about the character of the nominee and about his legal abilities and temperament. It is gathered through FBI interviews of men and women who know the candidate personally and professionally. After evaluation of the raw data, the candidate is either cleared or rejected by the Department of Justice.[59]

AMERICAN BAR ASSOCIATION'S COMMITTEE ON THE FEDERAL JUDICIARY   Since 1945, the American Bar Association (ABA), the major professional organization representing about half of the nation's lawyers, has played a role as screener of the professional qualifications of possible nominees of the president for positions on the federal bench. Made up of 14 members, including the chairman and others representing the 11 circuits (two each for the two largest circuits in the United States federal judicial system—the fifth and ninth circuits), the ABA's Committee on the Federal Judiciary carefully examines these persons in light of its well-defined criteria.

Applying its criteria, discussed below, the Committee reports to the Senate and to the Department of Justice on its findings. Generally, the Department of Justice will solicit the views of the ABA before formally submitting the name of the candidate to the Senate. After an examination of the candidate's professional background, the Committee will judge the person to be "well qualified," "qualified," or "not qualified" for the judicial position. A "not qualified" rating will generally mean that the person's name will not be placed in nomination by the president. "Needless to say, the committee has a profound impact on the selection

---

[59]See generally Chase, *Federal Judges*, pp. 21–23.

process."[60] After the Carswell ("qualified" ranking) nomination met with intense criticism, the ABA in 1970 changed its ratings as follows: "high standards of integrity," "not opposed," and "not qualified."[61]

If the FBI examines the personal proclivities of potential candidates for federal judicial posts, the ABA examines their professional lives. Since its inception, Republicans have dominated the Committee and their attitudes have colored the process somewhat.[62] The basic criteria developed over the years by the ABA are as follows: age, trial experience, honesty, intelligence, competence, judicial temperament, character, and sound legal training.[63]

Although the committee has been charged with gathering information about the candidate from federal and state judges and lawyers practicing in the candidate's community, it rarely functions in that manner. Studies indicate that "the sources tend to be cut from the same cloth as the committeemen, lawyers highly active in Bar Association activities."[64] Although some of the criteria are fairly objective ones—for example, age and trial experience—evaluations on the other factors such as character and judicial temperament are highly subjective. (For example, the ABA opposed the nomination of Louis Brandeis in 1916 on the grounds that he lacked judicial temperament!)[65]

Given the conservative leanings of the ABA and especially the members who serve on this very important committee, it is no wonder that many persons involved in the judicial selection process are highly critical of the role of the professional bar association in the selection of federal judges. Ratings of the ABA tend to reflect the ideological bias of the committee, and Democratic presidents have been extremely wary of ABA reviews and have passed this concern on to their initiators and screeners. Of course, the ABA cannot defeat the candidate for that is the constitutional prerogative of the Senate. But it is extremely difficult to affirm a candidate after the ABA has argued publicly that he or she has been judged not qualified by the person's peers.

THE UNITED STATES SENATE   The informal arrangements between the senators and the Department of Justice lead to the formal nomination of the candidate by the president, based on favorable reviews of the candidate's background by the FBI and the ABA's Committee on the Federal Judiciary. At this point, the Senate becomes the formal screener by having the nomination brought to the Senate Judiciary Committee. With

[60]Ibid., p. 20.
[61]Abraham, *Justices and Presidents*, p. 28.
[62]Chase, *Federal Judges*, pp. 148–50.
[63]Ibid., pp. 150–52.
[64]Ibid., p. 153.
[65]Abraham, *Justices and Presidents*, p. 30.

respect to lower court judgeships this committee will hold hearings on the qualities of the candidate but, given the senatorial courtesy tradition in the form of the "blue slip" tactic, these generally are brief and perfunctory—especially so when it is a district court vacancy that is being filled.

The Judiciary Committee's work is done in earnest when the vacancy to be filled is a seat on the United States Supreme Court. Hearings are scheduled, witnesses are heard, and deliberations take place behind the closed doors of the Senate subcommittee that is responsible for examining the credentials of the nominee. The Senate committee becomes the watchdog of the Senate and the committee can affect the process in three ways: (1) by delaying the Senate confirmation process in the hope of "embarrassing the president or to test his determination to make a particular appointment."[66] (2) by rejecting the nominee of the president in committee, and (3) after a judgment by the committee, by having a general debate on the floor of the Senate that "affords still another opportunity for senators to seek to embarrass the administration by questioning the wisdom of a particular appointment."[67] In sum, in addition to initiation functions, the Senate performs the screening function in accordance with Article II, Section 2 of the United States Constitution.

INTEREST GROUPS   Still another participant in the selection of federal judges are the major pressure groups in the United States. On occasion they play a major role in the confirmation or rejection of candidates for federal judgeships. Officials of these groups—labor, business, civil rights, legal—on occasion uncover information that has not been uncovered by other screeners.

Additionally, these groups might know things about the candidate that other screeners could not possibly know. Also, given the narrowness of the ABA screening procedures, other pressure groups often provide obvious information about candidates that simply was not gleaned by the ABA. For example, the ABA gave Judge Carswell, a 1970 nominee for the Supreme Court seat vacated by Abe Fortas, a "qualified" rating whereas civil rights organizations uncovered a great deal of information relative to Carswell's performance on and off the court to cast serious doubts on the Nixon candidate's overall legal competency.[68] All in all, the attempts by various pressure groups to influence the selection process "has long been characteristic of American politics."[69]

---

[66]Chase, *Federal Judges*, p. 21.
[67]Ibid., p. 23.
[68]See Richard Harris, *Decision* (New York: E. P. Dutton, 1971).
[69]Schmidhauser, *The Supreme Court*, p. 21.

Affirmers

Constitutionally, the affirmer in the judicial selection process is the United States Senate. After all the negotiations and all the screening by the FBI, the ABA, and the various pressure groups interested in the defeat or affirmal of the candidate, it is the U.S. Senate that has to "advise and consent." A simple majority vote of the Senate will lead to the formal appointment of the nominee to the position on the federal bench.

As has been suggested, beneath the constitutional requirement of presidential nomination and senatorial advice and consent, their lies a fundamental political process that reflects the character of our political system. Since the very first rejection of a nominee to a federal judicial position in 1795 the system has been this way. All attempts to modify the process notwithstanding, the judicial selection process will continue to remain an essentially political process.

CHARACTERISTIC ATTRIBUTES OF NOMINEES

General Observations

The chapter thus far has indicated that, apart from legal training, the major characteristic of all judicial appointees is party ideology. Lower federal judges are chosen because they have, in some way, "rendered service to the President's party."[70] This party orientation of nominees is one of three sets of attributes that come into play in the selection process. In addition to this very basic *representational* characteristic (which would also include religion, race, geographic factors), there are two other sets, *professional* and *doctrinal*, that are present in the process.[71]

Although party affiliation is the major factor in the representational set, if the district court is a multijudge tribunal, there will be chosen federal judges who have characteristics found in that jurisdiction. For example, in the Illinois northern U.S. district court (which includes Chicago and the populous Cook County) there are 13 judges. Given the politics and ethnic/religious nature of the region, there will be appointed judges who are Jewish, Catholic, and Polish-American. When a vacancy occurs, regardless of party, the selection process will take these other *representational* factors into account.

[70]Chase, *Federal Judges*, p. 28.
[71]Rohde and Spaeth, *Supreme Court Decision Making*, pp. 99–103.

Professional attributes refer to the legal training—law school, legal experiences—of the nominee. The ABA generally examines these qualities and renders its judgment based on a review of the quality of work the nominee has produced while a lawyer, judge, prosecutor, and so forth.

Doctrinal attributes are those attitudes the nominee has with respect to public policy issues. Presidents generally want their kind of person on the federal bench; a conservative president will want to appoint conservative judges whereas a liberal president will attempt to select men and women whose views on the issues parallel his perceptions. The following passage from a letter written to (Democratic) Attorney General Robert Kennedy indicates the importance of this doctrinal attribute:

> In the great run of cases it does not matter whether a judge is liberal or conservative if he is a good judge. There are a handful of cases, however—and, Heaven knows, they always seem to be the important ones!—where the judicial mind can go either way, with probity, with honor, self-discipline, and even with precedent. This is where the 'liberal' cast of mind . . . can move this nation forward, just as the conservative mind can and does hold it back. This is intangible truth, but every lawyer knows it as reality! (Candidate X) would go forward, (Candidate Y) would hold back.[72]

It is the mix of these representational, professional, and doctrinal attributes that initiators, screeners, and affirmers review and evaluate before making the judgment to nominate and to affirm a person for a seat on the federal bench. All candidates, whether for a U.S. district court or for the Supreme Court of the United States, are nominated and selected based on these considerations. The following brief segments look at certain attributes of lower federal court judges and of justices of the Supreme Court.

Lower Federal Judges

As Table 5-6 indicates (see also the data on Tables 5-2 and 5-3) there is very little to distinguish federal judicial appointees other than the political factor: Over 9 out of 10 of these presidential appointments have been members of the president's party at the time of appointment.[73] Federal district court judges generally come to the federal bench from private law practice, from the state judiciary, or from government legal work (Justice Department, U.S. attorney). A majority of the court of

---

[72]Quoted in Thomas P. Jahnige and Sheldon Goldman, *The Federal Judicial System* (New York: Holt, Rinehart and Winston, 1968), p. 21.
[73]Goodman, "Picking Federal Judges," p. 20.

TABLE 5-6   MAJOR OCCUPATION AT TIME OF APPOINTMENT OF APPOINTEES TO FEDERAL DISTRICT AND APPEALS COURTS, 1953-1972 (in percents)

	DISTRICT COURTS				COURT OF APPEALS			
	EISENHOWER	KENNEDY	JOHNSON	NIXON	EISENHOWER	KENNEDY	JOHNSON	NIXON
Large law firm	42.4	32.0	21.3	38.2	22.2	19.0	20.0	29.4
Judiciary	18.4	29.1	31.1	33.3	55.6	47.6	57.5	47.1
Individual or small law firm	12.8	21.4	22.9	18.7	4.4	4.8	10.0	8.8
Government lawyer	14.4	5.8	13.9	6.5	13.3	4.8	—	—
Politics-government	7.2	10.7	7.4	2.4	2.2	9.5	10.0	2.9
Other	4.8	1.0	3.3	0.8	2.2	14.3	2.5	11.7
Total number of appointments	125	103	122	123	45	21	40	34

Sources: Sheldon Goldman, "Characteristics of Eisenhower and Kennedy Appointees to the Lower Federal Courts," *Western Political Quarterly, 18* (1965), 758; "Johnson and Nixon Appointees to the Lower Federal Courts," *Journal of Politics, 34* (1972), 936.

appeals judges come to the federal appellate court from the federal district courts.

As a class, these lower federal court judges are:

1. white
2. Protestant
3. male
4. politically active
5. middle- to upper-class
6. educated in a law school in state/region of judicial appointment
7. middle-aged.[74]

Basic differences between Republican and Democratic judges are not that noticeable, with the obvious exception of party and doctrinal orientation. However, as already suggested, these are important factors in controversial cases argued before these judges.

Supreme Court Justices

Table 5-7 indicates the major occupations of the men chosen to be justices of the United States Supreme Court. It clearly indicates the politically active character of the appointees.

Table 5-8 presents a closer look at the backgrounds of the sitting justices of the Supreme Court in 1978 and it, too, suggests that the backgrounds of these men are similar in that they all were involved in public life—politically, legally—prior to their elevation to the Supreme Court.

Beyond this view of the major occupation at the time of appointment, a profile of the more than 100 men who have sat on the Supreme Court would look like this:

1. native born (only six exceptions);
2. white (Justice Thurgood Marshall, appointed in 1967, is the first black to serve);
3. Protestant (six Roman Catholics, five Jews are exceptions);
4. mid-50s at time of appointment;
5. Anglo-Saxon ethnic stock (except six);
6. upper middle to high social status;
7. reared in an essentially urban environment;
8. member of civic minded, politically active family;
9. B.A. and LL.B. degrees (from prestigious institutions);
10. service in public office (only one exception).

[74]Early, *Constitutional Courts*, p. 85.

TABLE 5-7   MAJOR OCCUPATION[1] AT TIME OF APPOINTMENT OF APPOINTEES TO THE UNITED STATES SUPREME COURT, 1789-1978

Federal officeholder in executive branch	22
Judge of inferior federal court	22
Judge of state court	21
Private practice of law	18
U.S. senator	8
U.S. representative	4
State governor	3
Professor of law	3
Associate justice of U.S. Supreme Court[2]	2
Justice of the permanent court of international justice	1

[1]Many of the appointees had held a variety of federal or state offices, or even both prior to their selection.

[2]Justices White and Stone were *promoted* to the chief justiceship in 1910 and 1930, respectively.

Source: Henry Abraham, *Justices and Presidents (New York: Oxford University Press, 1977),* p. 53.

In sum, the men chosen to sit on the Supreme Court share certain basic religious, social, and ethnic characteristics. The major difference, as with the lower federal court judges, is the *doctrinal/political* factor. It is, as already indicated, a significant difference that will determine the manner in which major public policies will be decided by the majority of the Court.

JUDICIAL RETIREMENT: A POLITICAL DECISION?

Discussion of the politicization of the federal judicial selection process leads, inevitably, to the question of judicial retirement and retirement politics. We have already examined the process of dealing with vacancies when they develop; from 1945 to 1975 vacancies on the federal bench created the opportunity for 71 percent of *all* federal appointments since 1789![75] What has not been fully examined is the "strategic importance of the creation of vacancies."[76] Does a federal judge decide to retire or resign his seat on the bench for political reasons? Does he or she vacate the seat on the federal bench when his or her party occupies

[75]Schmidhauser, *The Supreme Court;* Abraham, *Justices and Presidents*, ch. 1.
[76]R. Lee Rainey, "The Decision To Remain a Judge: Deductive Models of Judicial Retirement," paper delivered at the 1976 Southern Political Science Association Meetings, Atlanta, Georgia, November 4-6, 1976, p. 1.

TABLE 5-8   U.S. SUPREME COURT JUSTICES, 1978 (in order of seniority)

NAME	YEAR OF BIRTH	HOME STATE	LAW SCHOOL	PRIOR EXPERIENCE	APPOINTED BY	YEAR OF APPOINT- MENT
Warren Burger	1907	Minnesota	St. Paul College of Law	Assistant attorney general, federal judge	Nixon	1969
William Brennan	1906	New Jersey	Harvard	State judge	Eisenhower	1956
Potter Stewart	1915	Ohio	Yale	Federal judge	Eisenhower	1958
Byron White	1918	Colorado	Yale	Deputy attorney general	Kennedy	1962
Thurgood Marshall	1908	Maryland	Howard	Counsel to NAACP, federal judge	Johnson	1967
Harry Blackmun	1908	Minnesota	Harvard	Federal judge	Nixon	1970
Lewis Powell	1907	Virginia	Washington and Lee	President, American Bar Association	Nixon	1972
William Rehnquist	1924	Arizona	Stanford	Assistant attorney general	Nixon	1972
John P. Stevens	1916	Illinois	Chicago	Federal judge	Ford	1975

Source: *Kenneth Dolbeare and Murray Edelman,* American Politics *(Lexington, Mass.: D. C. Heath, 1977), p. 253.*

the White House? If there is in office a president not of his party, does a federal judge wait for his party to win the White House before he retires?

In an unpublished study of these and other questions, Professor Rainey came up with some interesting answers to these kinds of questions. He argued that there are three models that reflect various reasons for leaving the federal bench: the *ambition* model (where a judge leaves the bench for purely personal ambitions); the *career* model (where a federal judge departs from the bench for essentially nonpolitical reasons when the person reaches retirement age); and the *political* model (where the judge retires or resigns for fundamentally politically partisan reasons).[77] Using data on all federal judges who sat from 1937 to 1976 (36 justices and 265 judges) Rainey came up with not too surprising answers to these questions.

Rainey found that ambition and career models do not satisfactorily explain departure from the federal bench. Resignations are very rare; judges do not resign to find jobs elsewhere. The career model does not fit the data very closely either. However, the career model, with variations between the various courts accounted for below, did seem most closely to fit the data. "Of those who reached eligibility for retirement prior to 1975 and who had a known party identification, 35% of Supreme Court justices, 45% of Court of Appeals judges, and 51% of District Court judges took retirement while their party was in office."[78]

Examining the three federal courts, it is clear that the lower federal court judge who is most keenly aware of the political nature of the appointment process is the federal judge who retires for partisan reasons. "Among the Appeals and District judges there is a substantial contingent who bring to the bench political loyalties that encourage them, more often than not, to maneuver their departure in such a way that will maximize the chance for the appointment of a replacement by a president of their party."[79] One suggestion by the author of the study reaffirms what has been said about the process in earlier segments of this chapter: "Presidents (or senators) who want to maximize their patronage pool should (at least for the lower federal courts) appoint politicians to the bench. Such judges are more likely to return the seats to their party when they are through with them."[80]

What was not developed in this research was an ideology model that would account for judicial retirements. The Supreme Court justices did not score significantly on any of the three models developed by Rainey. Given the role and function of the Supreme Court in our po-

[77]Ibid., p. 7.
[78]Ibid., p. 11.
[79]Ibid., p. 16.
[80]Ibid., p. 17.

litical system, it might well be that ideological—*doctrinal*—reasons would account for the when and where of Supreme Court judicial retirements or the *lack* of retirements. Later chapters will focus on the nature of judicial decision making and will highlight this ideological dimension.

In sum, it has been suggested that lower federal court judges, much closer to the state and local political biases and pressures, more often than not follow the political model hypotheses when retiring: They retire and, in effect, return their seat to their party leaders.

THE SELECTION PROCESS AT WORK: FOUR CASE STUDIES

The segments that follow present three case studies that illustrate the nature of the federal judicial selection process, and one that points out by way of comparison, the politics behind the selection of United States attorneys, the prosecutors in the federal judicial system. These specific examples include: (1) the aborted Francis X. Morrissey nomination for a federal district judgeship in Massachusetts; (2) the J. P. Coleman nomination and appointment to the Fifth Circuit U.S. Court of Appeals; (3) the Nixon nomination, subsequently rejected by the U.S. Senate, of G. Harrold Carswell to fill the seat on the Supreme Court vacated when Justice Abe Fortas was forced to resign; and (4) the politics of selecting a federal judge, the firing of Republican U.S. Attorney David Marston by a Democratic president, Jimmy Carter.

A Friend of the Family as District Court Judge— Almost

Francis (Frank) Xavier Morrissey was a long time associate of Ambassador Joseph Kennedy and his sons. One of them became president of the United States in 1961. When John F. Kennedy took over the presidency, one of the tasks he set out to accomplish was to get his friend Frank a district court judgeship. The difficulty was that Morrissey would have a tough time with the American Bar Association due to his singularly lackluster legal background. For that reason, the president and his brother, the attorney general, delayed the nomination. In September of 1965, President Johnson formally nominated Morrissey at the urging of Senator Edward Kennedy (D-Mass), stating that he believed "that the late President made a private commitment to his father (Joseph P. Kennedy) to nominate Morrissey after the 1964 election."[81]

[81]Chase, *Federal Judges,* footnote 27, pp. 220–21.

Given the role of senatorial courtesy, the Senate Judiciary Committee voted six to three to affirm the nomination. This vote, with seven senators on the committee abstaining, came after the American Bar Association's Committee on the Federal Judiciary gave Morrissey a "nonqualified" rating. The ABA Committee had found that Morrissey's law degree came from a "quickie" nonaccredited law institution in Athens, Georgia; that he failed the bar examination at least two times; that he failed many important courses in the law school; and finally, that Morrissey's total legal experience was as a judge in the Boston Municipal Court (night session).

The media picked up the story and criticized the nomination; one newspaper labeling the selection "nauseous."[82] Calling Morrissey a political crony of the Kennedys, both the ABA and the press called for rejection of the nominee. But the Senate Judiciary Committee had voted favorably due to the fact that Senator Edward Kennedy strongly supported the nomination and that Kennedy had the support of Attorney General Nicholas Katzenbach, the Justice Department, and the White House.

Although the Senate was somewhat uneasy about the nomination, it was willing to vote to affirm a lackluster nominee due to the fact that one of their own had thrown his weight behind the nomination. However, barely a month after the name of Morrissey was introduced, Senator Edward Kennedy rose in the Senate and asked that body to send the name of the nominee back to the Judiciary Committee for further examination. After the name was sent back to committee, Frank Morrissey asked President Johnson to remove his name from consideration for the federal district court judgeship. Johnson complied with Morrissey's wish and the name was withdrawn.

The Morrissey incident illustrates the potency of senatorial courtesy. Regardless of the ABA position and the judgment of one of the senior federal district judges in Massachusetts that Morrissey was unqualified to be a federal judge, Morrissey would probably have been confirmed by a reluctant Senate because a senator wanted "his man" on the federal bench. The fact that the incident was widely publicized, and led to political embarrassment for Senator Kennedy, more than anything else led to the resubmittal and withdrawal. Had Kennedy not been concerned about his public reputation, Francis X. Morrissey would have been appointed to the federal bench. This exception proves the rule with respect to federal district court judgeships: Senatorial courtesy has a profound impact in the selection of federal trial judges.

[82]Ibid., p. 174.

The Appointment of a "Segregationist" to the Fifth Circuit

The nomination of James P. Coleman to a seat on the United States Fifth Circuit Court of Appeals was (along with the Morrissey nomination) the second controversial selection made by President Johnson in 1965. The nomination of a person who had been identified with racial segregation for his entire life (Coleman was governor of Mississippi from 1956 through 1960) so inflamed feelings in some parts of the nation that "for the first time in this century an Attorney General of the United States gave public testimony to a Congressional committee on behalf of an appointment to the Federal judiciary."[83]

The attorney general acknowledged the fact that Coleman was a firm supporter of racial segregation while governor of Mississippi but that Coleman's segregationist attitude was legal rather than emotional; that Coleman attempted to modify Mississippi's Constitution so as to remove mention of race (he failed in that attempt); that he supported Kennedy in Mississippi in 1960; that he prevented White Citizens Councils from obtaining tax money; that he called in the FBI to investigate a lynching in Mississippi; and that he supported a moderate congressman, Brook Hayes, of Little Rock, Arkansas (who was ultimately defeated by a segregationist). By the end of Coleman's tenure as governor, Katzenbach pointed out, he was branded by incoming Governor Ross Barnett as a "moderate," and as a "Kennedy liberal." Katzenbach concluded by stating that

> when the full picture is considered, we see not the caricature of an unyielding white supremacist but a man who was frequently willing to take great political risks to support moderation and respect for law and order when the opposite course would have been the politically expedient one.[84]

Katzenbach's comments did not soothe the anger of civil rights organizations and liberal senators; they condemned the nomination of such a segregationist and they feared the consequences of putting such a person on an appeals court that would be hearing so many civil rights appeals from federal courts in the deep south. NAACP leaders, law professors, and liberal congressmen all testified against the Coleman nomination.

[83]Ibid., p. 171.
[84]Ibid. See also Tip H. Allen, Jr., "Mississippi Votes: The Presidential and Gubernatorial Elections, 1947-1964," *Social Science Research Center*, Mississippi State University, May 1967, p. 10.

During the hearings before the Senate Judiciary Committee, Coleman was asked directly whether or not he would have difficulty in obeying the opinions of the Supreme Court and the Civil Rights Acts of Congress. He stated he would not have any difficulty "whatever in doing that. I wouldn't allow my name to be considered for a judgeship, Senator Kennedy, if I did have any difficulty."[85] The Senate Judiciary Committee voted to approve Coleman by a vote of 13 to 2 and the full Senate voted to affirm the nomination by a vote of 76 to 8.

The important factor in this particular nomination was that the Justice Department had to choose someone from the state of Mississippi to replace Judge Ben Cameron, the Mississippian judge on the fifth circuit who had died. After intense conversations with Mississippi Senators John C. Stennis and James Eastland, Coleman's name emerged. For Johnson, Katzenbach, and for the Justice Department, his name was the most moderate one on the list of possible candidates for the position. The Coleman appointment is an example of the "residual power" of the Senate over court of appeals appointments.[86] And when the chairman of the Senate Judiciary Committee (Eastland) is from the state of Mississippi, then the Justice Department and President Johnson had to be especially careful to work with the senators and the Senate. To have nominated a more moderate person not from Mississippi to fill the vacancy on the fifth circuit court of appeals would have been to risk defeat in the U.S. Senate. Johnson was unwilling to take that chance and, as a consequence, James P. Coleman became a federal appeals court judge.

The Nomination and Defeat of a "Mediocre" Candidate for Associate Justice of the Supreme Court

In the spring of 1969 Justice Abe Fortas of the United States Supreme Court resigned his seat on the Court. Accused by a news magazine of unethical and possible illegal activity and pressured by the Nixon administration (Attorney General John Mitchell) through intermediaries on the Court such as Chief Justice Earl Warren, Fortas resigned under a cloud of suspicion. He did so in order to avoid embarrassing the Court by staying on the bench and running the risk of legal action being commenced against a sitting justice.[87]

---

[85]Chase, *Federal Judges*, p. 172.
[86]Richardson and Vines, *Politics of Federal Judiciary*, pp. 69–70.
[87]See for example Abraham, *Justices and Presidents;* Simon, *In His Own Image;* and especially Harris, *Decision*.

In August of 1969, Nixon nominated Clement Haynesworth, chief judge of the fourth circuit court of appeals (from South Carolina), to succeed Fortas.[88] Haynesworth's nomination was rejected by the Senate in November 1969 because of his allegedly unethical actions while serving on the federal bench. (It was alleged, and some facts were presented to make the case against the judge, that he participated in a number of cases in which he had some personal stake in the outcome. For example, he was a stockholder in a vending machine company that did three percent of its business in a Deering-Milliken cotton mill. Haynesworth did not excuse himself from a case that came to his court involving that cotton manufacturer.)

Incensed at the Senate rejection of his nominee, President Nixon, in January of 1970, nominated G. Harrold Carswell, from the state of Florida, to fill the Fortas seat. Attorney General John Mitchell emphatically assured the Senate that the nominee did not have any ethical conflicts in his past; that Carswell was not antilabor and that he was a moderate on civil rights.

Almost immediately afterwards, the country (and the Senate) found out the truth about Carswell. First the press uncovered a statement of Carswell's to the effect that he would always be a white supremacist. Then the country learned of other stories of how Judge Carswell treated civil rights attorneys in his federal court; of how Judge Carswell had one of the worst overturn records on the entire fifth circuit; and of how, while in the employ of the United States as a federal attorney, he participated in the drawing up of restrictive covenants to allow a golf club to evade the civil rights laws. After the hearings, when the information was in, Senator Hiram Fong, Republican from Hawaii, stated to a colleague: "If you want my opinion, he's a jackass!"[89]

Senator Roman Hruska, Republican from Iowa, went even further, but in defense of Carswell's nomination. In mid-February 1970, the Senate Judiciary Committee voted 13 to 4 in favor of Carswell's nomination and sent his name to the floor of the Senate. After strategic delays that gave the opposition more time to develop a plan of attack in hopes of defeating the nominee, the hearings began in mid-March. After a day of intense debate, Hruska made a statement that is without precedent:

> Even if Carswell were mediocre, there are a lot of mediocre judges and people and lawyers. They are entitled to a little representation, aren't they,

[88]For an informative examination of the Haynesworth nomination to the Supreme Court, defeated in the Senate in November 1969, see John L. Steele, "Haynesworth vs. the United States Senate," *Fortune Magazine,* March 1970, pp. 90–96, 155–62.
[89]See generally Harris, *Decision.*

and a little chance? We can't have all Brandeises, and Frankfurters, and Cardozos and stuff like that there.[90]

This remark "was to go down as one of the greatest political blunders in the history of the Senate, and, in the opinion of those most intimately involved in the battle over the nomination, it contributed as much as any other factor to Carswell's defeat."[91]

After the Hruska statement, the tide turned against Carswell. Law school professors, the media, labor groups, civil rights groups, and religious organizations all joined to oppose Carswell. The White House was notified by Republican senators that the mood had shifted away from approval of Carswell, but the White House refused to believe these reports. President Nixon's letter to Republican Senator William Saxbe (already discussed in an earlier section of this chapter), written just before the vote, provoked the senators into intense anger. The president had argued that the U.S. Senate was merely a rubber stamp with respect to presidential nominations for judicial positions!

In early April 1970, after four long months of carefully examining the qualities of Carswell (and finding mediocrity), the Senate voted to reject the nomination. The vote was 45 for the nominee and 51 opposed. The primary reason for the Senate rejection was the judgment by that body that Carswell lacked basic skills and the intellectual acumen necessary to serve as a member of the United States Supreme Court. In response to this second rejection, President Nixon indignantly responded by arguing that the Senate would never confirm a southerner; he proceeded to nominate a Minnesotan, Harry Blackmun, who was then a member of the eighth circuit federal court of appeals (and a close personal friend of Chief Justice Warren E. Burger). The Senate, in rapid order, voted 94 to 0 to confirm the nomination. After a long year of oftentimes acrimonious debate and the rejection of two nominees in succession, the Abe Fortas seat was finally filled.

By Way of Comparison: The Firing of a U.S. Attorney

This case study of the firing of a United States attorney is presented to illustrate by comparison the nature of selection and dismissal of another key agent in the federal judicial system, the federal prosecutor. Although not a part of the federal judicial system and therefore not subject to the constraints of Article III with respect to appointment and

[90]Ibid., p. 110.
[91]Ibid.

tenure, the politics of the selection and firing of these federal prosecutors place the politics of the selection of the federal judges in better perspective. In this selection process, as in the others already presented, the politics of the person as well as the qualities and merit of the person are weighed and evaluated.

The office of attorney general was created in 1789 by the first Congress; in that same Judiciary Act of 1789 the office of United States attorney was also created. This symbiotic relationship between the national government's chief law enforcement officer and his prosecutors has continued since that enactment. The United States attorneys, with their staffs of assistant United States attorneys, clerks, etc., now number 94. There is an office of the U.S. attorney in each of the United States district courts in the 50 states and in the territories.

The U.S. attorney is responsible for enforcing the federal civil and criminal codes and does so by prosecuting persons who have been accused and arraigned in federal court. Much of this activity is discretionary activity on the part of the attorney and his staff. To the extent that the attorney decides what kinds of cases to develop, what kinds of criminality to pursue, he performs the basic kind of gatekeeping function that federal judges perform.

The position of U.S. attorney is considered a "piece of patronage."[92] They are appointed to four-year terms of office and can be removed at the discretion of the president. Generally, when a new administration entered the White House, "the lights went out in U.S. Attorney's offices everywhere," stated Attorney General Griffin Bell.[93] Presidents want to select their own kind of prosecutor in order for administration policy in civil and criminal areas to be enforced in the proper manner. The attorneys are members of the president's party and go through the same advice and consent process that federal district court judges go through in the U.S. Senate (with senatorial courtesy playing a major role in their selection).

Generally, these attorneys are partisan politician/lawyers who have supported the party's views on policy issues. They were born and educated in the district to which they were appointed to serve as attorney and many of these attorneys use the position as a stepping stone to higher federal positions: district court judgeships, congressional seats, Justice Department positions.[94] A U.S. attorney does not have as much

[92]Fred Schrum, "Fired: The Hiring and Firing of United States Attorneys," *New Times*, February 20, 1978, p. 34. See also Dorothy Samuels and James A. Goodman, "Party Favors: The Politics of Picking U.S. Attorneys," *Juris Doctor*, Oct./Nov. 1978, pp. 17–24.
[93]John Saar, "The Philadelphia Story," *New Times*, February 20, 1978, p. 31.
[94]See Goldman and Jahnige, *Federal Courts as a Political System;* and Herbert Jacob, *Justice in America* (Boston: Little, Brown, 1977).

prosecutorial independence as does his popularly elected counterpart on the local level, the district attorney, for the federal attorney is a part of the Department of Justice bureaucracy and, on occasion, carries out the orders of the departmental policy makers in Washington, D.C.

For example, the attorney might be instructed to prosecute antiwar radicals, or a labor union leader, or a major business (for antitrust violations). On occasion, Washington, D.C., will send down an attorney to argue these important cases in the district court. Under no circumstances will a U.S. attorney take the case on appeal to the federal circuit court in his area: the decision to appeal and to argue the case on appeal rests with the policy makers in Washington, D.C.[95]

David Marston was appointed United States attorney, eastern district, Pennsylvania (located in Philadelphia), by President Gerald Ford in July 1976. He was the fourth U.S. attorney in five years due to the dramatic political pressures on federal prosecutors in Pennsylvania. Marston was a 33-year-old lawyer who had been legislative counsel to Senator Richard Schweikert (Republican-Pa.) for three years. When the attorney's post opened up Marston indicated his interest and, on the basis of Schweikert's recommendation, got the job.[96]

When he arrived in Philadelphia, Marston was confronted by a corruption-ridden political system complete with fraud, bribery, kickbacks, payoffs, and obstruction of justice by various public figures in local and state government. Given the politics of the area, Marston, a Republican, was soon prosecuting local Democratic leaders—and getting convictions. By this time, a new administration had come into the White House—the Democratic administration of President Jimmy Carter. Given Carter's preelection campaign rhetoric (which called for the merit selection of federal judges *and* U.S. attorneys), given the fact that Marston had another three years left on his four-year commission, and given the fact that he was, after all, doing a good job, Marston felt that he would not be dismissed.

And for a time he was correct. Pleas to the Carter administration from Democratic congressmen to replace the Republican with a Democratic U.S. attorney were initially ignored by the attorney general and his assistants. The picture changed dramatically when Marston's staff began investigating the activities of two Democratic congressmen from Pennsylvania, Joshua Eilberg and Daniel Flood. A Philadelphia hospital had added a new wing, financed in part through federal funds. The U.S. attorney's office found out that Eilberg's Philadelphia law firm had been retained by the hospital as counsel and had received over $500,000

[95]Jacob, *Justice in America,* pp. 81–83.
[96]Saar, "The Philadelphia Story," p. 26.

in fees—part of this money received by Eilberg. The firm worked with Congressman Flood to get a $14.5 million federal loan for new construction. (Flood was the Chairman of the House Appropriations subcommittee on Labor, Health, Education, and Welfare.) Flood, in turn, convinced the hospital administrators to retain a Baltimore, Maryland, outfit, Capital Investment Development Corporation, to oversee the construction of the new wing for a fee of over $1 million. This information was gathered by Marston during the summer and early fall of 1977 and his staff was, in November 1977, seriously reviewing the possibility of criminal action.[97]

On November 4, 1977, two days after the U.S. attorney's office asked the FBI to participate in the investigation, Congressman Eilberg called President Carter and asked Carter to get rid of Marston. Because of Eilberg's power in Congress (Chairman of a House Immigration subcommittee), Carter immediately telephoned Attorney General Bell and instructed him to expedite the removal of Marston.

In mid-November, Marston was informed by Associate Attorney General Michael Egan that although "you're doing a good job, we may have to make a move on you next spring. When pressure comes from on high, it has to be relieved."[98] At that point, Marston met with his immediate superior, Assistant Attorney General Russell Baker, Criminal Division of the Department of Justice, and informed his boss of the ongoing hospital investigation and the possible criminal linkage between the two congressmen, the hospital, the law firm, and the construction firm.

This was to no avail, however, because on January 20, 1978, Marston was summoned to Washington, D.C., and personally fired by Attorney General Griffin Bell. After an hour of discussion, Bell stated, simply, that "you are being fired because you are a Republican and we are Democrats."[99] The "Marston Massacre," as it was labeled by Republicans who recalled the "Saturday Night Massacre," of October 1973 (when President Nixon fired Archibald Cox as Special Watergate Prosecutor), touched off a great outcry against the Carter administration. The White House received over 12,000 telephone calls and almost 25,000 letters in the next week. Over 99 percent of these communications condemned the Carter administration for the Marston firing. It mattered little; Marston was gone within days after the January meeting with Bell and Congressman Jonathan Eilberg had a role in the selection of the replacement—a loyal Democratic party attorney.

[97]Ibid.
[98]Ibid., p. 29.
[99]Schrum, "Fired," p. 33.

The importance of this case lies in the fact that it clearly points out the political environment in which the U.S. attorney functions and the political nature of the appointment and of the dismissal of these federal prosecutors. As a Kennedy administration aide once said to a Republican attorney who was complaining about leaving office: "Look pal, your party lost the election."[100]

This brief look at the politics of hiring and firing U.S. attorneys illustrates, much like the preceding case studies of the selection of federal judges, that there is in both kinds of positions within the federal judicial system, (the judges and the federal prosecutors) the intermix of politics, legal qualities, and representational qualities. While the selection of judges might be somewhat more muted than the selection of federal prosecutors, politics and political representations are present in both situations.

SUMMARY

This chapter has focused on the staffing of the federal judicial system. It has emphasized the joining of law and politics, as have the preceding chapters in part two. Gaining access to the federal judicial system is dependent to a certain extent upon the actions of the federal prosecutors (the U.S. attorneys) and the actions and judgments of the federal judges. This is essentially a gatekeeping function of these agents in the federal judicial system. Their judgments reflect, as the next portion of the book will suggest, the values and policy orientations of these federal judicial actors.

Policy and doctrinal attitudes and party affiliation of candidates are the major characteristics of the selection process. Whether the judicial vacancy is a U.S. attorney's position or a position on the United States Supreme Court, these variables are present and are dominant. Selection determines not only the outcome of cases and controversies; it also can determine whether an action or a case will be brought or heard in the federal judicial system.

Part III of this book, "The Politics of the Federal Judiciary," will continue this discussion of law and politics by examining the nature of judicial decision making in the federal courts. The decision-making process, however, is but the final stage in the process that begins with selection, jurisdiction, and justiciability.

[100]Ibid., p. 35.

THE POLITICS OF THE FEDERAL JUDICIARY

Part III

Part I has examined the role and functions of the federal judiciary and portrayed the essentially political character of much of the judiciary's business. Part II has examined jurisdiction, justiciability, access, and the selection process. It also indicated that values, attitudes, politics, and doctrinal positions on public policies are central factors in understanding *who* staffs the federal judiciary and *why* the selection process is so intimately linked with role, function, determination of jurisdiction, and access to the federal courts.

Part III examines *how* the judges operate in the various federal courts and what kinds of intra- and intercourt relationships exist between the district courts, the courts of appeals, and the Supreme Court of the United States. Chapter 6, "The Decision-Making Process: The Lower Federal Courts," examines the mechanics of the decision-making process in the United States district courts and in the United States courts of appeals. It will examine as well the relationships between the trial court and the appeal court in the federal system and will generally depict the "goings on" in these lower federal courts.

Chapter 7, "Judicial Decision-Making Process: The United States Supreme Court," will examine the process of bringing appeals to the Supreme Court, the mechanics of Court work, the intragroup relationships among the justices of the Supreme Court, and the general relationship between the Supreme Court and the lower federal courts.

Figure III-1 presents an overview of the general stages in the federal judicial process. Chapters 6 and 7 will examine the interrela-

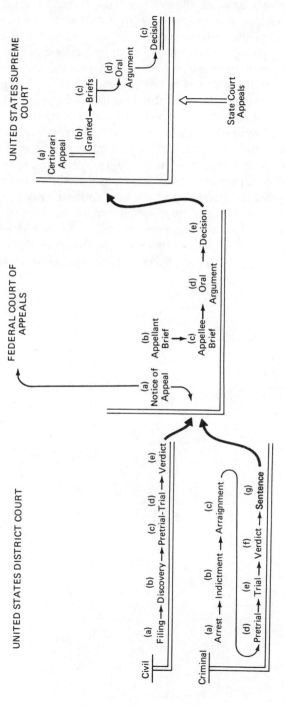

FIG. III-1   FEDERAL JUDICIAL PROCESS: FROM TRIAL TO FINAL APPELLATE REVIEW

tionships between these three basic federal constitutional courts. It will be pointed out that most filings and criminal arrests end in the trial courts of the federal system: the United States district courts. Less than five percent of the civil and criminal cases that commence in the federal trial courts ever go beyond that trial court.

Of the cases that are appealed to the federal courts of appeals, most never get beyond this first level of appeal. As chapter 6 will illustrate, the courts of appeals are, in effect, courts of last resort in the federal system: 9 of 10 cases end in these appeals courts. Since the Judges Bill of 1925, perhaps as early as the creation of the courts of appeals in 1891, the United States Supreme Court has been freed of the ordinary appellate review tasks. Instead, the nation's highest tribunal has used its discretionary powers to hear only those cases which a majority of the Supreme Court determined were of sufficient public importance for that Court to examine. To the extent that the Supreme Court uses its powers of review in this very discretionary manner, the courts of appeals have become the final appeals forum for many litigants.

the decision-making process: the lower federal courts

6

This chapter will investigate and examine the nature of judicial decision making in the federal district courts and courts of appeals. The chapter will differentiate and distinguish between the quiet world of the court of appeals judge and the whirring reality of the trial judge in the federal judicial system—the district court judge.

Figure 6-1 illustrates one of the basic points that will be discussed in subsequent segments: the transformation of the character of a case as it travels from the trial court to the appeals courts in the federal system. This "metamorphosis"[1] radically changes the case so that a non-civil liberties trial in a federal district court—an antitrust case, for example—is appealed on grounds that the vice president of the business firm has been denied "due process of law." The federal judicial system and the constitutional and statutory safeguards that have been developed over the years permit litigation to undergo "significant transformation"[2] as it moves within the appellate process.

For various reasons the business executive appeals his conviction: For example, the trial judge committed an error in interpreting statutes and precedent; there should have been a continuance, change of venue; the jury was unfairly impaneled; the judge ignored relevant Supreme Court instructions, etc. How this comes about and how the federal ap-

[1]Richard J. Richardson and Kenneth Vines, "Review, Dissent, and the Appellate Process: A Political Interpretation," *Journal of Politics*, vol. 29, no. 3 (August 1967).
[2]Ibid.

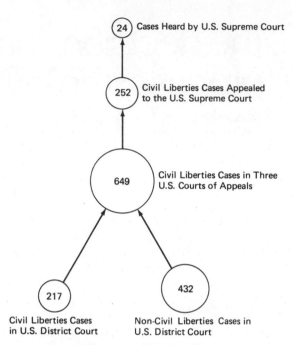

24 — Cases Heard by U.S. Supreme Court

252 — Civil Liberties Cases Appealed to the U.S. Supreme Court

649 — Civil Liberties Cases in Three U.S. Courts of Appeals

217 — Civil Liberties Cases in U.S. District Court

432 — Non-Civil Liberties Cases in U.S. District Court

FIG. 6-1   THE FLOW OF CIVIL LIBERTIES CASES IN THE FEDERAL JUDICIAL SYSTEM

Source: *Richard J. Richardson and Kenneth Vines, "Review, Dissent and the Appellate Process: A Political Interpretation,"* Journal of Politics, *vol. 29, no. 3 (August 1967).*

peals courts deal with this and other issues is the focus of the subsequent portions of this chapter.

DECISION MAKING IN THE DISTRICT COURTS

The Localism of the District Court Judges

As the chapter on selection of federal judges indicated, the overwhelming majority of federal district court judges were born, grew up, went to school (including law school), practiced law, and got involved in politics in the jurisdiction they sat in as federal judge. These various local experiences and the legal and political socialization that would-be judges go through prior to their nomination have a major impact on the judicial behavior of the federal district court judge.

The influence and impact of localism and the parochialism inher-

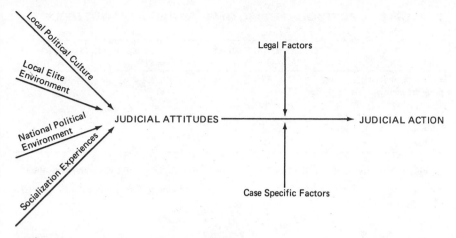

FIG. 6-2   MODEL OF JUDICIAL BEHAVIOR

Source: *Herbert Kritzer, "Political Correlates of the Behavior of Federal District Judges,"* Journal of Politics, *vol. 40, no. 1 (February 1978).*

ent in that general concept is seen most vividly when one examines the way in which southern federal district judges handled race relations cases in the 1950s and 1960s. Vines and Peltason have written separate classic works that illustrate the impact of local values on federal district court decision making.[3] The conclusions they and others have reached are reflected in Figure 6-2.

State political experiences correlate with southern values. If the southern political, economic, and social systems emphasized segregation, and if intergration was anathema to the white population in the south, then the southern federal district judge will probably reflect that essential characteristic in his judgments from the bench.

Table 6-1 indicates that prior state political or legal experience is linked significantly with segregationist rulings from the federal bench. It is also interesting to note that the more the local person was pulled away, centripetally, from the local environment, the broader his thinking (and, subsequently, his legal rulings) became. Integrationists very infrequently held state political positions; they were therefore not potential candidates for federal judgeships.

Although these factors play a role in the development of a framework for judicial action, there are other variables at work on the federal judge that make for difficult judicial decisions for such judges. These

[3]Kenneth Vines, "Federal District Judges and Race Relations Cases in the South," *Journal of Politics,* vol. 26 (1964); Jack Peltason, *Fifty-Eight Lonely Men* (Chicago: University of Chicago Press, 1958).

TABLE 6-1   PREVIOUS PUBLIC OFFICES HELD BY SOUTHERN JUDGES

PUBLIC OFFICE	SEGREGATIONISTS (N = 14)	MODERATES (N = 12)	INTEGRATIONISTS (N = 11)
State political office	57.1%[1]	41.7%	9.1%
Federal political office	42.9	8.4	45.5
State judicial office	50.0	33.3	9.1
Federal judicial office	28.6	8.4	45.5
State and local judgeship	35.7	33.3	0.0

[1]Columns do not add up to 100.0 percent because some judges held more than one office.

Source: *Kenneth Vines, "Federal District Judges and Race Relations Cases in the South,"* Journal of Politics, *(Spring 1964), 338.*

variables account for the fact that not all of the federal district judges were classified as segregationist. If these local and parochial factors motivate the judge in one direction, there are other (professional) factors that pull in the opposite direction. One such variable is the fact that judges have been socialized in a manner that suggests deference to a higher court and few federal judges would, other factors not present, "reject the authority of these courts."[4] Another such motivational factor is the fact that the federal district judge's rulings are reviewed by his peers in the federal court of appeals and that, under ordinary circumstances, reversal is a significant sanction.[5]

The upshot of the matter is that the federal district court judge, torn between sanctions from one community (his judicial peers and superiors) or from another (his political, legal, social, religious groupings in his jurisdiction), and confronted by a host of legal, factual, and other kinds of data relevant to the case at hand, must decide how to rule on the many questions that are raised in the trial he is presiding over. It is not the least bit surprising that Professor Peltason's classic work on federal district judges and race relations cases in the south is entitled *Fifty-Eight Lonely Men.*

In the final analysis, Peltason wrote, "observation of federal judges leads us to appreciate how powerful certain social and political factors are in the operation of the courts. Never was it in doubt that judges were responding to a variety of social factors in the complex desegregation litigation rather than to the intricate skeins of the law. Most critical

---

[4]Lawrence Baum, "Lower Court Response to Supreme Court Decisions: Reconsidering a Negative Picture," *Justice System Journal,* vol. 3, no. 3 (Spring 1978), p. 211.
[5]Ibid.

of all were the backgrounds and socializing experiences of judges which linked them to southern segregationist values."[6]

Given the overpowering force of a value such as segregation, as but one example of the impact of localism on judging, the average federal district judge—resentful of higher court mandates, orders, values—will do what he can to evade and avoid actions that would go against the very basic principles and values of *his* community. Those judges who, in the name of the law, go against these local values, find themselves harrassed and ostracized from the community. In some cases these jurists were forced to move from the jurisdiction for their own safety.[7]

When the Congress drew up the Voting Rights Act of 1965, which had a major impact on black voting in the south,[8] the legal remedies available to plaintiffs in case there was state reluctance to modify voting arrangements in local southern towns and cities were to be found only in the District of Columbia!

If a black citizen wanted to challenge the voting procedures of his local community, procedures that were allegedly diluting black voting strength, he had to go either to the federal district court in the District of Columbia or to the Justice Department in the District of Columbia. Evidently the national legislators knew or felt they knew what would happen if local blacks had to go to the average federal district court judge in their jurisdiction to remedy illegal voting processes.[9]

This is not to suggest that all southern federal judges acted in this manner with respect to questions of race relations; however, given the nature of the selection process and the conflicting factors at work on the judicial mind, the majority of judges could not help but act in a manner that could only be described as prejudiced—some more so than others. Over time, this behavior has diminished, in part because of new personnel on the court and also because of slowly changing societal values in the south.

Judicial behavior and actions from the bench are linked to variables—political, social, cultural—external to the judicial system.[10] Given the nature of the process of selecting judges and the decentralized struc-

[6]Peltason, *Fifty-Eight Lonely Men*, p. 267.

[7]Ibid.

[8]See, generally, Howard Ball, Dale Krane, and Thomas P. Lauth, "Judicial Impact on the Enforcement of the 1965 Voting Rights Act," paper presented for delivery at the Southern Political Science Association meeting, November 1977, New Orleans, Louisiana.

[9]Ibid.

[10]Herbert Kritzer, "Political Correlates of the Behavior of Federal District Judges," 40 Journal of Politics, No. 1, February 1978, p. 28.

ture of the federal judicial system, there is "little to encourage judicial independence from surrounding pressures."[11] Until process and structure change, federal district court judges will act, at critical times, in a parochial manner.

Federal District Courts As Organizations

Judge and Company

Federal district courts are miniature organizations within the larger economic, legal, political, and demographic environment. There exists in the federal trial court an organized network of relationships centering around the federal judge. These other persons, the U.S. magistrate, the U.S. attorney and his staff, the chief clerk, the law clerks of the federal judge, the lawyers for the plaintiffs and defendants, the bailiffs, the jurors, all perform "quite specialized functions and their activity fits into a broader pattern and is constrained by it."[12] Given other factors such as increased caseload that affect this organization (see Figure 6-3) a harmonious courtroom workgroup can deal with the caseload much more efficiently and effectively than can a disharmonious group of participants who cannot interact well.[13]

THE DISTRICT COURT JUDGE   The federal district court judge is a trial judge. "The responsibility of the judge is to be superintendent of the production of justice" in his court.[14] He must be able to deal almost instantaneously with a wide assortment of technical questions that arise during the time the litigation is in his court. He is primarily engaged in the enforcement of norms established by higher courts and the Congress regarding adjudication of disputes that fall within his court's jurisdiction. District court judges see themselves as judicial administrators;[15] they must constantly make rulings from the bench, consistent with Supreme Court decisions and/or with the Federal Rules of Civil and Criminal Procedure, regarding pretrial motions, change of venue, continuances, admissibility of evidence, directed verdict, demurrers, and sentencing.

At times they must act in this manner in an emotionally charged environment. In sharp contrast to the serenity of the appeals courts in

---

[11]Peltason, *Fifty-Eight Lonely Men,* p. 267.
[12]J. Eisenstein and H. Jacob, *Felony Justice* (Boston: Little, Brown, 1977), p. 10.
[13]Ibid.
[14]Steven Flanders and Alan Sager, "Case Management Methods and Delay in Federal District Courts," In Russell Wheeler and Howard Whitcomb, *Judicial Administration* (Englewood Cliffs, N.J.: Prentice-Hall, 1977), p. 232.
[15]Austin Sarat, "Judging in Trial Courts: An Exploratory Study," *Journal of Politics,* vol. 39, no. 2 (May 1977), p. 368.

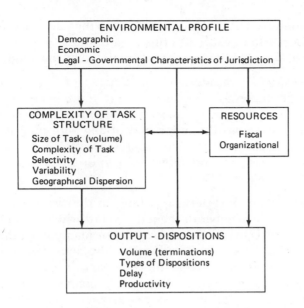

FIG. 6-3   FOUR DIMENSIONS OF DISTRICT COURT DECISION MAKING

Source: *Wolf Heydebrand, "The Context of Public Bureaucracies: An Organizational Analysis of Federal District Courts,"* Law and Society Review, *vol. 11, no. 5 (Summer 1977).*

the federal system, the trial judge must make quick decisions before and during the trial based on his perceptions of the facts and the law. Most of the district court judge's career is spent enforcing technical and procedural rules about which there is little disagreement.[16] Although some federal district judges have taken on broader policy-making roles, even the federal trial judge who is action oriented spends the great part of his time issuing rulings on motions brought to him by his lawyers involved in the civil and criminal litigation.

Judging in the district court is the individual stage of judicial decision making in the federal judicial system. A single judge, sitting alone, issues rulings and announces judgments from his bench. Most of these rulings and judgments are not challenged by litigants in the federal appeals courts. The trial judge is free to act, consistent with these parameters developed by others—as he interprets these parameters—in his courtroom with his subordinates. For the most part, the district court is a self-contained conflict resolution environment.[17]

The judge must know the rules of civil and criminal procedure and he must be able to control the trial court organization so that things

[16]Stephen Early, *Constitutional Courts*, (Totowa, N.J.: Littlefield, Adams, 1977), p. 5.
[17]Ibid.

can get done in his court. The judge establishes the pace, direction, and goals in his court. He is assisted in this organizational task by subordinates who have, in some instances, been appointed by the judge himself.

LAW CLERKS   District court judges select, annually, one or two outstanding law school graduates as their clerks. These young men and women, generally born and educated in the society bounded by the jurisdiction of the district court, assist the judge by working with him on various briefs and requests for motions. They do research for the district judge and handle some basic administrative tasks in order to free the judge for more substantive judicial work.

THE COURT CLERK   The court clerk, appointed by the district court judge, is "potentially the key member of the judge's staff when it comes to case management."[18] He is primarily responsible for maintaining the judge's calendar and for handling all the administrative arrangements for the court. Lawyers communicate with the court clerk for scheduling; the clerk keeps records of case proceedings, and prepares orders and judgments resulting from court decisions and acts. For many district court judges, the court clerk is more akin to an administrative assistant.[19]

A top-notch court clerk is an invaluable asset to a federal district court. Efficient management of cases by this key aide makes the increased caseload easier to deal with by the judge and others in the federal trial court. However, "while it is clear that courtroom deputies can keep cases from rotting in the starting gate and can push some cases further along the track, if a judge is not strongly committed to case management, the deputy's role is necessarily quite limited."[20] In sum, the court clerk is responsible for making sure that the basic operations of the court run smoothly and that things happen in the trial court when they are supposed to happen (in accordance with the Federal Rules of Civil and Criminal Procedure). If, however, the federal judge is reluctant or unwilling to redirect or change the nature of the district court operations, nothing will occur. The courtroom, after all, belongs to the federal district court judge.

U.S. MAGISTRATES   This quasi-judicial officer, appointed by the senior administrative judge in the district court for a six-year period, handles certain basic legal tasks formerly dealt with by the federal judges. Like the court clerk the magistrate has a wide variety of tasks. He participates in pretrial conferences, holds preliminary hearings, and makes rulings in certain kinds of pretrial motions. He also examines prisoner petitions

[18]Flanders and Sager, "Case Management," p. 229.
[19]Ibid.
[20]Ibid., p. 230.

and habeas corpus motions and makes recommendations on these matters to the federal judge. In addition, the magistrate conducts a certain number of minor criminal trials thus freeing the judge for more substantive trial work, if the district court judge is willing to allow this to occur.

The responsibilities of the magistrates are based on the legislation passed by the Congress in 1968, the Federal Magistrates Act, and fully implemented (as determined by district court judges) in 1971 in all the federal districts.[21] Table 6-2 depicts the types and numbers of dispositions handled by these judicial officers. "In fiscal 1974 magistrates heard 82,705 trials; these trials accounted for 34 percent of all matters heard by magistrates."[22]

However, because there has been a lack of clarity in the congressional statute and because the Supreme Court has not gotten involved in the question of the parameters of magistrate's work, "the magistrates' ability to assist district judges in many ministerial and decisional duties is delayed pending a further congressional definition of their power."[23] When final clarification of the role of magistrates is announced, the magistrate will play an even more important role in the district court decision-making process.

THE UNITED STATES ATTORNEY   This legal officer, appointed by the president with the advice and consent of the Senate (and senators from the state in which the U.S. attorney works), is responsible for prosecuting defendants in the district court and for defending the United States when it is party to a civil suit brought into the federal district court. He selects his staff of assistant United States attorneys and, with their help, functions as the prosecuting attorney for the federal government in that particular jurisdiction.

DEFENSE ATTORNEYS

Legal Aid Services   The federally created and funded Legal Services Corporation, created in 1976, has taken over many of the functions of an earlier legal assistance program funded by the U.S. Office of Economic Opportunity. Legal services "were located in many of the poorest neighborhoods and in centers of rural poverty.... Approximately 1,800 full-time attorneys each handled 500 cases per year and altogether served nearly 300,000 clients."[24] The Legal Services Corporation has

---

[21]Stephen Puro, "United States Magistrates: A New Federal Judicial Officer," *Justice System Journal*, 2 (Winter 1976), 144.

[22]Ibid., pp. 148–49.

[23]Ibid., p. 156.

[24]Herbert Jacob, *Justice in America* (Boston: Little, Brown, 1975), p. 66.

TABLE 6-2 MATTERS DISPOSED OF BY UNITED STATES MAGISTRATES DURING THE FISCAL YEARS 1972 TO 1974[1]

ACTIVITY	FISCAL YEARS			PERCENT CHANGE	
	1972	1973	1974	1974 OVER 1972	1974 OVER 1973
Total, all matters (a + b + c + d)	237,522	251,218	242,929	2.3	−3.3
a) Trial jurisdiction cases (Total)	72,082	84,580	82,705	14.7	−2.2
Petty offenses[3]	62,915	72,746	71,463	13.6	−1.8
Minor offenses other than petty offenses	9,167	11,834	11,242	22.6	−5.0
b) Preliminary proceedings in criminal cases (Total)[3]	120,723	115,121	100,152	−17.0	−13.0
Search warrants	7,338	5,961	5,649	−23.0	−5.2
Arrest warrants	36,833	33,149	27,029	−26.6	−18.5
Bail proceedings	64,518	66,095	58,034	−10.0	−12.2
Preliminary exams	9,554	7,628	7,124	−25.4	−6.6
Removal hearings	2,480	2,288	2,316	−6.6	1.2
Total, additional duties (c + d)	44,717	51,517	60,072	34.3	16.6
c) Criminal proceedings (Total)	22,336	24,337	28,028	25.5	15.2
Pretrial conferences and omnibus hearings	5,279	5,327	6,313	19.6	18.5
Motions	5,870	6,684	7,118	21.3	6.5
Post-indictment arraignments	10,799	12,093	13,996	29.6	15.7
Other matters[4]	388	233	601	54.9	157.9
d) Civil proceedings (Total)	22,381	27,180	32,044	43.2	17.9
Prisoner petitions	6,786	7,604	7,455	9.9	−2.0
Pretrial conferences	7,168	11,819	15,743	119.6	33.2
Motions	6,077	4,434	5,985	−1.5	35.0
Special master reports	256	306	367	43.4	19.9
Social security reviews	334	284	277	−17.1	−2.5
NARA proceedings[2]	705	740	320	−54.6	−56.8
Other matters[4]	1,055	1,993	1,897	79.8	−4.8

[1]Source: *1974 Annual Report of the Director of Administrative Office of United States Courts*, Table 2, p. vi–3.

[2]Narcotic Addict Rehabilitation Act.

[3]Activity within authority of former commissioners.

[4]Could not determine if activity was within authority of former commissioners.

Source: Stephen Puro, "United States Magistrates: A New Federal Judicial Officer," Justice System Journal, 2 (Winter 1976), 147

provided "more adequate legal services for indigents than had been provided ever before in American history."[25]

Private Counsel   Attorneys for defendants who are involved in lit-igation in the federal district court generally come from the immediate area of the federal court. They are, quite often, "regulars" who appear before the federal district judge on many occasions and who might possibly be close personal associates and friends of the federal judge prior to his elevation to the federal bench.

JURORS: GRAND AND PETIT   Yet another group in the district court work-shop are the men and women who serve as grand jurors and who sit in on trial juries. The grand jurors, convened by the United States attorney, are responsible for handing down an indictment after a showing by the federal prosecutor that there was probable cause to believe that the person has committed the federal crime for which he stands accused. In many federal district courts, the grand jurors are chosen for one year and meet bimonthly to hear the charges brought by the U.S. attorney.

Petit jurors are those persons chosen at random from the geo-graphic community in which the federal district court has jurisdiction who hear and decide guilt or innocence in criminal and civil trials. Federal rules allow fewer than 12 jurors in civil cases and call for 12 jurors in criminal cases. At one time, in certain areas of the federal system, there was systematic exclusion of blacks and other minorities from the juror rolls. This is, however, no longer the case in the federal and state legal systems.

OTHER SUPPORT PERSONNEL   In addition to the persons mentioned above, there are additional personnel, hired by the chief clerk and others, who provide the necessary support for the federal district court operation. There are the U.S. marshalls who provide security, and the clerks, stenographers, and other administrative support personnel who are needed for the smooth operation of the federal district court.

The Caseload Crisis in the Federal District Courts

REASONS FOR THE INCREASE   There has been in recent decades an increased demand for governmental service while at the same time there has been a relative decline in the resources of the state to deal with the increased demand.[26] Courts, especially since the Warren Court's efforts to expand the scope of "due process of law" and "equal protection of the laws," have had more and more demands placed on them by litigants

[25]Ibid.
[26]Wolf Heydebrand, "The Context of Public Bureaucracies: An Organizational Analysis of the Federal District Courts," *Law and Society Review*, vol. 11, no. 5 (Summer 1977), p. 761.

who had not used the federal judicial system to redress grievances—perceived and real—before.

The number of filings in the lower federal courts "has increased more dramatically than any time since the creation of the courts of appeals in 1891."[27] The statistics presented in an earlier chapter clearly show the dramatic nature of the increase. Federal district court judge Jack Weinstein remarked of this dramatic increase:

> As the law has become more compassionate and guarantees of equality and due process have begun to be realized, the quantitative problems of the courts have increased. The increased load on the courts because of the fact that we are doing more than merely paying lip service to the Constitution and our democratic ideals is great.[28]

Average filings per judge have increased from 77 in 1964 to over 175 in 1977 in the court of appeals; a similar increase exists in the number of terminations per district court judge (over 380 per judge in 1976). The reasons for this increase, as suggested above, are at least two: (1) Supreme Court interpretations of constitutional and criminal procedures, and (2) congressional legislation that has (a) created certain basic civil rights and has provided citizens denied these rights a forum in the federal courts to rectify their alleged mistreatment by officials of the state or by private persons, and (b) expanded the welfare/regulatory state actions on behalf of citizens and has allowed citizens access to the federal courts to pursue these ends. The rights of citizens and the responsibilities of political agencies have thus been clarified in the past two decades—but at a cost: increased workloads for federal district court judges.

SOME SUGGESTED REMEDIES   Given the caseload increase in the federal courts, three possible remedies have been discussed: (1) Increase the resources by adding more judges and courts; (2) reduce the flow of cases by narrowing the scope of federal jurisdiction, and (3) adopt procedures, administrative in character, that "increase" the federal court's capacity to do justice without directly increasing the resources.[29]

Adding Resources   One suggestion made as early as 1800, in response to court caseload has been to add new judges to existing federal courts and to develop additional courts (including some special limited juris-

[27]Steven Flanders and Jerry Goldman, "Screening Practices and the Use of Para Judicial Personnel in a U.S. Court of Appeals," *Justice System Journal,* vol. 1, no. 2 (March 1975), p. 1.
[28]Jack Weinstein, "The Role of the Chief Judge in a Modern System of Justice," in Wheeler and Whitcomb, *Judicial Administration* (Englewood Cliffs, N.J.: Prentice-Hall, Inc., 1977), p. 145.
[29]Flanders and Goldman, "Screening Practices," p. 2.

diction courts) to assist the courts of appeals. Increasing the size of the judicial staff has some drawbacks. Such an increase would "tend to reduce the honorific quality of the position, making it difficult to draw to the bench the very best lawyers. Further, increasing the size of the court would seriously interfere with those aspects of court functioning that have a collegial quality." Finally, "the authority symbol of the judge in society depends to some extent upon having relatively few judges."[30]

Reducing the Intake of the Federal Courts   This remedy to overcrowded dockets in the federal courts calls for the redefinition of the jurisdiction of the federal courts by the Congress of the United States. The Congress would have to reduce the jurisdiction of the federal courts or increase the monetary amount necessary to get cases into the federal courts. By acting in that manner, the role of the federal courts would be dramatically reduced.

The intriguing and very difficult question that would have to be answered is: Which of the areas of federal jurisdiction are "unnecessary or undesirable?"[31] In an era of legislative activity that has broadened dramatically the jurisdiction of the federal courts to the point where the "case loads already outstrip the capability of court processes as now constituted,"[32] would Congress be willing to take away what it has just mandated the federal courts to do?

If the legislators were willing to reduce the jurisdiction in order to reduce the flow of cases to the federal courts, where would the Congress begin? Would it remove from district court jurisdiction civil rights issues and challenges? Diversity of citizenship? The point is that taking this route will surely involve the Congress in a great many years of debate and argument over how best to reduce jurisdiction of the federal courts.

Devise and Employ New Administrative Techniques   Developing new administrative techniques seems to be the course of action that would run into the least difficulty, for it involves doing something different to the cases as they enter the federal judicial system. Streamlining the process involves not only the introduction of new machine technology transferred into the judicial system, but also the introduction of organizational and management techniques into the federal judicial system. "In order to utilize the power that might be realized from the transfer of established technology into the courts, we must have far better information systems than we now have."[33] The Judicial Council of the United States

[30]William B. Eldridge, "Barriers and Incentives to Technology Transfer into the United States Courts," in Wheeler and Whitcomb, *Judicial Administration*, p. 265.
[31]Ibid.
[32]Ibid., p. 264.
[33]Ibid., p. 266.

has seen the advantages of such technology transfer into the courts, as have many judges, and the transfer of techniques and technology into the court system is now underway.

Many judicial scholars believe there should be an attempt to deal with the caseload explosion in the federal courts by borrowing successful technological and managerial techniques before reducing the jurisdiction of the federal courts or adding large numbers of judges and courts to the federal judicial system that seems to have reached the position of maximum size in the 1970s.[34] The following segments examine the case flow in the federal district courts.

Case Flow in the Federal District Courts

There are now over 170,000 filings annually in the federal district courts and the number of filings increases by as much as 10 percent each year (see Table 6-3). These cases fall into three general types:

1. private cases which involve no opportunity for broad policy statements but rather deal with torts, contracts, diversity of citizenship problems;

2. public cases in which the United States attorney initiates criminal actions against individuals or in which the federal government is a defendant in a civil proceeding;

3. there are a few public cases that come to the federal district courts that invite public policy innovation by the federal district court judge. Here, at the federal trial court level, one sees clearly the norm enforcement role of the federal judges. For example, federal questions will emerge in a federal district court for which there are no clear-cut answers in the existing body of law. Given a lack of precedent, the federal district judge—forced to act—will be free to innovate and create judgments that attempt to resolve the conflict in his court.[35]

Almost 400 federal district judges have to deal with these filings. They preside in the federal courts of first instance and more than 90 percent of these cases end in the district court. The initial phase in the case flow process is the *filing* of the complaint in a civil proceeding and the handing down of the indictment or information in a criminal proceeding. Disposition of the case is the other end of the cycle that began with the filing or indictment. Very few of the cases are disposed of by trial by judge (or jury). Only about 8 percent of the civil and criminal

---

[34]See, for example, William C. Mack, "Settlement Procedures in the U.S. Courts of Appeals," *Justice System Journal*, vol. 2, no. 2 (March 1975).
[35]Early, *Constitutional Courts*, p. 54–55.

TABLE 6-3   UNITED STATES DISTRICT COURTS—NATIONAL STATISTICAL PROFILE

			ALL DISTRICT COURTS					
			1976	1975	1974	1973	1972	1971
OVERALL WORKLOAD STATISTICS	Filings		171,617	160,602	143,284	140,994	145,227	136,553
	Terminations		153,850	148,298	139,159	141,715	143,282	126,145
	Pending		159,945	142,178	129,874	125,749	126,470	124,525
	Percent Change in Total Filings— Current Year	Over Last Year	6.9					
		Over Earlier Years		19.8	21.7	18.2	25.7	
ACTIONS PER JUDGESHIP	Number of Judgeships		399	400	400	400	400	401
	FILINGS Total		430	402	358	352	363	341
	Civil		327	294	259	246	240	233
	Criminal		103	108	99	106	123	108
	Pending Cases		401	355	325	314	316	311
	Weighted Filings		432	400	350	343	335	307
	Terminations		386	371	348	354	358	315
	Trials Completed		49	48	46	49	47	44
MEDIAN TIMES (MONTHS)	From Filing to Disposition	Criminal	3.1	3.6	3.8	3.9	3.4	3.0
		Civil	9	9	9	10	9	9
	From Issue to Trial (Civil Only)		11	11	11	12	11	11
OTHER	Number (and %) of Civil Cases Over 3 Years Old		9,414 (6.9)	7,563 (6.4)	7,352 (7.0)	7,602 (7.6)	8,684 (8.8)	9,022 (9.2)
	Triable Defendants in Pending Criminal Cases Number (and %)		8,028 28.9	2,083 (18.5)	3,465 (26.6)	3,441 (28.2)	2,909 (27.6)	2,769 (31.9)
	Vacant Judgeship Mos.		240.6	190.2	215.6	156.7	230.7	604.8
	Juror Usage Index		19.73	19.32	19.12	20.16	20.96	23.31
	% of Jurors Not Serving		39.7	39.9	41.7	43.5	44.5	45.8

CASE CLASS	AS A GENERAL RULE THE WEIGHTS FOR THESE CLASSIFICATIONS ARE		
	LIGHTER THAN AVERAGE	AVERAGE	HEAVIER THAN AVERAGE
CIVIL	A - NARA and Social Security B - Commerce (ICC) C - Prisoner Petitions D - Forfeitures and Penalties and Tax Suits	E - Real Property F - Labor Suits G - Contracts H - Torts	I - Copyright, Patents, and Trademark J - Civil Rights K - Antitrust	L - All Other Civil Cases
CRIMINAL Original Proceedings Only	A - Immigration B - Embezzlement C - Auto Theft D - Weapons and Firearms	E - Selective Service F - Liquor, Internal Revenue G - Burglary and Larceny H - Drug Laws	I - Forgery and Counterfeiting J - Fraud K - Homicide, Robbery, Assault and Sex Offenses	L - All Other Criminal Cases

Source: Management Statistics for United States Courts, *p. 127, 1976.*

cases ever get to the trial or adjudication end of the judicial cycle.[36] (Of those filings and indictments that reach trial, 32 percent of the civil cases are jury trials and 64 percent of criminal trials are jury trials—the rest are trials before the district court judge.) Between the filing and final disposition, then, there are many stages that will be discussed in the following segments (see Figure 6-4).

Civil Cases in the Federal District Courts

Assuming that there is no informal negotiating or actual settlement of private disputes or civil disputes involving the federal government, the federal district court first becomes aware of civil litigation when the plaintiff files a *complaint* with the federal court and a *summons* is issued to the defendant (see Figure 6-5).[37]

The plaintiff's complaint against the defendant is presented to the court in the *pleadings;* part of the pleadings consists of the defendant's response to the plaintiff's complaint. In addition, the pleadings indicates the nature of federal court jurisdiction to hear the case as well as the type of relief sought by the plaintiff.

In 1938 the Federal Rules of Civil Procedures were developed by the Congress in order to assist both parties in a civil dispute. Two basic

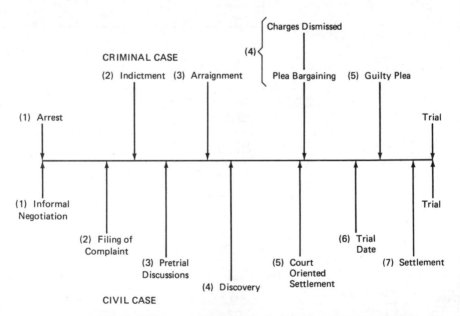

FIG. 6-4   FEDERAL CRIMINAL AND CIVIL CASES IN DISTRICT COURT: INITIAL PROCEEDINGS TO FINAL DISPOSITION

[36]Jacob, *Justice in America,* p. 153.
[37]*Federal Rules of Civil Procedure,* 28 USC, revised.

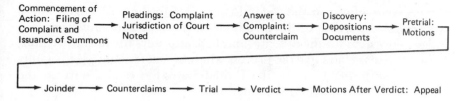

FIG. 6-5   U.S. DISTRICT COURT: CIVIL CASE FLOW

rules, which lead to settlement of claims rather than continuation of litigation to trial, are *discovery* and the *pretrial conference*. The former device allows both sides, under court supervision, to engage in a total review of the facts and examination of witnesses in order to find out what both sides are dealing with in the litigational effort.

Rule 16 of the Civil Procedures authorizes a pretrial conference between the judge and the attorneys for both parties to the dispute. It was incorporated in the hope that such a phase would lower the number of civil trials and increase the percentage of out of court settlements.[38] It is seen as a "common sense method of shifting the issues and reducing the delays and expenses of trials so that a suit will go to trial only on questions on which there is an honest dispute of fact or law."[39]

At this point in the civil case flow process, if the facts are fairly clear, the attorneys will attempt—with or without the federal district judge—to settle the question in order "to avoid the costs and perils of a trial."[40] If there is no settlement, then the civil case goes to trial.

Trial necessitates the calling of jurors if the parties opt for jury trials in the federal district court. In 81 of the 94 federal district courts, there are six-person juries to hear civil disputes. The Rules of Federal Civil Procedures provide for a judge-conducted *voir dire* proceeding at which time potential jurors are interviewed and either selected or rejected. After the impaneling of the jury, the trial commences. At the conclusion a verdict is rendered followed by motions after the verdict and, finally, in a very small percentage of cases, appeals filed with the court of appeals.

Criminal Cases in the Federal District Courts

Criminal cases seldom reach the trial stage; generally there is either a dismissal of charges or a guilty plea (as a consequence of plea bargaining in some jurisdictions). Only about eight percent of criminal

[38]Kenneth M. Holland, "William J. Campbell: A Case Study of an Activist U.S. District Judge," *Justice System Journal,* vol. 3, no. 2 (Winter 1977), p. 148.
[39]Wheeler and Whitcomb, *Judicial Administration,* p. 166.
[40]Ibid.

actions commenced in the federal courts get to the trial stage. There has been a great deal of discussion about the plea bargaining process; judges, attorneys for the defense, and U.S. attorneys for various reasons have come to use and like the process whereby a defendant pleads guilty to a lesser offense. In 1971, the United States Supreme Court, in the *Santobello v. New York* opinion, stated that

> disposition of charges after plea discussions is not only an essential part of the process but a highly desirable part for many reasons. . . . Prompt and final disposition of most criminal cases, . . . avoidance of enforced idleness during pre-trial confinement, . . . protects the public, and, by shortening the time between charge and disposition, it enhances whatever may be the rehabilitative prospects of the guilty when they are ultimately imprisoned.

In 1973 the Congress passed the Speedy Trial Act which called for the narrowing of time between arrest and the commencement of the trial to a period of no more than 100 days (see Figure 6-6). After arrest or issuance of the summons, the United States Attorney has 30 days to prepare the case for presentation to the grand jury or to the district court judge. This requirement ostensibly ensures that disinterested third parties—the grand jurors or the judge—will investigate the charges and the evidence accumulated by the federal prosecutor in the preliminary hearing. If the grand jury finds probable cause that the defendant committed the action, an *indictment* is handed down. If the judge agrees with the judgment of the attorney for the government, an *information* is handed down. "In either case, the stated purpose of the independent review of the prosecutor's behavior is largely illusory, with the prosecutors winning most requests for indictment or information."[41]

Assuming that an indictment has been forthcoming, the defendant is then formally charged with the criminal offense and, within 10 days, must be formally *arraigned* in federal district court at which time the defendant formally responds to the charges against him or her.

Within days there is an omnibus pretrial hearing held in the federal court, serving much the same purpose as discovery and pretrial in civil pleadings. At this time, defense and prosecution evidence is disclosed, motions to challenge the admissibility of evidence are introduced, continuances are asked for, change of venue requested, and so forth. It is at this point in the formal proceedings that plea bargaining begins between the two attorneys, assuming that charges have not been dropped. Nationally, at least 90 percent of all criminal cases in federal and state courts end up with pleas of guilty as a result of plea bargaining. In the

---

[41]Wheeler and Whitcomb, *Judicial Administration*, p. 163.

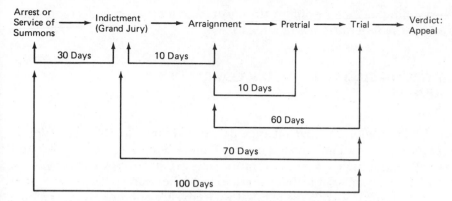

FIG. 6-6   U.S. DISTRICT COURT: CRIMINAL CASE FLOW

federal district courts, the judges generally do not play a major role in the negotiations "owing to a strong conviction that it would be improper for a judge to induce pleas, or decide sentences before presentence reports have been rendered by probation officers."[42]

If the charges have not been dismissed and if there is no guilty plea, then the trial must commence in the federal district court no later than 70 days after the indictment has been handed down. Voir dire and jury trial (or trial with the judge rather than jury) follow. Finally, there is the verdict and, if the defendant is found guilty, sentencing, followed by a motion for reviewing the verdict and then, if it is requested, an appeal to the federal court of appeals covering that jurisdiction.

Appeals to the U.S. Courts of Appeals

Federal law allows an automatic appeal by convicted defendants to the court of appeals. Given the factors present in the district court environment, there are occasions where there is a challenge to the federal district judge's sentencing procedures, or the way in which the judge impanelled the jury, or interpreted a congressional statute or opinion of a federal appellate court, and so forth. As indicated earlier, the way in which the federal judge handled the case determines the character of the appeal to the federal court of appeals. It is quite common, as the introduction suggested, for a federal district judge to so botch up an appellate precedent so as to deny the defendant due process of law. The

[42]Martin Levin, "Urban Politics and Judicial Behavior," *Journal of Legal Studies,* 1 (1972), 203.

upcoming segments examine the nature and mechanics of decision making in the federal courts of appeals.

DECISION MAKING IN THE U.S. COURTS OF APPEALS

The federal courts of appeals were created in 1891 in order to reduce the appellate burden on the United States Supreme Court and to allow the high Court to be more selective in the reviewing process. (It is interesting to note that the creation of the courts of appeals allowed the Supreme Court, in the 1960s, to selectively examine various criminal justice questions associated with constitutional rights and to create standards for defendants in criminal and civil trials that created a major caseload burden for the federal courts of appeals.)

The federal courts of appeals must hear all appeals brought to them from the federal district courts, although the judges do not devote equal time to all cases. There is a symbiotic relationship between the trial courts and the courts of appeals. The actions of the federal district judge establish the character of the litigation as it moves to the court of appeals.[43] The U.S. courts of appeals deal with procedural-technical questions that arise due to the way in which the trial judge dealt with the case at the pretrial, trial, and posttrial stages.

For example, the federal appeals judges do not examine whether Howard Smith smuggled heroin into the United States; rather, they examine questions associated with whether or not the evidence was properly admissible in the trial or whether it should have been suppressed because it might have been seized without a proper search warrant, and so forth. In other words, they deal with questions of law rather than with the facts of the case.

Cases coming to the federal courts of appeals have already been screened; motions have been made to trial judges and these have been rejected. Every case that comes to the federal courts of appeals is an attempt to "undo a previous judicial or administrative decision."[44] The following segments portray the nature of federal court of appeals decision making, the caseload problem, and the nature of the case flow in these courts. It must be pointed out that the district court/court of appeals relationship is a "self-contained conflict-resolution process for the most part" because the few cases (about four percent) that go on to the

[43]Richardson and Vines, *The Politics of the Federal Courts* (Boston: Little, Brown, 1971), p. 117.
[44]Ibid.

courts of appeals from the district courts usually end their litigational travels in these intermediate courts.[45]

Although courts of appeals judges might have a more glamorous role in the federal judicial system than do the district judges and although they might "show a distinctly panoramic outlook,"[46] their values and their attitudes on policy issues are just as important a set of variables to them as to their federal colleagues in the trial courts. Judicial behavior of the federal courts of appeals judges is linked to political variables external to the judicial system.[47]

Courts of appeals judges are appointed on the basis of a modified senatorial courtesy; politics and ideology are major variables in the selection of these judges. These variables are determinants in the selection process because the selectors believe that these patterns of behavior will emerge on the occasions when judges must establish or validate major public policy for the community. It is not surprising that the perceptions of judicial role held by these federal judges are "heavily influenced by official (political) and professional prescriptions."[48]

In studies conducted by political scientists about the behavior of federal court of appeals judges, it has been shown that political and professional values have a major impact on the role perceptions held by these federal jurists. Party affiliation is a significant determinant of the voting pattern of the federal court of appeals judge. "Many of the policy choices of judges affiliated with the Democratic party tended to differ from those made by Republican affiliated judges."[49] Also, liberal or conservative leanings prior to elevation to the federal court of appeals emerge in the decisions of these federal judges.

The federal appeals court judge, in sum, is a captive of his past political, professional, and social development. He is selected, in part, because of his prior record on the important policy issues affecting the society. He cannot avoid his professional and political socialization experiences. If he takes an oath to do justice to rich and to poor alike, he "does" justice under the influence of these variables.

What kinds of perceptions of judicial role are held by these federal jurists? Professor Howard has identified three basic types of perceptions of judicial role: innovators, realists, and interpreters.[50] The *innovator* is

---

[45]Early, *Constitutional Courts*, p. 48.

[46]Sarat, "Judging in Trial Courts," p. 368.

[47]Kritzer, "Federal District Judges, p. 28.

[48]J. Woodford Howard, "Role Perceptions and Behavior in Three U.S. Courts of Appeals," *Journal of Politics*, vol. 39, no. 3 (November 1977), p. 918.

[49]See Ibid.; Kritzer, "Federal District Judges"; Flanders and Goldman "Screening Practices," and Sheldon Goldman, "Voting Behavior on the U.S. Courts of Appeals, 1961–1964," *American Political Science Review*, 60 (1966), 374–83.

[50]Howard, "Role Perceptions," pp. 918–21.

the judge who is not afraid to make law and launch new ideas based on his perceptions of the policy issue under discussion in his court. The *interpreter,* on the other hand, is the jurist who is opposed to the judicial activism of the innovator. Statist oriented, he is only willing to interpret the words of the statutes in question so as to validate the existing procedures and legal standards. The majority of judges, according to Howard, are classified as *realists.* These federal jurists take the middle position on the question of the propriety of judicial intervention in policy making. On occasion these jurists can see themselves making law in the absence of clearly defined precedents developed by their court of appeals or by the United States Supreme Court. On the other hand, they are very reluctant to act consistently in this policy-making role and prefer to act as traditional interpreters and validators of existing policy.

Based on the judge's prior legal experiences, political experiences, ideological perspectives, view of the role and function of the federal judges in the society, he will respond to appeals from the district courts in a certain way. Lawyers for plaintiffs and defendants are aware of this basic fact of judicial life and if at all possible, as the following segments illustrate, attempt to find a court whose judges (or a majority of them) are amenable to their legal arguments.

Caseload in the Courts of Appeals

The caseload of the federal courts of appeals has gone up dramatically in the past decades, for reasons already presented. The 97 judges in the 11 courts of appeals have seen the caseload increase from just over 6,000 filings in 1964 to over 18,000 in 1976. In 1976, appeals from the 94 federal district courts totaled over 15,000; almost 10,500 were civil appeals and 4,600 were criminal appeals.[51] If the caseload increase was 159 percent from 1964 to 1974, the increase in the number of judges, from 78 to 97, was a minimal 24 percent. "The per judgeship workload average now easily surpasses what were only lately considered the upper limits of individual judicial activity"[52] (see Table 6-4).

Court size has been increased to deal with the increase caseload; judicial positions in a particular circuit are a function of the existing caseload and geographic considerations.[53] The largest federal court of

---

[51]Report of the Director of the United States Courts, 1976, p. 157.
[52]Mack, *Settlement Procedures,* p. 17.
[53]Justin J. Green and Burton Atkins, "The Role and Behavior of Judges Sitting By Designation on the United States Courts of Appeals," paper delivered at annual Southern Political Science Association Meeting, November 1977, New Orleans, Louisiana, p. 1.

TABLE 6-4   UNITED STATES COURTS OF APPEALS—NATIONAL STATISTICAL PROFILE

			ALL COURTS OF APPEALS					
			1976	1975	1974	1973	1972	1971
OVERALL WORKLOAD STATISTICS	Filings		18,408	16,658	16,436	15,629	14,535	12,788
	Terminations		16,426	16,000	15,422	15,112	13,828	12,368
	Pending		14,110	12,128	11,470	10,456	9,939	9,232
	Percent Change in Total Filings — Current Year	Over Last Year ▶		10.5				
		Over Earlier Years ▶			12.0	17.8	26.6	43.9
	Number of Judgeships		97	97	97	97	97	97
ACTIONS PER JUDGESHIP	APPEALS FILED	Total	190	172	169	161	150	132
		Prisoner	25	25	29	29	27	26
		All Other Civil	91	80	75	69	66	52
		Criminal	48	43	42	46	41	33
		Administrative	26	24	23	17	16	14
	PENDING APPEALS		145	125	118	108	102	95
	APPEALS TERMINATED	Total	169	165	159	156	143	128
		Consolidations & Cross Appeals	19	20	20	16	14	14
		Without Hearing or Submission	54	51	52	41	40	35
		After Hearing or Submission	96	94	87	99	88	78
	OPINIONS	Per Curiam	29	24	33	40	38	32
		Signed	39	37	33	36	36	34
OTHER	% Reversed or Denied		17.9	17.8	18.6	17.5	19.4	18.1
	Median Time (Mos.) from Filing Complete Record to Disposition		7.1	7.4	6.8	6.4	6.6	7.6
	CASE PARTICIPATIONS	Total	26,342	25,945	18,464	19,800	17,520	17,653
		% by Active Judges	79.6	77.4	75.6	74.1	75.7	79.9
		% by Senior Judges	10.0	10.8	12.3	12.3	13.4	9.5
		% by Visiting Judges	10.4	11.8	12.1	13.6	10.9	10.6
	Matters Filed on Misc. Record		3,129	3,003	2,528	2,701	3,064	3,183
	No. of Senior Judges Sitting		39	42	42	44	42	34
	No. of Vacant Judgeship Months		16.0	36.2	31.0	50.6	55.1	113.2

Source: Management Statistics for United States Courts, *p. 13, 1976.*

appeals, the fifth circuit (deep south), covers the most geography and has 15 judges. (The *Omnibus Judgeship Bill* [Public Law 95–486], signed into law by President Carter on October 20, 1978, will enlarge the fifth circuit to 26 judges in 1979.) The smallest court of appeals, the first circuit (northeast) has only three federal judges. However, as indicated above, the increase has been minimal and suggestions for additional judges get caught up in the political infighting of the appointment process between the president and Congress.

Some remedies to alleviate this heavy caseload include the following: use of parajudicial personnel,[54] development of settlement procedures in the courts of appeals that are similar to those in the district court process,[55] and the use of retired federal judges sitting "by designation" on courts of appeals.[56] Short of the addition of new judges and the creation of additional courts of appeals, which seem highly unlikely, or the reduction of federal jurisdiction to hear cases on appeal, the courts of appeals have to deal with the caseload crisis administratively and creatively by establishing new procedures for consolidating, reviewing, and disposing of most of the appeals as quickly and as fairly as possible.

Case Flow in the Courts of Appeals

Three-Judge Panels

Of the more than 18,000 cases that come to the federal courts of appeals, only about one-third ever get to the oral hearing stage of the case flow process. In 1976, there were 6,102 oral arguments. The vast majority of these (6,048) were heard in three-judge panels created by the chief judge of the court of appeals (the other 54 were *en banc* proceedings, a process that will be discussed in the next segment).[57]

Most of the cases that are heard on the merits will be heard by panels of three judges. In those courts of appeals with more than three judges, the chief judge chooses the judges for a particular panel. On some occasions, he will intentionally create certain kinds of ideological panels so as to get a majority of two on the three-judge panel.

For example, during the 1960s, Chief Judge John Minor Wisdom of the fifth circuit court of appeals, often created three-judge panels consisting of himself, Judge Tuttle, and a third judge so that there would be at least two judges, Tuttle and Wisdom, who were moderate to liberal

[54]Flanders and Goldman, "Screening Practices," p. 2.
[55]Mack, *Settlement Procedures*, p. 18.
[56]Green and Atkins, "The Role and Behavior of Judges," p. 2.
[57]Report of Director, p. 157.

in civil rights policy questions and who would form a majority on that panel. Thus, even though a majority of the court of appeals judges of the fifth circuit might have been "segregationists," given the power of the chief judge to form the panels, "majority domination in a court of appeals is possible but not certain."[58]

Chief judges are determined solely on the basis of seniority and tenure of the court of appeals. Based on the values, concern, and commitment of the chief judge, there will be random selection or intentionally structured three-judge panels. In any event, these three-judge panels are changed frequently.[59] While together, the three judges act collegially on the cases that come to their panel. Generally these three-judge panels meet in various spots throughout the particular circuit. For example, the fifth circuit federal appeals judges meet in three-judge panels in Jackson (Mississippi), Montgomery (Alabama), as well as in New Orleans, the home city of the fifth circuit court of appeals.

En Banc *Proceedings*

When an issue of national importance comes to the federal court of appeals from the district court, or if the court of appeals decides that there is a basic need for uniformity on an issue, an *en banc* panel will be formed at the call of the chief judge. The *en banc* panel consists of all the judges in that circuit sitting and deciding the case at hand in a collegial manner.

An example of an *en banc* proceeding (as indicated above these are rarely convened) would be the Nixon Watergate tape litigation in 1973. The Sirica judgment was appealed to the court of appeals in the District of Columbia. Because of the dramatic importance of the issue (presidential confidentiality and the power of the judiciary to issue compulsory orders to a sitting president) the court of appeals met in *en banc* proceedings.[60] These judgments by the entire court of appeals are rarely reversed by the United States Supreme Court whereas court of appeals panel judgments are often reversed by the high court.[61]

Dissents in the Courts of Appeals

Dissenting opinions on the Supreme Court of the United States have sometimes been harbingers of future legal rulings; in any event it is not uncommon for the Supreme Court to produce nonunanimous

---

[58]Richardson and Vines, *Politics*, p. 122.
[59]Jacob, *Justice in America*, p. 214.
[60]See Howard Ball, *No Pledge of Privacy* (New York: Kennikat Press, 1977).
[61]Richardson and Vines, *Politics*, p. 123.

opinions. In recent years more than half of all Supreme Court judgments have been nonunanimous. Dissents on the courts of appeals are much rarer, however, and are "usually seen as an expression of non-libertarianism."[62]

Generally the dissenting judge will be in agreement with the federal district court judge who has been reversed by the other two judges on the panel. "Since in all circuits the reversal of cases by the appeals courts is largely directed toward turning non-libertarian decisions into liberal ones," the dissenting judge is, as suggested above, a conservative jurist: "dissent is an almost exclusive expression of non-libertarianism."[63]

Moreover, given the fact that three-judge panels are being continuously created and then recreated, there is the phenomenon called the "shifting context of dissent."[64] The dissenting judge on one panel will inevitably become part of a majority of two or three on another panel—or on that same panel given a different set of legal questions. Still another fact to consider is that the dissenting judge acts alone and this "intrinsic loneliness of dissent on the circuits may well act as a deterrent to a single judge who faces the possibility of lone disagreement with the majority judges in contrast to the Supreme Court judge who more frequently dissents in company with colleagues."[65] In sum, dissent in the courts of appeals is rarer and much different from dissent on the Supreme Court.

Given the nature of the three-judge panel, the way it is put together by the chief judge, a judge's views may be either in the majority or the minority. It is this element of chance that unnerves even the best of lawyers who is preparing to take his or her cases to the court of appeals. There may be 10 liberal judges in the group of 15 jurists on that circuit court of appeals but, given the nature of the process, the lawyer might very well draw a panel of two conservatives and one liberal!

BRIEFS FILED IN THE COURTS   After an adverse judgment in the district court or in the federal administrative agency, the person must file papers in both the trial jurisdiction and in the court of appeals informing the courts of the intent to appeal. Generally the case flow process in the federal courts of appeals (see Figure 6-7) is less time consuming than in the federal district courts and in the administrative agency judicial processes. If the defendant so wishes, after the district court judge has denied a new trial motion, the appeal brief will be filed by his counsel. This is accompanied by a transcript of the trial proceedings so that the court of appeals judges will know with certainty what took place at the trial.

After the briefs (which state the reasons for the appeal and suggest

[62]Richardson and Vines, "Review, Dissent," p. 621.
[63]Ibid.
[64]Ibid.
[65]Ibid.

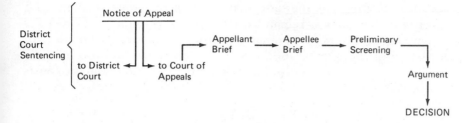

FIG. 6-7   CASE FLOW: U.S. COURTS OF APPEALS

remedies the court of appeals may apply to that case) are filed there are discussions held between counsel for both parties to the dispute and officers of the court of appeals. Many cases can be screened out in this fashion; settlements occur much in the same fashion that they occur in the federal district courts.

> Attorneys may "settle" the case before court consideration, or they may withdraw the appeal, or the court may dismiss it on one party's motion that the court does not have jurisdiction. In 1975, for example, 16,000 cases were "terminated," but of those, 4,998 (almost a third) were disposed of, prior to submission, either by the court or by the parties.[66]

In addition to cases being dropped, other cases will be consolidated (one case joined with another) in order to use the time of the courts of appeals judges more efficiently.

ORAL ARGUMENTS   The presubmission screening in the federal court of appeals has set aside those appeals called consensual, i.e., where there is general agreement on how the case ought to be disposed of by the court of appeals.[67] Those cases will be disposed of summarily by the court of appeals.

Those cases that are not dropped or settled are then scheduled for oral argument before the panel of three federal courts of appeal judges. During this proceeding counsel for both parties elaborate upon points made in their written briefs and respond to interrogations by the judges sitting on that panel. It is the difficult issue—the complex, difficult, and unusual legal question—that is fully heard by the courts of appeals. (This screening is done by the professional staff working in that particular court of appeals: the chief clerk, law assistants to the judges, etc.)

It is these questions that lead to intracourt conflicts. In the Howard study of three federal courts of appeals, he found that only 7.7 percent of federal district court judgments were reversed on appeal. More than

[66]Wheeler and Whitcomb, *Judicial Administration*, p. 173
[67]Early, *Constitutional Courts*, p. 102

two-thirds of the time, the lower trial court action was affirmed (67.4 percent) or the case was remanded (19.9 percent) to the trial court for further action. Reversal and remand decisions accounted for more than 25 percent of the activities of these courts of appeals and it is in these areas that one encounters dissenting opinions from judges on the courts of appeals.

DECISION   In many instances, the court of appeals will announce its judgment immediately after oral argument without meeting in conference session to vote and write an opinion. For those cases that are not decided that quickly, yet are not complex enough or important enough to warrant full, deliberate judgments (about 25 percent of the cases heard in oral argument), there is the "per curiam" opinion or brief unsigned order of the court.

For the remainder, a very small portion of the total number of cases heard on the merits, there is some discussion in conference session, the formal vote, and then the writing of an opinion which is the justification of the panel's decision, based on case law, in that case. After the opinion has been written and signed, it is then announced by the court of appeals.

A criminal appeal, from time of filing to final disposition via a written opinion of the court of appeals, will take some federal courts approximately four months to dispose of under ordinary circumstances.[68] Given the fact that many cases are consolidated, dropped, or dealt with summarily, this does not seem to be an inordinately long time.

However, the cost involved in these various administrative screenings (often made by legal personnel and not the judge himself) and so forth, which speed up the process by dealing with so few cases on the merits, is the essence of the issue of justice. Is justice served when most cases are dealt with in this summary fashion? Especially when, as the next segment illustrates, the federal courts of appeals are in effect the court of last resort for federal cases? This is still an unsolved question and will become an even more important issue as the caseload continues to increase and more and more of these cases are dealt with in an assembly line fashion.

Courts of Appeals as Final Reviewers

Federal courts of appeals in effect serve to allow the Supreme Court to fulfill its broad policy-making role. They were created to relieve the Supreme Court of the mundane, workaday appeal that comes up

[68]Marianne Stecich, "Speeding Up Criminal Appeals In the Second Circuit," *Justice System Journal*, vol. 1, no. 2 (March 1975), p. 45.

from the federal district courts. Since 1925, the Supreme Court has become an even more selective policy maker, choosing only a very small number of cases to review for their policy implications: It is simply not a typical Court of review. To the extent that the Supreme Court is not the court of last resort for federal appeals, the court of appeals are. Cases do not move all the way up to the Supreme Court. If only four percent of the cases move from the district courts to the courts of appeals, an even smaller number move from the courts of appeals to the United States Supreme Court. What justice one gets in an appeal from an adverse judgment in federal district court generally must be found in the court of appeals.

THE WEARING OF A BLACK ARMBAND: A CASE STUDY[69]

The Facts and the Legal Issues (1969)

In November 1969 there was a major antiwar protest in America known as the moratorium days. People all across the nation opposed to the war in Vietnam met in Washington, D.C., to voice their grievances to the president and to the Congress. In Elmira, New York, a small group of Quakers planned their moratorium day activities, and thus began the five-and-a-half-year journey of Charles James (at the time a 41-year-old English teacher at a local high school).

After attending the meeting, for religious and moral reasons, James decided to wear a black armband to his high school to protest the war. For this action he was suspended from school the very day he showed up with the black ribbon on his arm. He was, however, allowed to return to the school on the condition that he not participate in such political actions in the future.

In December 1969 James wore the black armband again and was summarily fired by the school board. Summoning help from the American Civil Liberties Union (ACLU) in March 1970, James and his counsel, along with counsel for the school board appeared in the office of the New York State Commissioner of Education, Ewald B. Nyquist. James argued that he was denied freedom of religion and expression and that his dismissal violated due process of law. The school board argued that James's actions in school disrupted ordinary school procedures and that the board was within its rights in firing the war protester.

In September 1970 Nyquist ruled against James. The commissioner

[69]See Richard Harris, *Freedom Spent: Tales of Tyranny in America* (Boston: Little, Brown, 1976).

concluded that the English teacher had violated basic educational principles and that his actions were thus not constitutionally protected. The ACLU suggested filing a civil action in federal district court against the school board and James, somewhat reluctantly, agreed to take this legal action.

The questions raised were these: Was James's action a legitimate one under the Constitution's First Amendment or did the educational system have the power to prevent such an expression of religious and moral opinion—even though it was nondisruptive?

Civil Suit Filed in Federal District Court (1971)

The civil complaint was filed in the federal district court in Buffalo, New York. The complaint argued that James was denied his basic constitutional rights, due process of law, and equal protection of the laws. He asked for damages in the amount of $25,000 to cover the lost teacher salary since his dismissal. Responding to the pleading, the school board submitted 11 defenses including arguments that there was no federal question raised, that the dismissal was lawful, and that there was no exhaustion of state remedies.

In September 1971 a hearing was set in the district court in Rochester, New York, one of the divisions in the western district, New York, United States district court. An old, hard-of-hearing, conservative judge presided. Judge Harold P. Burke had a reputation as an unpredictable jurist whose legal actions often led to reversals or remands by the court of appeals of the second circuit—frequently on the grounds that his rulings violated elementary constitutional safeguards.

After James's attorney made the case for the plaintiff, the attorney for the school board argued that the case was *res judicata,* that is, that it had already been judged and thus could not be legally raised again in another legal setting. The school board argument was that the Nyquist hearing and judgment was a legal judgment although Nyquist was not a judge and it was an administrative ruling!

In December 1971 Judge Burke handed down his opinion. It was a short, two-page opinion that rejected the arguments of the plaintiff James. The questions raised are *res judicata,* he concluded, and the complaint was dismissed on the merits. After rejection by Judge Burke of requests for a new trial and reversal of verdict, the ACLU took the case to the court of appeals.

Appeal of Judgment to the Court of Appeals
(1972)

The argument made by the ACLU in the brief written for the three-judge panel rebuked the *res judicata* reasoning of Judge Burke and argued the free speech, denial of due process substantive points. The school board's written brief argued the *res judicata* argument and the fact that James did not have the free speech protection because he was in the employ of the school board.

The oral arguments were made in the federal court in May 1972 before a three-judge panel headed by the senior judge, Irving R. Kaufman. The three judges responded well to the James arguments but fairly well rebuked counsel for the school board with their hard questions about *res judicata* and the scope of free speech.

Within three weeks the panel handed down its verdict. In a unanimous ruling, the panel reversed (and remanded) the judgment of the district court judge. The case was sent back to the lower trial court for proceedings "not inconsistent with this opinion." The court had found that, on balance, the free speech argument in the James case outweighed the argument of the school board. The court found no disruption, therefore James was free to express his feelings. As for the *res judicata* argument that had been used as the technical device to dismiss James's complaint in district court, the panel stated that "we consider this point to be wholly without merit."[70]

The school board immediately appealed to Chief Judge Henry J. Friendly of the court of appeals for an *en banc* hearing before all nine judges of the second circuit. The request was denied. An appeal was made to the Supreme Court for a writ of certiorari but, in December 1972, the high court denied certiorari. The court of appeals judgment was the final ruling on the matter although the case did go back to court again.

When the case was remanded to the trial court, the federal judge ordered James reinstated to his teaching position in the high school. However the school board refused to give James his back pay.

Results (1973–1975)

James and his attorney went back to federal district court in 1973 to collect back pay. A judgment was made in 1974 for about $20,000

[70]Ibid., p. 106.

plus costs for legal and other fees, including damages to reputation. This judgment was appealed to the court of appeals once again in April 1975. A court referee called the parties together in a preliminary screening to discuss negotiation. As a result of these conferences, the school board offered $51,000 as a settlement. After five-and-a-half years of bitter struggles, ostracism, frustration at court delays, the legal matter was resolved. The mental anguish the English instructor and his family had suffered would not be as easily repaired.

In this short examination of a very complex legal and moral issue one sees the interaction of the lower federal courts and the fact that, in most cases, the court of appeals is the court of last resort in the federal judicial system. The technical error of the federal district judge, a jurist with a reputation for such legal errors, led to a unanimous, almost instantaneous reversal at the appellate level. Justice was done, although it took five years of hard and patient legal action plus five years of patience and motivation on the part of the plaintiff Charles James.

SUMMARY

This chapter has focused on the interactions of the lower federal courts. Throughout the discussion of the activities of federal judges in the district courts and courts of appeals, there appeared the political and doctrinal variables that have been discussed in earlier segments of this book.

Judicial decision making in the lower federal courts reflects the legal training and professional skills of the judges; it also reflects the politics and ideology of these men and women. The discussion of the Supreme Court's decision-making process will reveal the presence of the same variables: political values and doctrinal positions on public policy issues. Politics and ideology are present in every stage of the federal judicial process and, as Chapter 7 will indicate, at every level of the federal judicial system.

judicial decision making: the united states supreme court

7

Preceding chapters have presented a portrait of the men who have participated in the judicial decision-making process in the United States Supreme Court. The justices of the Supreme Court are public figures who have shared similar background characteristics. They were chosen by presidents because it was believed that they had certain professional, representational, and doctrinal characteristics.

It has also been pointed out that *who* makes the decisions affects the types of decisions that will be made; that it is "the private attitudes of the majority of the court which become the public law."[1] This chapter's focus is on the normative and structural dimensions of Supreme Court decision making: it will examine (1) *what* it is the justices of the Supreme Court do; (2) *how* they go about doing their work; and finally, views will be presented as to (3) *why* the justices of the Supreme Court act in the manner they do when they carry on their business.

Although the Supreme Court, in the words of a president forced to resign from office in great part because of a Court decision, is "the fastest track" in America, insofar as the justices are motivated by their deeply held values and by their past political, personal, and professional socialization experiences, they are not unlike lower federal judges.[2]

[1]C. H. Pritchett, "Division of Opinion Among Justices of the United States Supreme Court, 1939-1940," *American Political Science Review*, 35 (1941), 890.
[2]David J. Danelski, "Values as Variables in Judicial Decision Making," *Vanderbilt Law Review*, vol. 19 (1966).

However, because of the nature of their unique function and role in the political and legal systems in America, the values expressed by a majority on the Supreme Court have a greater impact than those reflected by any other court in our society. The following segment examines the nature of the Supreme Court's role and function in our system.

THE NATURE OF SUPREME COURT DECISION MAKING

Sources Of Power

As already discussed, the Supreme Court's power to hear and decide cases and controversies is found in the Constitution and in appropriate statutes passed by the Congress of the United States. Since the 1925 Judges Bill passed the Congress, the discretionary powers of the Supreme Court have been almost complete. Thousands of petitions arrive at the Supreme Court annually (the figure topped 5,000 in the 1973 term of the Supreme Court) but only a handful are examined and evaluated by the nine justices: more than 90 percent of the petitions for review are denied (certiorari) or dismissed (appeal).

The justices of the Court alone decide whether or not to use the reviewing jurisdictional power that they have in the Constitution and in the statutes. The 1925 Judges Act gave the Court complete control over petitions to the Court for a *writ of certiorari,* the source of more than 90 percent of the petitions to the Court.

With regard to the *appeal as of right,* a 1928 congressional statute gave the Supreme Court justices the power to evaluate these otherwise automatic appeals to the Court to determine whether a "valid issue is a 'substantial' federal question."[3] If the justices think that an appeal is not a *substantive* federal issue, then the "automatic" right of appeal is dismissed for "want of a substantial federal question."

The justices of the U.S. Supreme Court are, in their own way, vigilant gatekeepers. They determine the cases they wish to hear and in this determination "the line between law and policy is often blurred."[4] The justices of the Court, as will be depicted later in this chapter, use this discretionary power to take only those cases they wish to hear for policy reasons.

Based upon personal judgments, rather than random selection,

[3]Pritchett, *The American Constitution* (New York: McGraw-Hill, 1975), p. 27.
[4]Archibald Cox, *The Role of the Supreme Court in American Government* (New York: Oxford University Press, 1976), p. 3.

the justices of the Supreme Court choose to hear only those cases they are willing to hear and to evaluate policy or to hear and to make policy for the society. The gatekeeping function of the Supreme Court allows only those cases into the Court that the justices want in; there are no uninvited guests in the Supreme Court's marble palace.

The number of appeals sent to the Supreme Court has tripled since 1951 while the number of cases actually reviewed has remained the same. This increased load has led to long days and nights for justices and their clerks (and 70-hour weeks). In the 1977 term of the Court, 76 of the 129 signed opinions came in the last two months. "It's bizarre, a panic. It comes to a point in May where you just hope you aren't making any serious mistakes," stated a clerk.[5]

As a consequence the percentage of cases the Supreme Court has been examining in recent years has declined due to these increases in the number of petitions received by the Court. In 1941, the justices reviewed 17.5 percent of the petitions on the merits; in 1951, it was down to 11.1 percent. In 1961, the number reached a low of 7.4 percent and by 1971, the number reviewed had declined to 5.8 percent. By the mid-1970s, the justices were reviewing less than 5 percent of all petitions received in a given term.

In sum, when the justices decide to take a case under review, they do so for particular and important reasons. Most of the cases that come up to the Court are not there because the justices were obliged to hear them; they are up for review because the justices *wanted* to hear these cases. Why they are chosen for review is a matter that will be discussed in this chapter; for now it is enough to recall the late Chief Justice Earl Warren's words: "the standards by which justices decide to grant or to deny review are highly personalized and necessarily discretionary."

The Primary Business of the Supreme Court: Policy Formulation

Technically the Supreme Court is the final appellate court in America; if an appeal fails before the Court there is no higher court to hear the case. However, given the Court's almost total control of its business, through the granting of certiorari and the noting of probable jurisdiction, and the very small number of petitions fully reviewed on

[5]Stephen Wasby, *Continuity and Change* (Pacific Palisades: Goodyear, 1976), p. 34; S. Sidney Ulmer, "Upperdogs and Underdogs: Litigant Status As a Factor in the Selection of Cases for Supreme Court Review," paper presented at the Annual Meeting of the Southern Political Science Association, November 1976, Atlanta, Georgia. See also, "Supreme Court, Trials and Tribulations," *U.S. News and World Report,* March 26, 1979, pp.32–37.

their merits, in reality the final courts of appeal for most litigants are the federal courts of appeals and the state supreme courts. The Supreme Court is, however, the ultimate legal tribunal insofar as the resolution of major constitutional issues is concerned. The justices of the Supreme Court are very responsive to basic social, political, and economic issues as they develop in constitutional cases and controversies in our judicial system. A view of American history clearly indicates that the Supreme Court has played a major role in constitutional adjudication (and, consequently, policy formulation for the society) with respect to major economic, social, and political crises that have confronted our society.

Since the birth of the nation, Supreme Court decisions have provided our society's lawyers, politicians, and most important, our judges with authoritative guidelines for the resolution of conflicts in four important areas of substantive law: "(1) the delineation of governmental authority as against claims of individual liberty, (2) mark(ing) boundaries between state and national power, (3) interpret(ing) and clarifying the vast body of statutory and common law, and (4) supervis(ing) the operation of the federal courts."[6]

A look at some of the constitutional issues that the Supreme Court has examined in recent years illustrates without any doubt that the Court "is a public law court chiefly concerned with policy making and not with correcting lower court error or assuring justice for individuals."[7] In the past decade the Court has examined the legal and political questions associated with issues such as abortion, affirmative action programs, reverse discrimination in higher education, marital privacy, searches and seizures, presidential privilege, school property taxes, freedom of the press from compulsory processes of law, the death penalty and the question of cruel and unusual punishment, and so forth. Using the legal mechanisms and the power of judicial review, the Supreme Court has selected these and other equally hard and controversial issues generally "attuned to political factors."[8]

When the Supreme Court grants a writ of certiorari or hears an appeal as of right, it is not done to give the defeated party in the lower court (federal or state) another chance in yet another appellate hearing. The justices vote (and only four votes are necessary) to grant the request for the writ of certiorari so that they, if so motivated by the facts and constitutional or statutory questions raised in that controversy, can sub-

---

[6]Arthur D. Hellman, "The Business of the Supreme Court Under the Judiciary Act of 1925," 91 *Harvard Law Review*, June 1978, no. 8, p. 1716.
[7]Early, *Constitutional Courts of the U.S.* (Totowa, N.J.: Littlefield, Adams, 1975), p. 9.
[8]Richardson and Vines, *The Politics of Federal Courts* (Boston:Little, Brown, 1970), p.161.

stitute their view for those views developed in the lower federal or state courts. If it takes a case for review, the Supreme Court will "quite likely reverse the lower court."[9]

In one sample of cases that came to the Supreme Court for review from lower federal courts, 102 of the 150 were judgments where both the district court judge and the court of appeals panel were in agreement (68 percent). In these 102 cases of lower court agreement, the Supreme Court reversed the lower courts agreements 70 times (70 percent). Of the total number of federal cases reviewed, the Supreme Court "introduced conflict 47 percent of the time by reversing the lower court judgments."[10]

In effect, the justices of the Supreme Court were substituting their judgment for the agreement reached in the lower courts in this sample study. (Quite frequently there is much disagreement between federal judicial levels.)[11] Although it disrupted the "policy consensus" coming from these courts, the Supreme Court did stake out its own policy preferences and its own values and it did develop a national policy on those issues the justices felt were important enough to be reviewed by the Court.

It matters little whether or not there was consensus in the lower courts; if the Supreme Court wants to hear the controversy because they believe it is ripe for Supreme Court resolution, they will hear it. "What the justices do with their power depends in the last analysis upon what they individually perceive to be proper."[12] That is precisely why presidents take great care in the selection process; they want justices on the Supreme Court who will act in a certain way when these controversial cases come to the court on appeal. The fundamental task of the Supreme Court is policy formulation and clarification. In this effort, the justices of the Court *use* lower court decisions as the vehicle for this policy clarification and formulation.

The Relationship Between the Lower Courts and the Supreme Court

Given the policy orientation of the Supreme Court, i.e., the fact that the justices choose to hear only a handful of substantive public policy issues, the lower federal courts are not very dependent upon the high Court. Unless the policy pronouncement affects the lower courts

[9]Wasby, *Continuity and Change*, p. 37.
[10]Richardson and Vines, *Politics*, p. 153.
[11]Ibid.
[12]Early, *Constitutional Courts*, p. 138.

directly (as did the various search and seizure rulings or the school integration rulings), the lower courts will and are allowed to formulate and develop courtroom procedures and policy standards without review by the Supreme Court.

There is neither systematic appellate review nor random selection of cases from these federal courts for review by the Supreme Court to ensure that justice is being done on the lower court level. Nor is there necessarily Supreme Court review to evaluate disagreement between the trial and lower federal appellate courts. In simple terms, the Supreme Court hears cases in order to deal with what a majority of the justices on the Court believe are significant public policy issues (coming to them in the form of constitutional questions) which deserve a final resolution by the highest court in the land.

Given the existence of traditional legal perceptions held by all judges, judicial gatekeeping lets those cases into the Supreme Court that the justices want in for political and policy reasons. Couched in legal terminology, these legal disputes are the vehicle through which the Supreme Court majority pronounces its judgment on major societal issues. Since the creation of the federal courts of appeals in 1891 and especially since the passage of legislation in the 1920s which gave the justices total control of their docket, the Supreme Court has chosen those cases (regardless of lower court actions) that four of the Supreme Court justices wanted to hear and resolve.

Although the number of cases that come to the justices has increased dramatically in the past decades, the rationale for accepting and rejecting these petitions has not changed. Given the transiency of majorities, personalities, and the doctrinal positions of a Court "majority," petitions will or will not be granted. The following segment of the chapter examines the institutional setting and the structure of Supreme Court decision making.

THE STRUCTURE OF SUPREME COURT DECISION MAKING

Access to the Supreme Court

Although the Supreme Court has original jurisdiction, it has been already noted that the basic avenues to the Supreme Court are either by writ of certiorari or by an appeal as of right, both appellate procedures. The writ of certiorari is granted by the Supreme Court not to correct errors in lower court judgment but, in the words of former

Associate Justice Tom C. Clark, to "secure national rights and uniformity of judgment"[13] (however a particular Court majority defines these rights).

A denial of the certiorari petition means, stated the late Justice Clark, that the case did not come within the parameters of Rule 19 of the Supreme Court regulations. Denial does not mean that the result reached in the lower court was correct; it means that the Supreme Court justices did not think that the individual's case was an important federal question of law to be considered through the mechanism of judicial review.[14]

Rule 19 states that a review on the writ of certiorari "is not a matter of right, but of sound judicial discretion." However, these are "banana words," according to Professor Ulmer, i.e., words requiring interpretation by the justices of the Court.[15] As the late Chief Justice Earl Warren stated with respect to this judicial guide: Rule 19 is given life through the interpretation of that standard's words by the men on the Court; these interpretations are discretionary and "they cannot be captured in any rule or guideline that would be meaningful."[16] The Supreme Court will grant the petition for a writ of certiorari and will review the lower federal issue or the state case—if a federal question has been presented— only if enough justices sitting on the Court at that time think that the issue is one that the Court should review.

The appeal as of right, accounting for about 10 percent of the petitions to the high Court, is a more specialized form of appeal to the Supreme Court. An appellant is legally entitled to an appeal as of right from a state court judgment where a state law was upheld after being challenged on the ground that it violated the United States Constitution, or where the federal court declared a state law unconstitutional, or declared a federal law unconstitutional where the United States is a party in either a civil or criminal suit. However, as already noted, the Court can dismiss such a statutorally defined "automatic" right of appeal by determining that there was no "substantive federal question raised."

In sum, the Supreme Court completely controls its docket; the justices of the Court weed out those petitions they do not want to hear. All these cases have already been tried in federal or state trial courts and all have had appellate review in the lower federal appeals courts or in the highest state court (except for the small number of three-judge

---

[13]Alan F. Westin (ed.), *The Supreme Court: Views From Inside* (New York, Norton, 1961), p. 48.
[14]Ibid.
[15]Ulmer, "Upperdogs and Underdogs," p. 7.
[16]Westin, *The Supreme Court*, p. 25.

district court cases and the infinitely small number of cases heard by the Supreme Court under its original jurisdiction).

The Supreme Court is not an appellate tribunal in the traditional sense; justice is received by individuals in their respective state courts or in the lower federal courts. The fact that the Supreme Court reviews the case means that the justices have decided to use that particular case as a vehicle for making known their policy preferences on one of the issues raised in the litigation.

The Mechanics of the Decisional Process: An Overview

As Figure 7-1 illustrates, there are at least 10 stages in the Supreme Court's business of hearing, deciding, and disposing of the thousands of cases and controversies that come to the Court every year. The following segments sketch out the various manifestations facets of the process.

The Term of the Supreme Court

The Supreme Court meets from the first Monday in October through late June or early July of a given year in an ornate marble building in Washington, D.C. This is referred to as the "October Term" of the Court for that particular year, e.g., October 1980 would begin the 1980 term of the Supreme Court even though the period ends in 1981. During the summer months petitions continue to arrive at the Court daily; these await the return of the justices in the early fall for action. The early portion of the term is largely devoted to handling the backlog of cases that has arrived at the Court from July to September. In recent years more than 2,000 petitions were resting in the chief justice's office awaiting Supreme Court action when the justices began the term of the Court.

During the summer months and throughout the year, the justices are responsible for particular federal circuits (see Table 7-1). If a need arises in one of these areas, the justice responsible for that area will examine briefs and, if necessary, decide the case or controversy at that moment. Generally, the justice involved will hold the case over for a hearing by the full Court in the fall. If the case has to be dispensed with immediately, the justice can either act on behalf of the full Court or ask the chief justice to convene the full Court in special session. This is rarely done; cases coming to a justice when the Court is not in session are generally held over for action during the term of Court.

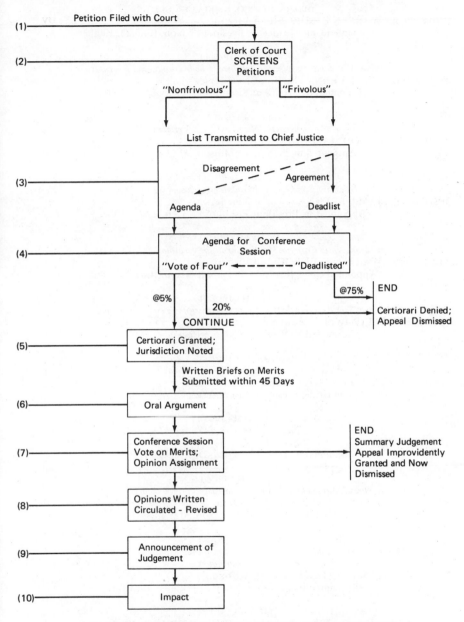

FIG. 7-1   JUDICIAL DECISIONAL FLOW CHART: SUPREME COURT

TABLE 7-1   ALLOTMENT OF THE JUSTICES

DISTRICT OF COLUMBIA CIRCUIT.
CHIEF JUSTICE WARREN E. BURGER, of Virginia.
Appointed Chief Justice by President Nixon, June 23, 1969.

FIRST CIRCUIT.
Maine, Massachusetts, New Hampshire, Rhode Island, and Puerto Rico.
JUSTICE WILLIAM J. BRENNAN, Jr., of New Jersey.
Appointed by President Eisenhower, October 15, 1956.

SECOND CIRCUIT.
Connecticut, New York, and Vermont.
JUSTICE THURGOOD MARSHALL, of New York.
Appointed by President Johnson, August 30, 1967.

THIRD CIRCUIT.
Delaware, New Jersey, Pennsylvania, and Virgin Islands.
JUSTICE WILLIAM J. BRENNAN, Jr., of New Jersey.
Appointed by President Eisenhower, October 15, 1956.

FOURTH CIRCUIT.
Maryland, North Carolina, South Carolina, Virginia, and West Virginia.
CHIEF JUSTICE WARREN E. BURGER, of Virginia.
Appointed Chief Justice by President Nixon, June 23, 1969.

FIFTH CIRCUIT.
Alabama, Florida, Georgia, Louisiana, Mississippi, Texas, and Canal Zone.
JUSTICE LEWIS F. POWELL, Jr., of Virginia.
Appointed by President Nixon, December 9, 1971.

SIXTH CIRCUIT.
Kentucky, Michigan, Ohio, and Tennessee.
JUSTICE POTTER STEWART, of Ohio.
Appointed by President Eisenhower, October 14, 1958.

SEVENTH CIRCUIT.
Illinois, Indiana, and Wisconsin.
JUSTICE JOHN PAUL STEVENS, of Illinois.
Appointed by President Ford, December 17, 1975.

EIGHTH CIRCUIT.
Arkansas, Iowa, Minnesota, Missouri, Nebraska, North Dakota, and South Dakota.
JUSTICE HARRY A. BLACKMUN, of Minnesota.
Appointed by President Nixon, May 14, 1970.

NINTH CIRCUIT.
Alaska, Arizona, California, Guam, Hawaii, Idaho, Montana, Nevada, Oregon, and Washington.
JUSTICE WILLIAM H. REHNQUIST, of Arizona.
Appointed by President Nixon, December 15, 1971.

TENTH CIRCUIT.
Colorado, Kansas, New Mexico, Oklahoma, Utah, and Wyoming.
JUSTICE BYRON R. WHITE, of Colorado.
Appointed by President Kennedy, April 12, 1962.

TEMPORARY EMERGENCY COURT OF APPEALS.
CHIEF JUSTICE WARREN E. BURGER, of Virginia.
Appointed Chief Justice by President Nixon, June 23, 1969.

Work Phases of the Court

There are two distinct general phases of Court work each term: the individual and the group work styles. During the term of the Court, the justices will be meeting together in the large courtroom to hear oral arguments in two-week cycles. In addition to this group activity (discussed below) the justices of the Supreme Court also meet in a group setting twice weekly during those weeks the Court hears oral arguments (about 20 to 23 such weeks). Called the conference session, this group setting provides the arena for a great deal of the Supreme Court's substantive and procedural activities and will be discussed below.

The individual phase of the business of the Supreme Court is that period of time when the Court is not hearing oral arguments and meeting in conference. During these periods each justice "works largely in isolation, except as he chooses to seek consultation with others."[17] He reads information about pending cases; he writes the opinions assigned to him by the chief justice; he researches in order to prepare himself for the oral arguments that are coming up in the next two-week cycle. In sum, the justice is generally doing his homework and his catch-up work during these two-week periods between the group phase. Although there will be an empty courtroom, the nine justices are hard at work in their chambers and in the Supreme Court's law library located on the third floor of the building.

The Conference Session

As Figures 7-1 and 7-2 illustrate, the conference session of the Supreme Court is the heart of the Court's decisional process. It is in this group meeting of the nine justices, held every Friday since 1953 during the weeks the Court hears oral argument, and more recently twice a week, that the justices make two kinds of very important decisions. (Prior to 1953, the justices met on Saturdays to decide these cases.)

Summoned to the conference by a buzzer rung by the chief justice, and after shaking hands with each other, the justices sit down to a full day of business. The agenda has been drawn up by the chief justice, who assumes the role of task and social leader (i.e., he is responsible for getting the men on the Court to do the tasks in an efficient, effective manner) of this small group of policy makers.[18] The day generally begins around nine in the morning and will go on until about six in the evening. There are no secretaries taking notes, there are no pages to run errands for the justices. (If anything is needed, the junior justice transmits the

---

[17]Early, *Constitutional Courts*, p. 36.
[18]David Danelski, "The Influence of the Chief Justice in the Decisional Process," paper delivered at the Annual Meeting of the American Political Science Association, September 1960, (New York City).

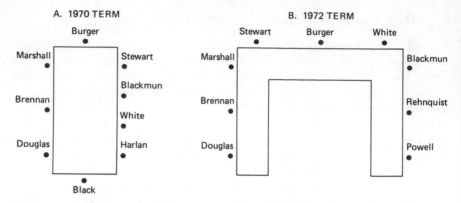

FIG. 7-2   SEATING ARRANGEMENTS: BURGER COURT CONFERENCES

Source: *Glendon Schubert,* Judicial Policy Making *(Glenview, Ill.: Scott, Foresman, 1977),* p. 134.

request to personnel outside the conference room.) At most, there are only the nine men of the Supreme Court in that conference room.

At one time, the conference session was held in a separate room and all nine justices entered this neutral space. Chief Justice Warren Burger changed this process by taking over the large conference room as his office and by then keeping the conference session in that room. The other eight justices now come to "his" office for their important meetings. In addition, as Figure 7-2 illustrates, Chief Justice Burger devised a new format for the conference by the simple expedient of sawing the mahogany table in three parts and arranging it so that his ideological opposition would not be sitting in a confrontational position—directly across the table from the Chief Justice. These two examples are indications that personality and ideology play a role in the decisional process in the Court.[19]

"It is in the conference that the mettle of a justice is tested, for here he must meet his colleagues in the rough and tumble of free discussion."[20] In this meeting of the justices (1) appeals petitions, (2) writs of certiorari, (3) *in forma pauperis* (indigent prisoner) petitions, and (4) cases argued that week in court are discussed in that order. Prior to the Friday meeting the justices receive the agenda from the chief justice. On it are listed the appeals and petitions for certiorari that will be discussed in the conference session as well as those petitions that have been deadlisted by the clerk of the Court and by the chief justice.

[19]Glendon Schubert, *Judicial Policy Making* (Glenview, Ill.: Scott, Foresman, 1977), p. 135.
[20]Loren Beth, *Politics—The Constitution and the Supreme Court* (New York, Row, Peterson, 1962), p. 41.

All petitions and appeals arrive at the clerk's office of the Supreme Court. The clerk of the Court, a person with legal experience, will make an initial screening of the material. After docketing these requests according to the nature of the appeal—(1) *original docket* for petitions under the Supreme Court's original jurisdiction, (2) *miscellaneous docket,* indigent petitions, and (3) *appellate docket,* all other certiorari and appeal petitions—the clerk then categorizes these cases as either "frivolous" or "nonfrivolous." They are then passed on to the chief justice and his law clerks who in turn prepare digests of all these cases to determine if the initial judgment of the clerk is a correct perception.

If the chief agrees with the clerk, then the case labeled frivolous is placed on a deadlist. This designation means that if no other justice believes that that particular case is important enough for further discussion, it will be dismissed or denied without any Supreme Court commentary. If, however, one of the eight justices believes that there should be a vote taken on that deadlisted case, it will be taken off the deadlist and placed on the calendar for discussion in the conference.

In this occasionally rough-and-tumble heated atmosphere,[21] the justices of the Court handle the two basic chores mentioned above: jurisdictional decisions and decisions on the merits of cases argued in Court that week.

JURISDICTIONAL DECISIONS   All the justices, each employing from two to four law clerks to assist him, must "screen cases and select for argument and decision only those which in our judgment, guided by pertinent criteria, raise the most important and far-reaching questions."[22] The appeals and the petitions for certiorari have been reviewed by each of the justices prior to their conference meetings, they have, with the help of their law clerks, made individual judgments as to the merits of these cases that appear on the agenda. It takes a vote of four of the nine justices to have that case accepted by the Court for further consideration. As Justice William J. Brennan stated, "only an exceptional case raising a significant federal question commands the review" of the Supreme Court.[23]

Ninety-seven percent of the petitions are dismissed or denied in any given term of the Court;[24] fully 75 percent may have been deadlisted and so a "vote of four" was not even necessary in about three-fourths of the petitions that come to the Supreme Court. Given the nature of the Court's work, policy formulation, the justices must quickly dispose

[21]Westin, *The Supreme Court,* p. 50.
[22]William J. Brennan, "Inside View of the High Court," *New York Times Magazine,* October 6, 1963.
[23]Ibid.
[24]Ulmer, "Upperdogs and Underdogs," p. 4.

of those nonessential cases in order to devote as much time as possible to the 120 or so cases that they examine and evaluate on the merits every term.[25]

A vote to deny the certiorari petition request is not necessarily the same as a vote on the merits. A justice of the Supreme Court might think that a particular case ought not to take up the Court's time. He makes his decision based on a number of considerations. Other justices, however, have reached the opposite conclusion. If there are four members of the Court who believe that the case raises significant public policy questions that the Court ought to examine, then certiorari will be granted or jurisdiction of the Court noted if it is an appeal as of right.

The justice who disagreed in the jurisdictional vote will then participate in the discussion of the case on the merits. "I have frequently voted to reverse cases where I voted against bringing them before our Court for review," wrote Justice Hugo Black. "This is because that for many reasons a vote to grant certiorari is not the equivalent of a final vote on the merits. And the same thing may frequently be true about dismissal of an appeal."[26]

After this procedural yet substantive decision is made by the Court (substantive in that the judgment of the lower court is upheld if there is no Supreme Court review of the case), letters are sent out informing petitioners of the results. If a case has been scheduled for further action, the Court will inform the party that he has 45 days to submit written briefs. Oral argument in the case is also scheduled at this time. (The other party to the dispute is given 30 days to respond to the written brief filed by the appellant's lawyers.) If the appellant is indigent, the Court will appoint counsel for him.

If there was a lack of a "vote of four," the petitioner will receive a short letter from the Court informing him that his petition for writ of certiorari was denied or that his appeal was dismissed for "want of a substantial federal question." There is nothing more in the letter; the Court does not give reasons for dismissing or denying requests for Supreme Court review.

There are times when the Supreme Court justices find themselves so committed to public policy positions that even with a vote of four the case is not heard. A classic example would be in the area of pornography. In recent years until the retirement of Justice William O. Douglas, the

---

[25]Ibid., p. 5.

[26]Personal communication, January 21, 1969. The significance of the Supreme Court's denial of certiorari was discussed by Justice Felix Frankfurter in *Maryland v. Baltimore Radio Show*, 338 *US* 912 (1950). The justice stated that "this Court has rigorously insisted that . . . denial carries with it no implications whatever regarding the Court's views on the merits of a case which it has declined to review."

Burger Court has taken hard and fast five to four positions on questions of pornography and free speech protections. Although there were four justices who could have voted to bring up the case—Brennan, Marshall, Douglas, and Stewart—there was no review on the merits due to the hardened positions on both sides. This however is a very rare occurrence; generally, when there are four justices who vote to hear a case it is then docketed for examination and discussion on the merits.

VOTE ON THE MERITS   Assuming that the petition for Supreme Court review has been granted, there will be the filing of written briefs by both parties to the disputes. In addition, Supreme Court Rule 42 allows interested parties to petition the Court if they wish to file an *amicus curiae* (friend of the court) brief. The power to grant or to deny such requests is a purely discretionary one and, given the workload of the justices, generally granted in those cases that are exceptionally significant.

After the briefs have been filed with the Court, oral argument takes place. As will be discussed below, this phase allows justices another view of the issues that emerge in the litigation. After oral argument, the conference session is devoted to a discussion of the case, and then there is a vote on the merits and the assignment of the majority opinion writing task.

In the discussion phase, the chief justice initiates the conversation by presenting his views on the case that had been heard in oral argument that week. (Given the time dimensions of oral argument, there may be 8 to 10 cases that must be discussed and voted upon on any given Friday conference session.) After the chief finishes his presentation, essentially observations and recommendations as to Court response to the legal question in the case, the associate justices, in order of seniority, present their views until the last justice—the most recently appointed justice on the Court—presents his views.

At this point the vote on the issue often takes place. (Often, especially in those cases where the Court is unanimous in its judgment, a direct vote is replaced by a consensus determination.) The most junior justice of the Supreme Court votes first and the chief justice casts the last and, if necessary, the deciding vote. This vote taken in conference is not a binding one. There have been numerous occasions where a justice voted one way in conference and then changed his mind at a later stage in the decision-making process. As Justice Black once said: "My votes at conference are never final. They are tentative and I am always ready to change the vote if I reach the conclusion that my vote was wrong."[27]

[27]Personal communication, January 21, 1969.

After the vote is taken, if the chief justice is in the majority he will determine who will write the opinion for the Court majority. If he is in the minority, the senior associate justice will make that often strategic decision.[28] Given the fluidity of judicial choice that has been suggested,[29] there are occasions when the writer for the majority turns out a dissenting opinion or vice versa. Justice Brennan has written of this fluidity that "I have had to convert more than one of my proposed majority opinions into a dissent before the final opinion was announced. I have also, however, had the more satisfying experience of rewriting a dissent as a majority opinion of the Court."[30] Justice Black has also commented that there "is nothing extraordinary in the fact that a Justice to whom an opinion is assigned to write one way may write it another way."[31]

This intense activity goes on after the assignments have been made in the conference session. On occasion during the conference session there is a lot of heat and, as the late Justice Clark remarked, "fur begins to fly."[32] This does not dissipate after the conference session but continues through the passage of memoranda, and so forth. Before the final judgments are made by the justices, there is a "constant interchange" (via the telephone, personal contacts, over the lunch table) that continues until "we hammer out the final form of the opinion."[33]

COURTROOM ACTIVITIES   With the cry of "oyez, oyez," the Supreme Court justices enter the ornate courtroom to hear oral arguments in cases before the Court. These oral arguments are scheduled from 10 A.M. to noon and from 1 to 3 P.M., Monday through Wednesday, of those weeks set aside for the oral arguments. (Thursdays and Fridays are set aside for the conference sessions.) Oral argument is another dimension of the decision-making process. Some justices, said Justice John M. Harlan, Jr., listen better than others and since the Court's role is to "search out the truth,"[34] oral argument gives these justices (and the others) an opportunity to discuss the case with counsel from both sides in this search for the correct way to decide the issues.

Each side is given a certain amount of time (30 minutes for each side in most cases, 60 minutes for each side in the major cases that come

[28]See Walter Murphy and C. Herman Pritchett, *Courts, Judges and Politics* (New York: Random House, 1975), pp. 511–12.
[29]J. W. Howard, "On the Fluidity of Judicial Choice," *American Political Science Review*, vol. 62, p. 43. (March 1968).
[30]Brennan, "Inside View," p. 22.
[31]Personal communication, January 21, 1969.
[32]Westin, *The Supreme Court*, p. 49.
[33]Brennan, "Inside View."
[34]Westin, *The Supreme Court*, p. 57.

to the Court) to present what they consider to be the salient issues raised in the litigation. Rule 44 of the Court regulations states that there shall be no readings of prepared notes during this period of oral argument. Instead, each counsel must be prepared to discuss what he and the justices think are the important aspects of the case.

There is a free-flowing quality to the Supreme Court's oral argument; justices can and often do interrupt the counsel with probing questions. Often these questions catch the counsel unprepared and the consequences can prove to be both embarrassing and fatal—embarrassing to the lawyer and fatal to the case. It has been noted that oral argument generally does not of itself win cases; however, poorly argued points of law have on occasion lost a case for the counsel and his client.[35] All this activity in the open courtroom is but another phase in the fluidity of judicial choice. "Judges," said Justice Felix Frankfurter, "are men, not disembodied spirits."[36] Impressions of the case culled from oral argument are but another facet of judicial decision making, and judicial decision making is an essentially personal activity. The way a justice perceives the oral argument can affect his final judgment.

OPINION-WRITING STAGE   The final, most exasperating phase of the judicial decision-making process is the drafting (and frequent redrafting) of the opinion for the Court majority. The assignment of the opinion in the conference session is the initial phase of this activity. The chief tries to take care in the selection of the opinion writer in order to ensure an even distribution of the work load on each of the justices as well as to ensure that the justice chosen to write the opinion is the best possible choice for that particular opinion-writing task.

Once the opinion is assigned to a justice, he must write the views of the Court majority in such a way as to make sure that he keeps at least four other justices with him until the final announcement of the decision of the Court. The opinion writer is formulating and circulating to all the other justices on the Supreme Court the policy—i.e., the response to the constitutional question—of the Court, not the personal policy of the opinion writer.

The opinion is an expression of collegial thinking on an important piece of public policy. The drafter of the opinion must make sure that the opinion meets with the approval of the other members of the majority coalition. He therefore discusses the case with them after the vote, sends them drafts of the opinion, revises these drafts in accordance with

[35]See Anthony Lewis, "High Drama in the High Court," in Murphy and Pritchett, *Courts, Judges,* pp. 501–4.
[36]Westin, *The Supreme Court,* p. 42.

their critiques, and finally works up a tolerable opinion for the majority. (Unless of course the justice loses his majority—in that case, he has written a dissenting opinion.) On major controversial cases, it is not uncommon for the opinion writer to circulate many drafts of an opinion before it is acceptable to the other members of the coalition.

While the majority opinion is being hammered out, other justices may be writing their dissenting opinions. These are statements that are oftentimes highly critical of the reasoning and judgment of the Court majority. In addition to these dissenting opinions that are being formulated because justices cannot agree on the merits or direction of an issue (and which are also circulated to each of the sitting justices on the Court), on occasion one or more of the justices in the majority cannot agree, under any circumstance, upon the reasoning or line of precedents employed by the majority opinion writer. Therefore, although they concur in the final decision in the pending case, they cannot concur in the rationale developed by the majority for that decision in the written opinion. They are forced to write a concurring opinion under these circumstances.

Once these activities are completed, the judgment of the Court is announced in open court. This, however, is just the beginning of the process because the opinion must now be implemented by the appropriate person or agency—federal judges, state judges, Congress, the president, etc. Given the nature of the opinion-writing phase, there will be cases that will come to the Court in the future in order to clarify the earlier judgment. In sum, judicial opinions of the Supreme Court are occasionally revised and updated through the judicial review process. The feedback factor is obvious and important in Supreme Court decision making.

Four Key Decision Points in the Supreme Court's Decisional Process

Political scientists have essentially agreed that there are four major decision points in the operation of the Supreme Court.[37] Three of the four critical phases of judicial activity occur in the conference session itself, making the conference session the very heart of the judicial decision-making process. These four key points are as follows: (1) vote on jurisdiction, (2) vote on the merits, (3) assignment of the majority opinion, and (4) bargaining over the content of the majority opinion.

[37]David W. Rohde, "Policy Goals and Opinion Coalitions in the Supreme Court," *Midwest Journal of Political Science*, vol. 26 (May 1972).

Vote on Jurisdiction

As already pointed out, it is at this stage that the justices function as gatekeepers—keeping out those many thousands of petitions that are not substantive public policy dilemmas and allowing into the court only that small number of cases that the justices consider to contain critically important policy issues.

Vote on the Merits

The second of the critical stages occurs after the reading of the written briefs on the merits and the justice's participation in the oral argument phase. It takes place in the conference session and it is the vote on the merits of the constitutional issue. Although there "are agonizing tensions at times"[38] during this phase, the result is the vote on the merits and the movement toward a collegial judgment on the public policy issue in the particular case.

Assignment of the Majority Opinion

If the opinion of the Court "is the core of the policy making power of the Supreme Court,"[39] then the person given the assignment of writing the majority opinion is faced with a very difficult task. He has to be able to formulate the policy for the majority of the judges and do so in a manner that marshalls the Court majority and holds it together throughout the creative process of molding the majority opinion.

The chief justice or the senior associate justice voting with the majority may write the opinion. However, given the necessity of equalizing the workload as much as possible among the nine justices, the chief justice may give the assignment to a justice whose view on that policy issue "is closest to his own on the issue in question."[40] As opinion assigner the chief justice plays a major role in the decision-making process. This, however, is an integral part of his job as task leader of the Supreme Court.

Formulation of the Majority Opinion Coalition

"All intra-court bargaining takes place with the understanding that if the opinion writer ignores the suggestions which his colleagues scribble

---

[38]Brennan, "Inside View."
[39]David Rohde and Harold Spaeth, *Supreme Court Decision-Making* (San Francisco: Freeman, 1976), p. 172.
[40]Ibid., p. 174.

on slip opinions, he risks the disintegration of his majority."[41] This statement is the bottom line with respect to the formulation of a majority opinion of the Supreme Court. Such an activity, done in isolation by the opinion writer, must meet with the approval of the other members of the majority coalition. His task is to write an opinion *for the majority*, which means in the end deferring to the wishes of the members of the coalition in order to arrive at an opinion that is tolerable to the other justices. As has been pointed out already, if the opinion writer cannot do the job well, the majority might very well dissipate.

Justices might break off and write a concurring opinion because their suggestions to the majority opinion writer were not acted upon by the author of the majority judgment. Enough of the justices may break away, either to concur or, worse yet, to dissent, so that there are not enough justices left to formulate an "opinion" of the Supreme Court.

Worst of all is the reality that if enough justices desert the majority position, the majority opinion writer turns into a dissenting justice writing a minority opinion. Therefore, to retain the majority, the majority opinion writer must act to please his colleagues. This accommodation involves modification of the author's own personal views and deference to the views of the other members of the majority coalition.

An Explanation of Supreme Court Decision Making

The justices of the Supreme Court are continuously asked to resolve disputes that involve federal questions. Thousands of petitions flood the Court annually. Litigants constantly ask the justices to review their case. They argue that the legal action taken against them violates their constitutional or statutory rights.

The justices of the Court, when they decide to hear particular cases, of necessity get into statutory and/or constitutional interpretation. As illustrated in the chapter on functions of the federal courts, the justices might have to interpret the meaning of the commerce clause, or determine, once again, the inexact dimensions of the Fourteenth Amendment's equal protection clause.

In this activity the justices are making *choices* between various possible interpretations of the statute in question or of the constitutional phrase that is present in the litigation proceedings. Given what H. L. A. Hart called the "open-texture" of the law,[42] judges must choose. In

[41]Walter F. Murphy, *Elements of Judicial Strategy* (Chicago: University of Chicago Press, 1960), p. 59.
[42]H. L. A. Hart, *The Concept of Law* (London: Clarendon Press, 1961).

sum, a judge "not only orders facts, states principles, and applies principles to facts; he also chooses among premises and is not oblivious to social norms and societal trends when doing so."[43]

From what has been said about the politics of the selection process and about the general characteristics of the justices of the Court, it is clear that every man on the high Court brings to the job his own personality, attitudes, values, and manner of approaching problems. In short, he brings with him his wisdom and his judgment. "The decisions in the case that really give trouble," wrote Justice Frankfurter, "rest on judgment and judgment derives from the totality of a man's nature and experience."[44]

When a judge has to choose among alternative courses of action, the value judgment of the judge is reflected in his selection. As will be discussed below, values are basic variables in the judicial decision-making process.[45] The justice of the Supreme Court is chosen, in great part, because of his doctrinal positions on important public policy issues. And, as Justice Frankfurter once stated:

> a man brings his whole experience, his training, his outlook, his social, intellectual, and moral environment with him when he takes a seat on the Supreme bench . . . (as well as) his rooted notions regarding the scope and limits of a judge's authority.[46]

These values that have been nurtured in a life filled with legal, political, and social activities cannot be discarded when the man puts on the robes of a Supreme Court justice. Instead, these attitudes and values of the majority of the justices become the public law of the land.[47] The Constitution, as Chief Justice Charles Evans Hughes once remarked, is what the judges say it is. The remaining segments of this chapter will illustrate these general remarks in greater detail.

Judicial Attitudes and Values

A justice of the Court votes the way he does in large measure because of the values he possesses. After three or so decades of public life and after 50 years or so of living and experiencing and of learning and growing intellectually, emotionally, spiritually, the justice on the Supreme Court is in possession of a fairly cohesive set of beliefs—some

---

[43]Ulmer, "Upperdogs and Underdogs," p. 1.
[44]Westin, *The Supreme Court*, p. 42.
[45]Danelski, "Values as Variables."
[46]Westin, *The Supreme Court*, p. 15.
[47]Pritchett, *The American Constitution*, p. 893.

stronger than others, some still in the process of developing—which he uses to determine the outcome of the case or controversy before the Court.

The values the justice possesses are basic variables in the judicial decision-making process; they are "central to the explanation of judicial decision making."[48] Members of the Supreme Court sharing a particular set of beliefs with respect to the concept of political equality, for example, will work toward the maximization of that shared concept. They do so by marshalling a majority of the Court to act in a cohesive manner in the case that offers them the opportunity to so maximize their beliefs and values regarding political equality.

As will be indicated below, an appeal or a petition to the Supreme Court is a stimulus to the justices; "responses are decisions of courts defined in terms of judges' behavior at the end of the decisional process."[49] If at least four justices of the Court are positively stimulated by the jurisdictional brief, the case will be brought to the Court for argument on the merits.

Given the incompleteness of value systems, the interposition of other factors in the decisional process such as the justice's needs, experiences, and perceptions of judicial role, there will be variations and degrees of commitment to these basic beliefs. The point is, however, that whenever the justice chooses to act in a certain way, he does so based in large measure upon the values he has developed.

Judicial blocs, groups of justices who join together in voting decisions because of their shared experiences and mutual commitments to particular values such as freedom, economic liberalism, political equality, or civil rights, do exist on the Supreme Court and have been identified by various political scientists. "All agree that the sets of justices who comprise the bench of relatively large appellate courts characteristically partition themselves into dissenting blocs that reflect the polarization of those courts into liberal, moderate, and conservative subsets."[50]

The justice, therefore, shares common values with others on the Court, and acts in a collegial group environment. Although he acts on the basis of his value system with its hierarchy of attitudes on issues, his goal-oriented activity is modified and blunted by the very existence of (1) other justices who may disagree with his perceptions of issues, (2) the fact that his choices are somewhat restricted by the existence of formal and informal rules of judicial behavior, and (3) the situational context within which the decision is made.

[48]Danelski, "Values and Variables," p. 722.
[49]Ibid., p. 739.
[50]John D. Sprague, *Voting Patterns of the U.S. Supreme Court* (Indianapolis: Bobbs-Merrill, 1968), p. 11.

Court behavior, wrote Joseph Tanenhaus, is a product of three factors. First of all, there are the *external forces* at work on the Court, that is, those economic, social, political factors outside the control of the justices of the Supreme Court. Next there are the *institutional factors* that affect Court behavior, that is, the formal rules and informal practices of the judicial branch that have been established by Constitution, Congress, and the justices of the Court themselves. These two combine to set limits and constraints on the third set of factors: the *personal dimension,* that is, the differences in personality and values which result in varying patterns of judicial behavior.[51] In sum, justices of the Supreme Court are political actors whose response toward cases and controversies brought to the Court is based largely but not entirely upon their attitudes about these policy issues.[52]

The actions of the justices of the Court, based on their accumulated wisdom and prejudices, are modified by the context within which they operate. The external and the institutional forces modify the personal proclivities of the justices of the Supreme Court. Judicial decision making must be viewed within the political, social, economic, and institutional contexts; the justices do not stand atop the mountain hurling thunderbolts down to the masses.

Maximization of Policy Goals

Throughout the book, great stress and emphasis has been placed on the *representational* (political party) and the *doctrinal* (ideology-value system) attributes of the men and women who staff the federal judiciary. The basic assumption made about judicial decision making is that because these persons are psychological products of their pasts, they cannot help but continue to express themselves on public policy issues and, ultimately, attempt to realize policy goals they favor. "Court made pronouncements closely approximate the justice's own personal policy preferences. He acts to accomplish this goal as efficiently and as effectively as possible" through bargaining, negotiation, and compromise with the other eight justices of the Supreme Court.[53]

The justices of the Supreme Court are rational political actors who are goal oriented. They must seek out the achievement of their goals

[51]Joseph Tanenhaus, "Supreme Court Attitudes Toward Federal Administrative Agencies," *Journal of Politics*, vol. 22, no. 3, (August 1960), p. 504.
[52]Victor Flango and Craig C. Ducat, "Toward an Integration of Public Law and Judicial Behavior," *Journal of Politics*, vol. 39, no. 1 (February 1977), p. 41.
[53]Gregory Rathjen, "A Theory of Intracourt Influence: The Supreme Court," paper presented at the 1973 American Political Science Association meeting, New Orleans, Louisiana.

in a collegial small group decisional process with various elements impeding the attainment of their goals. They seek to maximize their policy orientations through an appropriate case that appears on the jurisdictional docket. Political scientists have discussed this activity and have coined terms such as *cue theory* and *upperdog/underdog*.[54]

Cue theory suggests that the vote of four to hear a case on the merits before the Court is based on the justices' perceptions of the presence of certain cues in the jurisdictional brief that "separates the wheat from the chaff."[55] The cues tested for were: petitions in which the federal government seeks review; review of lower court decision where judges were divided; civil liberties issue present; economic issue present.

The conclusion of the researchers was that if three of these factors were present in a petition, there was an 80 percent chance that it would be brought up to the full Court for examination and judgment. "Conversely, where none of the cues are present, only 7 percent of the petitions should be granted."[56]

The *upperdog/underdog* theory suggests that Supreme Court justices "differ with respect to the treatment of canines"; that is, there are perceptible differences with regard to the treatment of *upperdogs*—for example, higher social status litigants who have power such as governmental agencies and business corporations. Conservative justices on the Court generally favor the arguments of these litigants whereas the liberal justices seem inclined to favor the *underdogs*, that is, labor unions, workers, civil rights groups, etc.[57]

The point to these and other theories concerning the granting or denial of writs of certiorari by the Court is that the justices responded to these stimuli based on their perceptions of the major public issues and how they ought to be dealt with by policy makers. Given the presence of a fairly stable bloc of justices who share some common values, at least enough to get the case onto the Court's dockets, the justice has a fighting chance of getting his goals achieved—if he is willing to work hard in the small group environment to achieve these goals.

If he is willing to compromise and bargain, an ethical dilemma for a principled jurist,[58] the justice of the Supreme Court can maximize his goals upon occasion. But he has to work hard at it; cementing past associations and developing, always trying to develop, new accommodations and associations with members of the Court.

The durability of these blocs of justices on the Court that share

---

[54]Ulmer, "Upperdogs and Underdogs"; Rohde and Spaeth, *Supreme Court.*
[55]Rohde and Spaeth, *Supreme Court*, p. 125.
[56]Ibid.
[57]Ulmer, "Upperdogs and Underdogs," pp. 14–16.
[58]Murphy, *Elements of Judicial Strategy*, p. 185.

common values depends upon certain variables: role perception, leadership of the bloc, personalities of the members of the bloc, and the intensity of the shared values.[59] There is always the presence of fluidity in the Court's decisional process. Justices reevaluate their views, develop a more mature or complete value hierarchy, develop a distaste for certain members of the voting bloc, lose respect for the leader of the bloc, and so forth.

All these factors make the task of the goal-oriented justice a difficult one and, when there are personnel changes on the Court, an often frustrating one when the bloc turns from majority to minority strength. It is at these times that a justice in dissent will comment that he hopes that "this or some future court" will rectify the terrible judgment that the Court majority has handed down.[60] In sum, maximization of policy goals takes time, effort, skill, and a great deal of patience and plain good luck.

Justices of the Supreme Court vote the way they do because of their perceptions of what public issue is important enough for the Court to hear and decide. The legal socialization process, the demands of the legal profession, the political reality of the place of the Court (and its role) in American politics, and their own predispositions about the use of judicial power all combine to aid the judge in his decision to act in that case. He is forced to choose to hear or not to hear a case; to choose one path to follow over another when determining the merits of the case; and so forth.

They must choose although "what is wise is not always discernible" to these fallible jurists.[61] This is the agonizing dilemma for the justices of the Supreme Court. In making their choices the justices are guided by their values and the arguments of their colleagues. The justices' common search is the search for truth; they vote the way they do because they believe sincerely that their perception is the correct one—although it just happens to coincide with their deeply held values and beliefs.

Mental constructs in the minds of jurists somehow affect their actions as justices of the Court. Justices of the Supreme Court do act with some degree of regularity and predictability; but "attitudes and ideologies are strictly hypothetical constructs which are invoked to explain the manifest observable regularities and discontinuities in the voting behavior of United States Supreme Court justices."[62]

There is the empirical reality of thousands of cases arriving at the

[59]See for example the classic by Eloyise Snyder, "The Supreme Court as a Small Group," *Social Forces*, 36 (1958), 232.
[60]See Black's dissent in *Dennis v. United States* (1951) for one such statement.
[61]Potter Stewart in *Boys Market v. Retail Clerks Union*, 398 *US* 235 (1970).
[62]Goldman and Jahnige, op cit., p. 282.

Supreme Court and being reviewed, dismissed, or denied by the justices. Since this is not a random selection process and since we have knowledge of the backgrounds of the justices of the Court, the assumption made is that decisions are grounded on the basic values that justices possess. Given the fact that justices have differing doctrinal orientations, there will be differences of opinion about the right way for the Court to travel. These differences must be rectified or else the work of the Court will come to a standstill.

Through bargaining, negotiations, and compromise, these differences are worked out (for the most part) and the decisions are announced—with concurring opinions and dissenting opinions at times. And this process continues every time the justices of the Supreme Court meet in conference, in the courtroom, in the chambers, over coffee and cake, and so forth.[63] Cases are presented to the justices for resolution; because of their importance, a small handful are examined by the justices of the Supreme Court. The justices must act and in that mandatory activity, there is the interplay of value, rule, personality, and environment. The outcome, for better or for worse, is the decision of the Supreme Court.

STONE V. POWELL— JUDICIAL "EVISCERATION" OF PRIOR JUDICIAL POLICY: A CASE STUDY ILLUSTRATING THE MAXIMIZATION OF POLICY GOALS

Congressional statutes from 1789 to the present (28 *USC* § 2254) have provided a procedure whereby a prisoner, whether in a federal or in a state penitentiary, can seek action from a federal district court judge under a *writ of habeas corpus*[64] to review the prisoner's conviction.

In the early 1960s the Supreme Court, under the leadership of Chief Justice Earl Warren, gave the broadest possible interpretation of these federal habeas corpus statutes; especially the 1867 Habeas Corpus Statute. The 1867 Statute allowed that a state prisoner, after exhausting state remedies including petition for certiorari to the Supreme Court, can secure another chance for federal judicial review by filing a habeas

---

[63]Ulmer, "Earl Warren and the Brown Decision," in Murphy and Pritchett, *Courts, Judges,* pp. 505–9.
[64]A *writ of habeas corpus,* if granted by the judge petitioned by the prisoner, is a judicial order to someone (warden, etc.) to bring the prisoner to the federal court so that the federal judge can determine whether or not the imprisonment is constitutionally valid.

corpus petition in the federal district court alleging that the state procedures that led to his/her conviction were in violation of the Constitution. (This procedure became fairly common; in 1941 there were only 127 such petitions filed, whereas in 1974, there were 7,626 petitions filed by prisoners in state penitentiaries.)[65]

In what one constitutional scholar suggested was the Warren Court's "promise of a radical reformulation of state procedural grounds doctrine"[66] by the high Court, in 1963 and 1965 the Supreme Court handed down two opinions that broadened federal jurisdiction of state criminal procedures by making direct federal review and federal habeas corpus review on collateral grounds more easily available to state prisoners. *Fay v. Noia*, 1963, and *Henry v. Mississippi*, 1965, were the two opinions that were "interpreted as the first move in the direction of a general program of increased Supreme Court scrutiny of state procedures affecting the assertion of federal claims."[67]

In *Fay v. Noia*, 372 *US* 391 (1963), the Warren Court majority stated that, absent a knowing and deliberate waiver of a federal constitutional contention during the state trial proceedings, the jurisdiction of the federal courts with regard to habeas corpus petitions was not affected by procedural defaults incurred by the applicant during the state court proceedings.[68]

Simply, the ruling meant that the fact that the defendant did not raise certain points in a timely manner (due, perhaps, to carelessness of counsel) did not prevent the state prisoner, *so long as the inaction was not deliberate,* from seeking federal habeas corpus relief. Fairness and equity, rather than sensitivity to the autonomy of state procedures, was the policy position of the Warren Court.

Two years later, in the case of *Henry v. Mississippi*, 379 *US* 443 (1965), this policy position was reiterated—much to the anger of those jurists in America who urged greater sensitivity to the needs and autonomy of state court systems by the federal courts. This case was, in the words of Lawrence Tribe, the "Supreme Court's most ambitious confrontation with the problem of state procedural grounds" for bringing federal judicial relief.[69] It was also to be, as Tribe put it bluntly, "the end of an era."[70]

In *Henry*, the Supreme Court reversed and remanded a state su-

[65]C. Herman Pritchett, *The Federal System in Constitutional Law* (Englewood Cliffs, N.J.: Prentice-Hall, 1977), p. 302.
[66]Lawrence Tribe, *American Constitutional Law* (Mineola, N. Y.: Foundation Press, 1978), p. 129.
[67]*Ibid.*, p. 126.
[68]*Fay v. Noia*, 372 *US* 391 (1963).
[69]Tribe, *American*, p. 126.
[70]Ibid., p. 129.

preme court decision upholding a conviction. Henry had appealed his conviction on Fourth Amendment grounds after the trial ended. Under Mississippi law, such an appeal was barred due to the failure of the defendant to comply with the state procedural rule that called for such an appeal during the trial itself. However, Justice Brennan for the Warren Court majority wrote that

> a litigant's procedural defaults in state proceedings do not prevent vindication of his federal rights unless the State's insistence on compliance with its procedural rule serves a legitimate state interest.[71]

Both *Fay* and *Henry* made the same basic point: "A state could not place any undue procedural burden on the assertion of federal rights."[72] The Supreme Court had jurisdiction on direct review from the highest state court, and the federal district court had collateral jurisdiction under federal habeas corpus to examine any state procedure that a defendant claimed denied fundamental constitutional rights.

Fairness was the primary policy of the Warren Court. Fairness was the promise of the Warren Court majority, even though it meant that, under certain circumstances, the concept of comity, i.e., deference to state criminal law procedures and the principle of federal judicial abstention in proceedings involving state procedures, had to be set aside.

A colleague of Chief Justice Earl Warren, Associate Justice Arthur J. Goldberg, wrote of the Warren Court's criminal justice opinions that "they introduced an entirely new principle—a new promise—that where there is a right, that right will not remain unenforceable because of the defendant's poverty, ignorance, or lack of remedy."[73] He could have added (indeed it was implied) the following additional factor in light of these two 1963 and 1965 opinions of the Warren Court: The right will remain enforceable regardless of the existence of state procedures and the concept of comity, which would in effect deprive a citizen of basic constitutional protections.

This "new principle and promise" of the Warren Court was not received very warmly by the public. Outcries were heard from police, prosecutors, congressmen, and judges, and the criminal justice policy of the Warren Court became a major campaign issue of the 1968 presidential election.[74]

[71]*Henry v. Mississippi,* 379 *US* 443 (1965).

[72]Tribe, *American,* p. 129.

[73]Arthur J. Goldberg, *Equal Justice: The Warren Era of The Supreme Court* (New York: Farrar, Straus, and Giroux, 1972), p. 20.

[74]See for example Harris, *The Fear of Crime,* and Theodore White, *The Making of The President, 1968* (New York: Doubleday, 1969).

By the October 1971 term of the Court, the recently elected president, Richard M. Nixon, had appointed four justices to the Supreme Court—and all four men were opposed to the criminal law principles and promises of the Warren Court. It was not long before the principles of the Warren Court majority became primary targets of the new and more conservative Supreme Court majority under the leadership of Chief Justice Warren E. Burger.

In the 1976 case of *Francis v. Henderson*, the Nixon Court, expressing a different principle, severely limited the 1963 *Fay v. Noia* decision of the Warren Court. Shortly thereafter (also in the 1976 term of the Supreme Court), *Stone v. Powell*, an opinion written by Justice Lewis Powell (one of the four Nixon appointees), severely narrowed the *Henry* case of 1965 as well as severely limited the use of a judicially created citizen protection that has come to be called the *exclusionary rule*.[75] These two 1976 holdings, in the words of Justice William J. Brennan, Jr.:[76] "portent a substantial evisceration of federal habeas corpus jurisdiction."[77]

The Nixon Court majority in the Louisiana case of *Francis v. Henderson*, 435 US 536 (1976), stated that if a defendant failed to follow appropriate state criminal law proceedings, he or she would be precluded from raising the claim later on in federal habeas corpus proceedings in the federal district court.

If there was this failure to raise specific procedures at a particular point in the criminal trial, the defendant had to either (1) *show cause* for failure to obey the state proceeding, or (2) show that there was actual prejudice against him or her due to a failure to comply with the state criminal law procedures. Raising the abstract constitutional right in the absence of either of these two characteristics, *contrary* to *Fay*, would no longer enable a state prisoner to raise the issue in federal habeas corpus proceedings in the federal district court.[78]

Stone v. Powell, for Justices Brennan and Marshall, was a far more ominous opinion of the Supreme Court. Powell had been stopped by police in a California town under an old vagrancy statute, one that he later claimed was unconstitutionally vague and therefore a denial of his

---

[75]The *exclusionary rule*, first enunciated by the Supreme Court in 1914 (*Weeks v. U.S.*), and again in 1961 (*Mapp v. Ohio*), extended to the states the ruling that any evidence seized in an illegal search and seizure cannot be used as evidence in any criminal proceeding.

[76]Brennan wrote the *Henry* opinion and was a central, pivotal member of the liberal Warren Court majority. In 1976 he was one of just two justices left over from the Warren Court—the other being Justice Thurgood Marshall—and it was Brennan who wrote the dissenting opinion in *Stone*.

[77]*Stone v. Powell*, 428 US 465 (1976).

[78]*Francis v. Henderson*, 425 US 536 (1976).

constitutional rights. In the course of the "stop and frisk," however, the police found a revolver. This revolver turned out to be the murder weapon Powell had used earlier that evening, and was the evidence for which he was subsequently convicted of second degree murder. When his conviction was upheld by the California Supreme Court, Powell then sought action in the federal district court by seeking a writ of habeas corpus.

The petition was granted, and the federal district court judge upheld the judgment of the California courts. The U.S. Court of Appeals reversed the lower federal court judgment, and the state of California appealed to the U.S. Supreme Court. Powell was arguing that because the vagrancy ordinance was unconstitutionally vague, the admission of the revolver into evidence was trial error because it was the result of an unlawful search incident to an unlawful arrest.

Furthermore, Powell's attorney argued, the Warren Court judgment in 1969, *Kaufman v. U. S.*, 394 *US* 217, was very relevant. *Kaufman* had stated that search and seizure claims raised by state defendants could be recognized in federal habeas corpus procedures and, if warranted, such violations of the Fourth Amendment could be rectified by the federal courts.[79]

In *Stone v. Powell*, a major opinion of the Nixon Court, joined in whole or in part by seven of the nine justices, Justice Powell overturned the *Kaufman* opinion of the Warren Court era and reversed the judgment of the court of appeals. The Powell opinion clearly stated that there was no collateral federal habeas corpus relief whatsoever available where the applicant was provided a full and fair opportunity to litigate the search and seizure issue in the state courts. Furthermore, the U.S. Constitution "does not require that a state prisoner be granted federal habeas corpus relief on the ground that the evidence violated the exclusionary rule."[80]

In an unusual response to Brennan's dissent that labeled Powell's opinion as a harbinger of "future eviscerations of the habeas statutes," Justice Powell stated that

> In sum, we hold only that a federal court need not apply the exclusionary rule on habeas review of a Fourth Amendment claim absent a showing that the state prisoner was denied an opportunity for a full and fair litigation of that claim at trial and on direct review.

[79]*Kaufman v. United States*, 394 *US* 217 (1969).
[80]*Stone v. Powell*, 428 *US* 465 (1976).

However, the policy position of the Nixon Court was a new and entirely different promise than that of the Warren Court. "We are unwilling to assume that there now exists a general lack of appropriate sensitivity to constitutional rights in the trial and appellate courts of the several states. . . . There is no intrinsic reason why the fact that a man is a federal judge should make him more competent, or conscientious, or learned with respect to the consideration of Fourth Amendment claims than his neighbor in the State courthouse."

In sum, the posture of the Nixon Court majority extolled the virtues of the *form* of federalism over the substance of a substantive question of possible state infringements of federally guaranteed rights in the form of defective state procedures. Justice William Brennan's dissent pointed to the fundamental shift in policy positions when he wrote that

> this denigration of constitutional guarantees and *constitutionally mandated procedures,* relegated by the Court to the status of mere utilitarian tools, must appall citizens taught to expect judicial respect and support for their constitutional rights. . . . Enforcement of *federal* constitutional rights that redress constitutional violations directed against the 'guilty' is a particular function of *federal* habeas corpus, lest judges trying the 'morally unworthy' be tempted not to execute the supreme law of the land. State judges popularly elected may have difficulty resisting popular pressures not experienced by federal judges given lifetime tenure. . . and the federal habeas statutes reflect the Congressional judgment that such detached federal review is a salutary safeguard against *any* detention of an individual "in violation of the Constitution or laws of the United States."(Brennan's italics)

The Warren Court era, however, is no more. In its place is the Court majority put together by a president who chose federal jurists and U.S. attorneys who would not coddle the criminal. The Nixon Court has maximized its values with respect to the issue of criminal justice. To the extent that they have maximized these goals, the Burger Court majority have, indeed, eviscerated the norms of an earlier more liberal Supreme Court majority.

SUMMARY

The Supreme Court justices, like their brethren who sit on the lower federal bench, act in a manner that reflects their legal, representational, and doctrinal characteristics. The Justices that sit, have sat, and will sit in the future, share common characteristics that lead to intense, agonizing moments in the Court's decision-making process. Motivated by their sets of values, their legal training, and jurisprudential frame of reference, and constrained by fellow justices, the situational context, and the formal and informal rules of legal conduct, these men on the nation's highest bench examine the most important of the thousands of petitions that come to the Court annually. They do so in order to resolve legal disputes, and primarily in an attempt to formulate or clarify important public policy for the American society.

conclusion: politics and the federal judges

Legal decisions are inescapably ethical or moral decisions.

Leif H. Carter

This book has presented a portrait of the federal judicial system and of the judges in the federal judicial system; it has emphasized the impact of politics and political ideology on both system and personnel in the system. Throughout the book, it has been shown that political ideology and political forces have molded and shaped the contours of the federal system. These forces have determined, to a large extent, the policy direction of the appellate courts in the federal system. The book, however, is not an ode to politics; it simply attempts to place things in perspective. Politics itself is neither good or bad. It is a process, a tool, through which goals of men and women in society can be reached. To the extent that the judges are affected by politics and political ideology, they mirror the mood and the attitudes of Americans. What follows are some final comments on what has already been discussed in this book.

THE IMPACT OF POLITICAL FORCES ON THE STRUCTURE OF THE SYSTEM

The development and growth of the federal judicial system since the Constitutional Convention of 1787 reflects the impact of political forces, especially the politics of sectionalism and the politics of nation-

275

alism versus localism. The creation of the three agencies of the central government created an ideological dilemma for those in America in 1787 who believed in the concept of state sovereignty. For almost a century the opponents of a central government opposed the expansion of a national judiciary and successfully blocked that growth of federal jurisdiction. For over 100 years, the U.S. courts of appeals legislation was not passed because of the basic political/ideological concerns of those who feared the usurpation of state judicial power by an enlarged national court system. Even after the creation of the courts of appeals, there was concern over the impact of the federal judiciary on state powers and prerogatives. To this day, whether in Boston, Massachusetts, or in Montgomery, Alabama, there is still heated discussion about the unconstitutional intervention of the federal courts in the affairs of the local communities.

The jurisdiction of the federal courts has been a political issue for these two centuries of democratic rule; the national legislature due to the intransigence of many of its members for almost 100 years was unable to muster enough votes to give the federal district court judges broad jurisdiction to hear cases. Even though today there is a commitment to the principle of comity, state judges are still very sensitive to the overseer's role that federal courts have over their actions, especially through the use of the habeas corpus writ. And it was not until 1925 that the United States Supreme Court was given fairly complete (discretionary) control over its appellate docket by the national legislature.

Certainly jurisdiction of the federal courts is in part a reflection of political forces at work in the national government; gaining access to the federal courts is the other side of the coin. Judges, whether in the federal district court or sitting on the Supreme Court bench, are gatekeepers. And this gatekeeping task involves choices and value judgments. These value judgments are not made by robots, said Justice William O. Douglas. They are made by men and women who wear robes, but prior to the robing process were active in political and legal environments.

The judge's past determines his perception of the role of the federal courts and, consequently, how wide or narrow the gates of federal justice should be opened in our society. His legal training, his perception of the taught traditions of the law, i.e., the spirit of the law, the role of precedent, the Anglo-Saxon legal heritage, the impact of cases, influence the judge in his judgments regarding access to the federal courts.

But beyond these very important legal socialization experiences, there is the personal, political, and social experiences that affect the future behavior of judges. The judge who ruled in favor of the miners in the Buffalo Creek litigation drew upon his perceptions of the law but also drew upon his own personal life experiences in that coal mine country. If the plaintiffs had drawn another judge, the jurisdictional rulings might very well have gone against them.

Is it an evil or malevolent situation? I think not, for that situation is the human situation. Absent a "clockwork orange" society, judges will honestly differ on questions of access.

Who selects and affirms the judges to a large extent determines the kinds of legal perceptions that will prevail in a given period of judicial history in America. And, as pointed out in the text, politics plays a major role in the judicial selection process. Presidents and attorneys general want "their kind of man or woman" on the federal bench. From the last days of the Adams administration in 1800 to the 1978 omnibus judge's bill that gave Democratic President Jimmy Carter the enviable task of nominating and, with the advice and consent of the Senate, appointing 154 federal judges, political factors have impacted on selection.

Marbury v. Madison, the 1803 watershed constitutional case, came about because of the fact that the Federalists were so busy creating new federal district courts and staffing these newly created federal courts (just as the Federalists were having to turn over the reigns of government to the dreaded Democrat-Republican, Thomas Jefferson) that Marbury's justice of the peace commission was never delivered by John Marshall. (The man who failed to deliver the commission, John Marshall, was soon to sit as the chief justice of the United States.)

Jurisdiction of the federal courts reflects political factors as does access to the federal courts and the selection process itself. Although the president chooses the men, he has to deal with yet another basic political factor in the judicial selection process: the concept of senatorial courtesy. This political custom is still another indication of the interplay of politics and the law.

In short, the structure and the dynamics of the federal courts and of the judicial process is grounded in politics. It is not the only factor that accounts for organizational growth, the dynamism of the "standing to sue" concept, the expansion of the "political question" doctrine, and so forth, but it is a major variable. Without such an understanding of the impact of politics on the federal judicial system, there can be no true awareness of the realities of the federal judicial system.

THE IMPACT OF POLITICAL FORCES ON THE ROLE AND FUNCTION OF THE FEDERAL JUDGES

Just as political factors affect the structure and dynamics of the federal system, these same factors also influence the perceptions of judicial role held by the federal judges themselves. The norm enforcement and policy-making perceptions that activate judicial behavior in the federal courts have their beginning as concepts created through the interplay of the person's legal and political training and experiences within his mind. Behavior, judicial or otherwise, is a consequence of such an interaction of person/mind and environment. For example, Judge Frank Johnson, U.S. District Court, Middle District of Alabama, due to his political-social-legal training and upbringing will respond to the arguments of black plaintiffs somewhat differently than, say, Judge J.P. Coleman, U.S. Court of Appeals, Fifth Circuit.

One judge may empathize with the legal dilemmas of poor people, women, blacks, etc.; another judge treats blacks and others disrespectfully and rules against them in such an obviously biased fashion that he is constantly overturned on appeal. Judges do not necessarily view a case before them in the same way; perceptions of precedent, facts relevant to the disposition of the case, and so on, differ and with these differences come distinct judgments. And this is essentially politics, for politics is choosing one among a number of courses of action that brings one closer to the good life.

On the question of whether or not the judge ought to redirect policy for the society there have been fundamental disagreements between judges since the time of John Marshall. If John Marshall argued for judicial review and (consequently) policy making by the judiciary in the guise of determining what the law was on a subject, others argued that judges did not constitutionally have the power to review and set aside acts of Congress. In *Colegrove v. Green* (1946) or *Baker v. Carr* (1961) one finds classic statements of judicial deference and judicial activism. How does one account for these attitudes and perceptions? In part by the impact of politics and the various political experiences of a lifetime that are reflected in the actions of the federal judges.

All judges attempt to steer a course between stability of the law (continuity) and the change in law. This dilemma is inherent in a democratic society. The pace and tempo of the change, in light of the force of stability, precedent, and tradition, are based to a large extent on the environmental forces that have shaped the thinking of the judges. The judges ought to be able to recognize the existence of these intellectual and emotive elements at work in their brains. However, they cannot tear them out and program themselves to act as unemotionally as a computer. An awareness of the character of the judicial process must begin with a recognition that the judges respond to cases and controversies by drawing upon their legal training and their social and political experiences and ideals.

All judges in the final analysis are goal-oriented political actors. They have views of the good life and visions of justice; these are given expression every time they are asked to determine the meaning of a constitutional phrase such as "search and seizure," "due process," "commerce," "freedom of conscience," or to decide whether the judges ought to hear that case in the first place.

Judges for the most part have actively pursued these goals prior to their elevation to the federal bench. Some were legislators on the state and national level and the pursuit of the good life is evident there. Others were prosecutors on the state and national level. Here too there is the element of pursuit of the good life through the effective and efficient enforcement of the criminal code. Still other federal judges were formerly governors or, in one instance, a president of the United States. Here too, their prior public activities involved pursuit of happiness and the good life for their constituents.

And when these men and women become judges on the federal courts they continue their pursuit of certain basic ideals. For a judge, the accomplishment of the good life might well be to validate the national legislation regulating the transportation in interstate commerce of prostitutes and sordid characters. To another judge, perhaps sitting on the same bench and therefore dissenting from the first view, the good life might well be achieved by allowing these kinds of people access to transportation. The point is that the pursuit continues, for how else can one explain the activities of the federal judges since the creation of the federal district courts and the staffing of the Supreme Court in 1789.

POLITICS AND THE ART OF THE POSSIBLE

Acting in this manner, the federal judges mirror the basic values of the community. Not for long are judges out of synchronization with the larger society on the basic questions of value. It is a realistic commentary (and not a sad one) on the state of humankind; it is a realistic view of the functioning of the federal judiciary. Judges cannot evade or avoid the political dimension of their decisions.

People wish for larger than life actions from the federal judges; they want to believe that the federal judges act impartially, fairly, and objectively. The people want to believe in the permanency of the law and the ease with which trained jurists can find answers and resolve difficult controversies. But life does not imitate these wishes very often. Judges are human; politics is a reflection of human nature. It was Madison who wrote that if men were angels there would be no need for government. And of course men, including judges on the federal bench, are not angels—therefore we have government and politics.

However, given the predispositions and commitment to the taught traditions of the law and given the commitment to act so as to balance the judicial function between change and continuity, federal judges generally act in a prudent manner. Whether acting as norm enforcers or as policy makers, the federal judges must justify their actions before their peers and, ultimately, before the American people. Judges cannot act too long without the support of the national community. Policy making, a reflection of judges' attitudes on an issue, is tempered by this factor.

We end as we began, by pointing to the paradox of judicial policy making. We talk of politics as the art of the possible, as the art of what is passable in the context of democratic politics. Lifetime appointed judges, however, play an important role in the determination of what is possible in our political and social life. And we have come to expect that role and function of the federal judges. Therefore, nonelected lifetime appointees, selected in great part for their political ideologies and because they supported the right party at the right time, come to sit in judgment with respect to the people's efforts to achieve the good life. It is paradoxical but we have in America come to live with the paradox of politicians becoming federal judges and bringing their views, attitudes, and predispositions with them to the federal bench.

bibliography

BOOKS

ABRAHAM, HENRY J., *The Supreme Court in the Governmental Process*. Boston: Allyn & Bacon, Inc., 1975.

ALLEN, TIP H., Jr., "Mississippi Votes: The Presidential and Gubernatorial Elections, 1947–64," *Social Science Research Center*. Mississippi State: Mississippi State University, May 1967.

American Law Institute, *A Study of the Business of the Federal Courts*, part II. Civil Cases, 1934.

Annual Report of the Director of the Administrative Office of the United States Courts. Washington, D.C.: U.S. Government Printing Office, 1976.

ASHMAN, ALAN, and JAMES J. ALFINI, *The Key to Judicial Merit Selection: The Nominating Process*. Chicago: The American Judicare Society, 1974.

AUERBACK, CARL, and others, *The Legal Process*. San Francisco: Chandler Publishing Company, 1961.

BALL, HOWARD, *Judicial Craftsmanship or Fiat? Direct Overturn by the United States Supreme Court*. Westport, Conn.: Greenwood Press, Inc., 1978.

BALL, HOWARD, *No Pledge of Privacy: The Watergate Tapes Litigation*. New York: Kennikat Press Inc., 1977.

BALL, HOWARD, *The Vision and the Dream of Justice Hugo Black*. University, Ala.: University of Alabama Press, 1975.

BALL, HOWARD, *The Warren Court's Conceptions of Democracy*. Madison, N.J.: Fairleigh Dickinson University Press, 1972.

BENVENISTE, GUY, *Bureaucracy*. San Francisco: Boyd & Fraser Publishing Company, 1977.

BERGER, RAOUL, *Government by Judiciary*. Cambridge: Harvard University Press, 1977.

BERGER, W., *Annual Report on the State of the Judiciary*, in SUPREME COURT REPORTER, vol. 96, no. 9 (March 1, 1976).

BETH, LOREN, *Politics, the Constitution, and the Supreme Court*. Evanston, Ill.: Row, Peterson, & Co., 1962.

BICKEL, ALEXANDER M., *The Least Dangerous Branch*. Indianapolis: Bobbs-Merrill Co., Inc., 1972.

CAHN, EDMOND, ed., *Supreme Court and Supreme Law*, New York: Simon and Schuster, 1954.

CHASE, HAROLD W., *Federal Judges: The Appointing Process*. Minneapolis: University of Minnesota Press, 1972.

CHASE, HAROLD W., and CRAIG DUCAT, *Constitutional Interpretation*. St. Paul, Minn.: West Publishing Co., 1975.

CORWIN, EDWIN, *Total War and the Construction*. New York: Alfred A. Knopf, Inc., 1945.

COX, ARCHIBALD, *The Role of the Supreme Court in American Government*. New York: Oxford University Press, 1976.

COX, ARCHIBALD, *The Warren Court*. Cambridge: Harvard University Press, 1968.

DANELSKI, DAVID J., *A Supreme Court Justice Is Appointed*. New York: Random House, Inc., 1964.

DUCAT, CRAIG, *Modes of Constitutional Interpretation*. St. Paul, Minn.: West Publishing Co., 1977.

EARLY, STEPHEN T., *Constitutional Courts of the U.S.* Totowa, N.J.: Littlefield, Adams & Company, 1977.

EISENSTEIN, J. and H. JACOB, *Felony Justice*. Boston: Little, Brown and Company, 1977.

ELDRIDGE, WILLIAM B., "Barriers and Incentives to Technology Transfer into the United States Courts," in *Judicial Administration*, eds. Russell Wheeler and Howard Whitcomb. Englewood Cliffs, N.J.: Prentice-Hall, Inc., 1977.

FAIRMAN, C., *History of the Supreme Court of the United States: Reconstruction and Reunion*, part I, (1971).

FLANDERS, STEVEN, and ALAN SAGER, "Case Management Methods and Delay in Federal District Courts," in *Judicial Administration*, eds. R. Wheeler and H. Whitcomb. Englewood Cliffs, N.J.: Prentice-Hall, Inc., 1977.

FRANKFURTER, FELIX, and JAMES M. LANDIS, *The Business of the Supreme Court*. New York: Macmillian, Inc., 1928.

FRIEDMAN, LAWRENCE M., *A History of American Law*, p. 120. New York: Touchstone Publishing Company, 1973.

FRIEDMAN, LEON, *Milestones*. St. Paul, Minn.: West Publishing Co., 1976.

FRIENDLY, FRED, *The Good Guys, the Bad Guys, and the First Amendment*. New York: Vintage Books, 1977.

FRIENDLY, HENRY J., *Federal Jurisdiction: A General View*. New York: Columbia University Press, 1973.

GINGER, ANN FAGAN, *The Law, the Supreme Court and the People's Rights*. New York: Barrow Publishing Company, 1973.

GOLDBERG, ARTHUR J., *Equal Justice: The Warren Era of the Supreme Court.* New York: Farrar, Straus, & Giroux, Inc., 1972.

GOLDMAN, SHELDON, and THOMAS JAHNIGE, *The Federal Courts as a Political System.* New York: Harper & Row, 1971.

GOULDER, JOSEPH C., *The Benchwarmers.* New York: Weybright and Talley, Inc., 1974.

GREENBERG, JACK, *Judicial Process and Social Change.* St. Paul, Minn.: West Publishing Co., 1976.

GRODZINS, MORTON, "Centralization and Decentralization in the American Federal System," in *A Nation of States.* Edited by Robert Goldwin. Chicago: Rand McNally & Company, 1963.

GROSSMON, JOEL V., *Lawyers and Judges: The Politics of Judicial Selection,* p. 31. New York: John Wiley & Sons, Inc., 1965.

HAINES, CHARLES G., *The American Doctrine of Judicial Supremacy.* (1932).

HAMILTON, A., *The Federalist Papers,* p. 494. New York: Random House Modern Library, 1937.

HARRIS, RICHARD, *Decision.* New York: E. P. Dutton & Co., Inc., 1971.

HARRIS, RICHARD, *Freedom Spent: Tales of Tyranny in America,* pp. 3–130. Boston: Little, Brown and Company, 1976.

HARRIS, RICHARD, *The Fear of Crime.* New York: F. Praeger Co., 1969.

HART H. and H. WECHSLER, *The Federal Courts and the Federal System* (2nd ed.). Mineola, N.Y.: The Foundation Press, Inc., 1973.

HECLO, HUGH, *A Government of Strangers.* Washington, D.C.: The Brookings Institution, 1977.

JACKSON, ROBERT H., *The Supreme Court in the American System of Government,* New York; Harper & Row, 1955.

JACOB, HERBERT, *Justice in America.* Boston: Little, Brown and Company, 1977.

JAHNIGE, THOMAS P., and SHELDON GOLDMAN, *The Federal Judicial System.* New York: Holt, Rinehart and Winston, Inc., 1968.

JAMES, HOWARD, *Crisis in the Courts.* New York: David McKay Co., Inc., 1967.

KLUGER, RICHARD, *Simple Justice.* New York: Random House, Inc., 1977.

LEVY, L., *Judicial Review, History and Democracy: An Introduction in Judicial Review and the Supreme Court,* (1967)

LEVY, LEONARD, *The Supreme Court under Earl Warren.* New York: Quadrangle Books, Inc., 1972.

McCLOSKEY, ROBERT, *The American Supreme Court.* New York: Random House, Inc., 1960.

McILWAIN, C., *Constitutionalism: Ancient and Modern,* (1947 ed.)

MAYERS, LEWIS, *The American Legal System.* New York: Harper & Row Publishers, 1964.

MITAU, G. THEODORE, *Decade of Decisions: The Supreme Court and the Constitutional Revolutions, 1954–1964.* New York: Charles Scribner's Sons, 1967.

MURPHY, WALTER F., *Elements of Judicial Strategy.* Chicago: University of Chicago Press, 1960.

MURPHY, WALTER, and JOSEPH TANENHAUS, *The Study of Public Law.* New York: Random House, Inc., 1972.

MURPHY, WALTER, and C. HERMAN PRITCHETT, *Courts, Judges, and Politics*, pp. 668–69. New York: Random House, Inc., 1971.

NAGEL, STEWART S., *Comparing Elected and Appointed Judicial Systems*. American Politics Series. Beverly Hills: Sage Publications, Inc., 1973.

NAGEL, STEWARD, *The Legal Process from a Behavioral Perspective*. Homewood, Ill.: Dorsey Press, 1969.

PADOVER, SAUL K., *To Secure These Blessings, the Great Debates of the Constitutional Convention of 1787*, p. 417. New York: The Ridge Press, Inc., 1962.

PELTASON, JACK, *Federal Courts in the Political Process*. New York: Random House, Inc., 1955.

PELTASON, JACK, *Fifty-eight Lonely Men*. Chicago: University of Chicago Press, 1960.

PRITCHETT, C. HERMAN, *The American Constitution*, p. 101. New York: McGraw-Hill Book Company, 1977.

PRITCHELL, C. HERMAN, *The Federal System in Constitutional Law*. Englewood Cliffs, N.J.: Prentice-Hall, Inc., 1978.

RATHJEN, GREGORY J., "Population Growth and the Federal Judicial System," in *Political Issues in U.S. Population Policy*, ed. Virginia Gray. Lexington, Ma.: Lexington Books, 1974.

ROHDE, DAVID W., and HAROLD J. SPAETH, *Supreme Court Decision Making*. San Francisco: Freeman, Cooper & Company, 1976.

RICHARDSON, KENNETH J., and RICHARD N. VINES, *The Politics of Federal Courts*. Boston: Little, Brown and Company, 1970.

RODGERS, HARRELL, and CHARLES BULLOCK, *Law and Social Change*. New York: McGraw-Hill Book Company, 1972.

ROSENTHAL, DOUGLAS, *Lawyers and Clients: Who Is in Charge?* New York: Russell Sage Foundation, 1974.

SCHMANDT, HENRY J., *Courts in the American Political System*. Encino, Ca.: Dickinson Pub. Co., Inc., 1968.

SCHMIDHAUSER, JOHN R., *The Supreme Court*. New York: Holt, Rinehart and Winston, Inc., 1960.

SCHMIDHAUSER, JOHN R., and LARRY L. BERG, *The Supreme Court and Congress: Conflict and Interaction (1945–68)*. New York: The Free Press, 1972.

SCIGLIANO, ROBERT, *The Supreme Court and the Presidency*. New York: The Free Press, 1971.

SHAPIRO, MARTIN, *The Pentagon Papers and the Courts*. San Francisco: Chandler Publishing Company, 1972.

SHELDON, CHARLES H., *The American Judicial Process*. New York: Dodd, Mead & Company, 1974.

SHERRILL, ROBERT, *Military Justice Is to Justice as Military Music Is to Music*. New York: Harper Books, 1970.

SIGLER, JAY A., *An Introduction to the Legal System*. Homewood, Ill.: Dorsey Press, 1967.

SIMON, JAMES F., *In His Own Image: The Supreme Court in Richard Nixon's America*, New York: David McKay Co., Inc.,1973.

SMITH, DAVID G., *The Convention and Constitution*. New York: St. Martin's Press, Inc., 1965.

SPRAGUE, JOHN, *Voting Patterns of the U.S. Supreme Court*. Indianapolis: Bobbs-Merrill Co., Inc., 1968.

STERN, GERALD, *The Buffalo Creek Disaster*. New York: Random House, Inc., 1976.

STRUM, PHILLIPPA, *The Supreme Court and Political Questions*. University, Ala.: University of Alabama Press, 1974.

SUTHERLAND, ARTHUR, *Constitutionalism in America*. New York: Blaisdell, 1965.

TANNENHAUS, JOSEPH, MARVIN SCHICK, MATTHEW MURASKIN, and DANIEL ROSEN, "The Supreme Court's Certiorari Jurisdiction: Cue Theory," in *Judicial Decision Making*. New York: McMillan Publishing Co., Inc., 1963.

THORSON, THOMAS, *The Logic of Democracy*. New York: W. W. Norton & Company, Inc., 1967.

WARREN, CHARLES, *The Supreme Court in United States History*. Boston: Little, Brown and Company, 1929.

WASBY, S., *The Impact of the United States Supreme Court*. Homewood, Ill: Dorsey Press, 1970.

WATSON, RICHARD, and RONDAL DOWNING, *The Politics of the Bench and the Bar*. New York: John Wiley & Sons, Inc., 1969.

WEAVER, JOHN D., *Warren: The Man, the Court, the Era*, p. 191. Boston: Little, Brown and Company, 1965.

WEINSTEIN, JACK, "The Role of the Chief Judge in a Modern System of Justice," in *Judicial Administration*, eds. R. Wheeler and H. Whitcomb. Englewood Cliffs, N.J.: Prentice-Hall, Inc., 1977.

WEISS, LEONARD, and ALLYN STRICKLAND, *Regulation: A Case Approach*. New York: McGraw-Hill Book Company, 1976.

WESTIN, ALAN, F., *The Anatomy of a Constitution Law Case*. New York: MacMillan, Inc., 1958.

WESTIN, ALAN F., ed., *The Supreme Court: Views from Inside*. New York: W. W. Norton & Company, Inc., 1961.

WHITE, H., *The Making of the President, 1968*. New York: Doubleday & Company, Inc., 1969.

WRIGHT, CHARLES, *Federal Courts* (2nd ed.). St. Paul, Minn.: West Publishing Co., 1970 (supp. 1972).

ARTICLES

ABEL, RICHARD, *A Comparative Theory of Dispute Institutions in Society*, 8 LAW AND SOCIETY REVIEW 217–347 (Winter 1974).

ALBERT, CHARLES, *Standing to Challenge Administrative Action: An Inadequate Surrogate Claim for Relief*, 83 YALE L.J. 425 (1974).

ALLEN, JOHN, *The Supreme Court, Federalism, and State Systems of Criminal Justice*, 8 DEPAUL L. REV. 213 (1959).

ALLISON, JOHN R., *Professional Sports and the Antitrust Laws: Status of the Reserve System*, 25 BAYLOR LAW REVIEW No. 1, 1 (Winter 1973).

ANDERSON, JACK, "Merit Selection May Choose Judges." *Mississippi Clarion-Ledger*, June 18, 1978, p. 9.

ATKINS, BURTON M., *Merit Selection of State Judges,* 50 FLORIDA BAR JOURNAL 203–11 (April 1976).

ATKINS, BURTON M., and GLICK, HENRY R., "Formal Judicial Recruitment and State Supreme Court Decisions," *American Politics Quarterly* 2 (1974), 427–49.

AUBERT, VILHELM, "Competition and Dissensus," *Journal of Conflict Resolution* 7 (1963), 25.

BALL, HOWARD, "Careless Justice," *Polity* (December 1978).

BARRON, WILLIAM, *The Ambiguity of Judicial Review: A Response to Professor Bickel,* DUKE LAW JOURNAL (1970).

BAUM, LAWRENCE, "Lower Court Response to Supreme Court Decisions: Reconsidering a Negative Picture," 3 *Justice System Journal* 3 (Spring 1978), 211.

BENNETT, JOHN, "Arnold Seen as Nominee for Judgeship," *Memphis Commercial Appeal,* June 28, 1978, p. 1.

BENNETT, JOHN, "Senate Delays Judges Nominations," *Memphis Commercial Appeal,* June 13, 1978, p. 3.

BERGER, RAOUL, *Standing to Sue in Public Actions: Is it a Constitutional Requirement?* 78 YALE L.J. 816 (1969).

BERGER, WARREN E., "Reducing the Load on Nine Mortal Justices," *New York Times,* August 14, 1975.

BLACK, CHARLES L., JR., *A Note on Senatorial Consideration of Supreme Court Nominees,* 79 YALE L. J. 659 (1970).

BRENNAN, WILLIAM J., "Inside View of the High Court," *New York Times Magazine,* October 6, 1963.

BUCHANAN, CHARLES, *Judicial Supremacy Reexamined: A Proposed Alternative,* 70 MICHIGAN LAW REVIEW 1279 (1972).

CANON, BRADLEY C., *The Impact of Formal Selection Processes on the Characteristics of Judges—Reconsidered,* 6 LAW AND SOCIETY REVIEW 579–93 (1972).

CARBON, SUSAN, "The U.S. Circuit Judge Nominating Commission: A Comparison of Two of its Panels," *Judicature,* 62 No. 5 (November 1978).

CASPER, JONATHAN, "The Supreme Court and National Policy Making," LXX *American Political Science Review,* No. 1 (March 1976).

CHASE, HAROLD, *Federal Judges: The Appointing Process,* 51 MINNESOTA LAW REVIEW 185, 211 (1966).

CHOPER, WILLIAM, *The Supreme Court and the Political Branches: Democratic Theory and Practice,* 122 U. PA. L. REV. 810 (1974).

COMMENT, *An Expanding Civil Role for United States Magistrates,* 26 AMERICAN UNIVERSITY LAW REVIEW 66 (1975).

CORWIN, EDWIN, *The Higher Law Background of American Constitutional Law,* 42 HARVARD L. REV. 149, 365 (1928–29).

COX, ARCHIBALD, *The Role of the Supreme Court in American Society,* 50 MARQ. L. REV. 575 (1967).

DANELSKI, DAVID T., *Values as Variables in Judicial Decision Making,* 19 VANDERBILT LAW REVIEW (1966).

DAVIS, KENNETH, *Standing: Taxpayers and Others,* 35 U. CHI. L. REV. 601 (1968).

DUCAT, CRAIG R., and FLANGO, VICTOR E., "In Search of Qualified Judges," Paper presented at annual meeting of American Society of Public Administration, 1975.

ECKHOFF, TORSTEIN, "Impartiality, Separation of Powers, and Judicial Independence," *Scandinavian Studies in Law* 9 (1965), 9.

EMERSON, THOMAS, *Malapportionment and Judicial Power*, 72 YALE L. J. 64 (1962).

ERVIN, SAM, *Separation of Powers: Judicial Independence*, 35 LAW AND CONTEMPORARY PROBLEMS 1081 (1970).

FIELD, OLIVER, "Ten Years of the Supreme Court: 1937–47—Separation and Delegation of Powers," 41 *American Political Science Review* 1161 (1947).

FLANDERS, STEVEN, and GOLDMAN, JERRY, "Screening Practices and the Use of Para Judicial Personnel in a U.S. Court of Appeals," 1 *Justice System Journal*, No. 2 (March 1975), 1.

FLANGO, VICTOR, and DUCAT, CRAIG C., "Toward an Integration of Public Law and Judicial Behavior," 39 *Journal of Politics* 1 (February 1977), 41.

FOOTLICK, JEROLD, "Too Much Law," *Newsweek*, January 10, 1977, pp. 42–47.

FRIEDRICH, CARL, "Separation of Powers," 13 *Encyc. Soc. Sci.* (1934): 663–66.

FRIENDLY, FRED, *In Praise of Erie—and of the New Federal Common Law*, 39 NEW YORK U. L. REV. 383 (1964).

GLAZIER, NATHAN, "Toward an Imperial Judiciary?" *The Public Interest* 41 (1975), 104–23.

GOLDMAN, JERRY, "Federal District Courts and the Apellate Crisis," *Judicature* 57 (1973), 211.

GOLDMAN, SHELDON, "A Profile of Carter's Judicial Nominees," *Judicature*, 62, No. 5 (November 1978).

GOLDMAN, SHELDON, "Characteristics of Eisenhower and Kennedy Appointees to the Lower Federal Courts," 81 *Western P.A. Q* 755 (1965).

GOLDMAN, SHELDON, "In Defense of Justice," 39 *Journal of Politics* (February 1977), 155.

GOLDMAN, SHELDON, *Judicial Appointments to the United States Court of Appeals*, WISCONSIN LAW REVIEW 186–187 (1967).

GOLDMAN, SHELDON, "Voting Behavior on the U.S. Courts of Appeals, 1961–1964," *American Political Science Review*, 60 (1966), 374–83.

GOLDMAN, SHELDON, "Voting Behavior on the U.S. Courts of Appeals Revisited," *American Political Science Review*, LXIX, No. 2 (June 1975).

GOODMAN, JAMES, "The Politics of Picking Federal Judges," 7 *Juris Doctor*, No. 6, June 1977, p. 20.

HALL, KERMIL L., "Social Backgrounds and Judicial Recruitment: A Nineteenth Century Perspective on the Lower Federal Judiciary," *Western Political Quarterly*, 29 (1976), 243.

HALL, KERMIL L., *101 Men: The Social Composition and Recruitment of the Antebellum Lower Judiciary, 1828–61*, RUTGERS-CAMDEN LAW JOURNAL 7 199–226 (1976).

HART, HENRY, *The Power of Congress to Limit the Jurisdiction of the Federal Courts: An Exercise in Dialectic*, 66 HARVARD L. REV. 1362 (1953).

HOWARD, J. W., "On the Fluidity of Judicial Choice," 62 *American Political Science Review*, 43 (March 1968).

HOWARD, J. WOODFORD, "Role Perceptions and Behavior in Three U.S. Courts of Appeals," 39 *Journal of Politics*, No. 3 (November 1977), p. 918.

HELLMAN, ARTHUR D., *The Business of The Supreme Court Under the Judiciary Act of 1925,* 91 HARVARD L. REV., No. 8 (June 1978).

HENKIN, NEIL, *Is There a Political Question Doctrine?* 85 YALE L. J. 597 (1976).

HERNDON, JAMES, *Appointment as a Means of Initial Succession to the State Courts of Last Resort,* 38 NORTH DAKOTA LAW REVIEW 60–73 (1962).

HEYDEBRAND, WOLF, *The Context of Public Bureaucracies: An Organizational Analysis of the Federal District Courts,* 11 LAW AND SOCIETY REVIEW 5 761 (Summer 1977).

HOLLAND, KENNETH M., "William J. Campbell: A Case Study of an Activist U.S. District Judge," 3 *Justice System Journal* 2 (Winter 1977), 148.

JACKSON, R. B., *The Political Question Doctrine: Where Does it Stand After Powell v. McCormack, O'Brien v. Brown, and Gilligan v. Morgan?* 44 U. COLO. L. REV. 477 (1973).

JAFFE, LOUIS, *Standing to Secure Judicial Review: Public Actions,* 74 HARVARD L. REV. 1265 (1961).

JAFFE, LOUIS, *Standing Again,* 84 HARVARD L. REV. 633, 636 (1971).

JAFFE, LOUIS, *The Citizen as Litigant in Public Actions: The NonHohfeldion or Ideological Plaintiff,* 116 U. PA. L. REV. 1033, 1037 (1968).

JEWELL, MALCOLM, *Minority Representation: A Political or Judicial Question,* 53 KY. L. J. 267 (1965).

KRITZER, HERBERT, "Political Correlates of the Behavior of Federal District Judges," 40 *Journal of Politics,* No. 1 (February 1978), p. 28.

LEVIN, MARTIN, "Urban Politics and Judicial Behavior." 1 *Journal of Legal Studies,* (1972), 203.

MACK, WILLIAM C., "Settlement Procedures in the U.S. Court of Appeals," 2 *Justice System Journal* 2 (March 1975).

MENDELSON, WALLACE, "Mr. Justice Douglas and Government by the Judiciary," 38 *Journal of Politics* 4 (November 1976), 937.

MILLER, ARTHUR S., *Statutory Language and the Purposive Use of Ambiguity,"* 42 VIRGINIA LAW REVIEW 23 (1956).

MISHKIN, PAUL, *The Supreme Court, 1964 Term, Foreword: The High Court, the Great Writ and the Due Process of Time and Law,* 79 HARVARD L. REV. 56, 77–92 (1965).

MONAGHAN, *The Supreme Court, 1974 Term, Foreword: Constitutional Common Law,* 89 HARVARD L. REV. 1, 13–14 (1975).

MURPHY, WALTER, and TANNENHAUS, JOSEPH, "Patterns of Diffuse Support: A Study of the Warren and Burger Courts," Paper presented at the 10th World Congress of the International Political Science Association, 1976.

NAGEL, STUART, *Multiple Correlation of Judicial Backgrounds and Decisions,* 2 FLORIDA STATE UNIVERSITY LAW REVIEW 258 (1974).

NAGEL, STUART S., "Political Party Affiliation and Judges' Decisions." LV *American Political Science Review,* No. 4 (December 1961).

NELSON and WESTBROOK, *Court Martial Jurisdiction over Servicemen for 'Civilian' Offenses: An Analysis of O'Callahan v. Parker,* 54 MINNESOTA L. REV. 1 (1969).

NOTE, *The Competence of Federal Courts to Formulate Rules of Decision,* 77 HARVARD L. REV. 1084 (1964).

NOTE, *Wyatt v. Stickney and the Right of Civilly Committed Mental Patients to Adequate Treatment,* 86 HARVARD L. REV. (1973).

NOTE, *Exclusive Jurisdiction of the Federal Courts in Private Civil Actions,* 70 HARVARD L. REV. 509 (1957).

NOTE, *Standing to Assert Constitutional Jus Tertii,* 88 HARVARD L. REV. 423, 428–30 (1974).

ORREN, KAREN, "Standing to Sue: Interest Group Conflict in the Federal Courts, LXX *American Political Science Review,* No. 3 (September 1976).

PRITCHETT, C. H., "Division of Opinion Among Justices of the United States Supreme Court, 1939–1940," 35 *American Political Science Review* (1941), 890.

PURO, STEVEN, "United States Magistrates: A New Federal Judicial Officer," 2 *Justice System Journal* (Winter 1976), 141.

RATNER, L., *Congressional Power over Appellate Jurisdiction of the Supreme Court,* 109 U. PA. L. REV. 157 (1960).

RATNER, LEONARD, *The Co-ordinated Warmaking Power—Legislative, Executive, and Judicial Roles,* 44 SO. CALIFORNIA L. REV. 461 (1971).

RICHARDSON, RICHARD J., and VINES, KENNETH, "Review, Dissent, and the Appellate Process: A Political Interpretation," 29 *Journal of Politics,* No. 3 (August 1967).

ROHDE, DAVID W., "Policy Goals and Opinion Coalitions in the Supreme Court," 26 *Midwest Journal of Political Science* (May 1972).

SARAT, AUSTIN, "Judging in Trial Courts: An Exploratory Study," 39 *Journal of Politics,* No. 2 (May 1977), p. 368.

SCHELLHARDT, TIMOTHY D., "Reshaping the Federal Judiciary," *Wall Street Journal,* February 23, 1978, p. 26.

SCHRUM, FRED, "Fired: The Hiring and Firing of United States Attorneys," *New Times,* February 20, 1978, p. 34.

SCOTT, K., *Standing in the Supreme Court: A Functional Analysis,* 86 HARVARD L. REV. 645 (1973).

SNYDER, ELOYISE, "The Supreme Court as a Small Group," 37 *Social Forces* (1958).

SORR, JOHN, "The Philadelphia Story," *New Times,* February 20, 1978, p. 31.

STECICK, MARIANNE, "Speeding up Criminal Appeals in the Second Circuit," 1 *Justice System Journal,* No. 2 (March 1975), p. 45.

STEELE, JOHN L., "Haynesworth vs. the United States Senate," *Fortune,* March 1970, pp. 90–96, 155–62.

STEWART, *The Reformation of American Administrative Law,* 88 HARVARD LAW REVIEW 1667, 1723–47 (1975).

STONE, C., *Should Trees Have Standing?: Toward Legal Rights for Neutral Objects,* 45 SO. CALIFORNIA L. REV. 450 (1972).

TANNENHAUS, JOSEPH, "Supreme Court Attitudes Toward Federal Administrative Agencies," 22 *Journal of Politics,* No. 3 (August 1960), p. 504.

TAYLOR, W., *Legal Action to Enjoin Legislative Malapportionment: The Political Question Doctrine,* 34 SO. CALIFORNIA L. REV. 179 (1961).

VELVEL, RICHARD, *The War in Vietnam: Unconstitutional, Justiciable, and Jurisdictionality Attackable,* 16 KANSAS L. REV. 449 (1968).

VINES, KENNETH, "Federal District Judges and Race Relations Cases in the South," 26 *Journal of Politics* (1964).

WARREN, E., "Let's Not Weaken the Supreme Court," 60 *A.B.A.J.* 677 (1974).

WHITTEN, *Federal Declaratory and Injunctive Interference with State Court Proceedings: The Supreme Court and the Limits of Judicial Discretion,* 53 N. CAR. L. REV. 581 (1975).

WRIGHT, LAWRENCE, "Atticus Finch Goes to Washington," *New Times,* December 9, 1977, p. 31.

INDEXES

case index

293

subject index